Study Guide

Jack Adams
University of Arkansas, Little Rock

Macroeconomics
Theories and Policies

Richard T. **Froyen**

PRENTICE HALL, Upper Saddle River, NJ 07458

Acquisitions Editor: *Rod Banister*
Assistant Editor: *Gladys Soto*
Production Editor: *Joseph F. Tomasso*
Manufacturer: *Quebecor Printing Inc.*

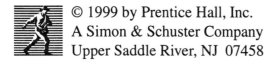
© 1999 by Prentice Hall, Inc.
A Simon & Schuster Company
Upper Saddle River, NJ 07458

All rights reserved. No part of this book may
be reproduced, in any form or by any means,
without permission in writing from the publisher.

Printed in the United States of America

10 9 8 7 6 5 4 3 2 1

ISBN   0-13-011236-4

Prentice-Hall International (UK) Limited, *London*
Prentice-Hall of Australia Pty. Limited, *Sydney*
Prentice-Hall Canada Inc., *Toronto*
Prentice-Hall Hispanoamericana, S.A., *Mexico*
Prentice-Hall of India Private Limited, *New Delhi*
Prentice-Hall of Japan, Inc., *Tokyo*
Simon & Schuster Asia Pte. Ltd., *Singapore*
Editora Prentice-Hall do Brasil, Ltda., *Rio de Janiero*

CONTENTS

PART I: INTRODUCTION AND MEASUREMENT

1. Introduction 1
2. Measurement of Macroeconomic Variables 9

PART II: MACROECONOMIC MODELS

3. Classical Macroeconomics (I): Equilibrium Output and Employment 16
4. Classical Macroeconomics (II): Money, Prices, and Interest 30
5. The Keynesian System (I): The Role of Aggregate Demand 42
6. The Keynesian System (II): Money, Interest, and Income 59
7. The Keynesian System (III): Policy Effects in the IS-LM Model 77
8. The Keynesian System (IV): Aggregate Supply and Demand 92
9. The Monetarist Counterrevolution 107
10. Output, Inflation, and Unemployment: Monetarist and Keynesian Views ... 119
11. New Classical Economics 134
12. Real Business Cycles and New Keynesian Economics 142
13. Macroeconomic Models: A Summary 149

PART III: EXTENSIONS OF THE MODELS

14. Consumption and Investment 158
15. Money Demand 168
16. The Money Supply Process 177
17. Long- and Intermediate-Term Economic Growth 184

PART IV: ECONOMIC POLICY

18. Fiscal Policy 192
19. Monetary Policy 202

PART V: OPEN ECONOMY MACROECONOMICS

20. Exchange Rates and the International Monetary System 211

21. Monetary and Fiscal Policy in the Open Economy 218

Answer Key 224

Preface

This Study Guide is designed to aid students in macroeconomics courses which use *Macroeconomics: Theories and Policies* as a text.

The Study Guide contains the following:

1. **Chapter Overviews**: A brief summary is given of the material covered in each chapter.

2. **Techniques in Depth**: In these sections, the technical aspects of many of the concepts and procedures used in the text are explained.

3. **Multiple-Choice Questions**: A number of multiple-choice questions are provided covering the material in each chapter. These problems are designed for self-testing on whether the material has been understood sufficiently to apply it in specific contexts.

4. **Problems and/or Essay Questions**: Several problems and essay questions are provided covering the material in each chapter. These problems are designed for self-testing on whether the material has been understood sufficiently to apply it in specific contexts.

5. **Answer Key**: Answers to all the multiple-choice questions and suggested approaches to answering problems and essay questions are provided at the end of the Study Guide.

Typically, in economics course such as intermediate macroeconomics, the amount of reading required of the student as measured in pages per week is, relative to may other courses, rather small. But to absorb the material covered requires more than one reading of the material. The student needs to devise methods for determining when he or she has mastered the material covered. It is to aid in this process that this Study Guide is intended.

In revising the Study Guide, we have added additional questions and revised and updated existing material.

PART I: INTRODUCTION AND MEASUREMENT

CHAPTER 1

INTRODUCTION

OVERVIEW

This brief introductory chapter begins with a discussion of the subject matter of macroeconomics. Macroeconomics is defined as the study of the behavior of the economy as a whole. The key variables studied in macroeconomics include total output in the economy, the aggregate price level, the levels of employment and unemployment, levels of interest rates, wage rates, and foreign exchange rates.

The second section of the chapter sketches the broad outline of U.S. macroeconomic performance over the post-World War II period. The behavior of the rate of growth in real output, the rate of inflation, and the unemployment rate are discussed. The values of these variables for the decades of the 1950s, 1960s, 1970s, 1980s, and 1990s are compared. The relationship between the unemployment rate and the inflation rate over this period is examined. It is shown in Figure 1.1 that there appeared to be a negative relationship between inflation and unemployment through the late 1960s, whereas, for the post-1970 period, there is no apparent relationship between these series. While the inverse relationship appeared to be restored in the early 1980s, it disappeared again in the latter 1980s and early 1990s. Between 1992 and 1997 both the inflation and unemployment rates declined.

On the basis of the data, several important macroeconomic questions are posed:

(1) Why has the behavior of output, employment, and inflation become so unstable in the period since 1970? In contrast, what factors explain the steady expansion of the 1960s or the price stability of the 1950s?

(2) Why have <u>both</u> the unemployment rate and the inflation rate been high during substantial portions of the post-1970 period? What became of the negative relationship that seemed to exist between inflation and unemployment during earlier years? What brought both inflation and unemployment rates down in the 1980s? What caused the inflation rate to fall between 1990 and 1997, and what will happen during the remainder of the decade?

(3) Why has there been an apparent secular increase in the unemployment rate over recent decades? Does the fall in the 1980s constitute a change in the long-term trend? If so, how can the increase between 1990 and 1994 be accounted for in terms of the trend?

(4) What explains the decline in the growth rate in output, as measured by real GDP, in the period since 1970?

Techniques in Depth

Presentation of Economic Data. In this chapter, several important macroeconomic variables were presented and analyzed. Since economic variables can behave quite differently from one another, and over time, there are several ways to present these data. We discuss some of these methods here.

Some economic variables show an unmistakable trend while others are largely trendless. For example, output, employment, and the price level show strong upward trends. Since 1953, real output rose fairly steadily. If we graph real output, the upward trend is readily apparent:

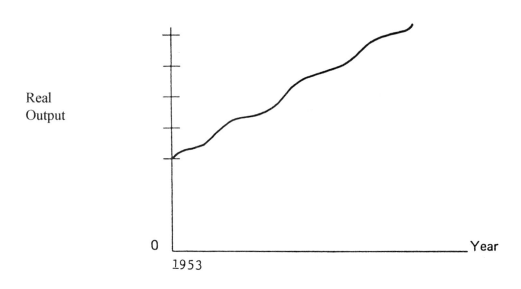

A graph of the price level and the number of individuals employed would show similar upward trends.

There is, however, important information that is obscured by concentrating on the trend. For example, economic cycles are hard to detect in the above graph. We can accentuate these cycles more by looking at rates of growth (percentage changes) instead.

A plot of percentage changes of real output looks more like the graph on the following page. From this graph, we see that real output has grown as fast as 10% in some quarters and has declined in others. Periods of economic expansion and recession are more clearly delineated. Of course, even percentage changes can obscure important facts. For example, it is difficult to see if there are any subtrends within all this variability. For the 1953-69 period, real output growth averaged about 3.5%. This was followed by average growth rates of 2.8% for the 1970-81 period, and 2.7% for the 1982-97 period. This decade-by-decade performance is not readily apparent in either of the graphs. What graph and what presentation of the data you choose will be dictated by your needs.

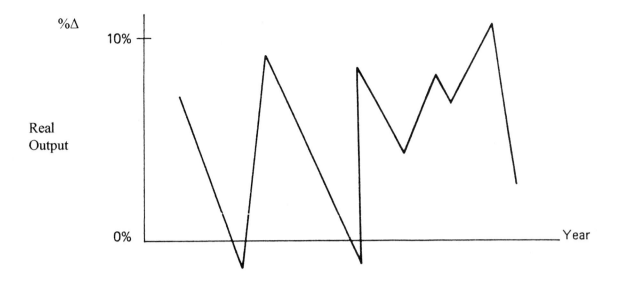

To see more clearly the cyclical components of prices, the percentage change in prices is often presented. This is called an inflation rate. To see the cyclical components of employment, however, we usually see the unemployment rate presented. This is not the percentage change in employment or unemployment. Rather it is the percentage of workers who are part of the labor force who cannot find jobs. If we think two or more economic variables are related in some way by cause and effect, we can sometimes learn more by graphing the two variables on a single chart. Then we can analyze if and how they relate to each other. For example, consider the following chart of the unemployment rate and the inflation rate during the 1950s:

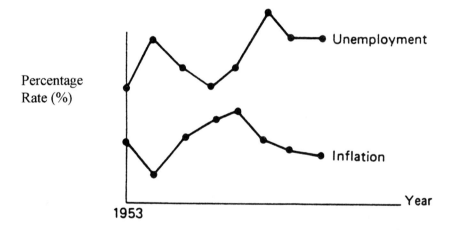

In 1954, 1955, 1956, and 1958, these two variables moved in opposite directions; when one rose, the other fell. In 1957 and 1959, they both moved together—first upward and then later downward. In 1959 they were both largely unchanged. This graph leaves the relationship between the two variables uncertain and suggests that looking at more data points is necessary. Although data points are never the ultimate proof of any theory, we can learn a great deal about economic relationships with them. Graphing economic variables in a variety of ways is useful, since each graph yields insights lost or minimized in the others.

Self-Tests

Multiple-Choice Questions:

1. The key variables that are studied in macroeconomics include:
   a. total output and aggregate price level
   b. employment and unemployment
   c. interest rates and wage rates
   d. foreign exchange rates
   e. all of the above

2. From 1992 to 1997:
   a. the inflation rate fell while the unemployment rate rose
   b. the unemployment rate fell while the inflation rate rose
   c. both the inflation and unemployment rates fell
   d. both the inflation and unemployment rates rose

3. The U.S. trade deficit and the federal budget deficit both ballooned in:
   a. the late 1970s
   b. the 1980s
   c. the early 1990s
   d. the early 1970s

4. The average unemployment rate for the 1982-97 period was:
   a. 6.7 percent
   b. 6.0 percent
   c. 8.0 percent
   d. 7.6 percent

5. The early 1980s were a period of:
   a. high inflation
   b. steady growth of GDP
   c. disinflation
   d. both a and b
   e. none of the above

6. The consumer price index (CPI) measures:
   a. the wholesale prices of about 3000 goods and services
   b. the retail prices of a selected "market basket" of one hundred goods and services purchased by households
   c. the retail prices of a fixed "market basket" of several thousand goods and services purchased by households
   d. changes in the prices of all currently produced goods and services

7. The roots of the Keynesian theory is an attack on:
   a. monetarism
   b. the classical economics
   c. the new classical economics
   d. the real business cycle theory

8. Between 1980 and 1997, the outstanding amount of federal government debt:
   a. doubled
   b. grew by over 500 percent
   c. increased by 200 percent
   d. declined

9. The merchandise trade deficit is:
   a. more exports than imports
   b. an excess of receipts over expenditures
   c. the excess of imports over exports
   d. a shortfall of exports over imports

10. The 1990s started off with a(n):
    a. boom followed by a recession
    b. recession followed by a boom
    c. instant recovery from a long depression
    d. mild recession followed by a long expansion

11. The public became much more interested in macroeconomic issues during the:
    a. late 1950s and early 1960s
    b. 1970s and 1980s
    c. 1980s and early 1990s
    d. during the 1990s

12. Challenges to Keynesian economics are:
    a. monetarism and classical economics
    b. new classical economics and business cycle theory
    c. monetarism and new classical economics
    d. business cycle theory and monetarism

13. According to economic data, real GDP:
    a. has steadily increased over the last twenty-eight years
    b. has declined in six of the last twenty-eight years
    c. has slowly declined over the last twenty years
    d. has declined in fourteen of the last twenty-eight years

14. Between 1982 and 1997, the average inflation rate was:
    a. 5 percent
    b. just under 6 percent
    c. 3.4 percent
    d. below 3 percent

Introduction   6

15. Even so the economy had settled down, in some respects, by the mid-1980s, with low inflation and declining unemployment, the two structural imbalances that emerged were:
   a. a small federal government budget deficit and a skyrocketing merchandise trade deficit
   b. a large federal government budget deficit and a small merchandise trade deficit
   c. both a small federal government budget deficit and a small merchandise trade deficit
   d. a large federal government budget deficit and a skyrocketing merchandise trade deficit

16. Accompanying the decline in the growth rate in output, as measured by GDP, in the post-1970 period were:
   a. declines in labor productivity growth
   b. declines in real wages
   c. increases in the real wage
   d. both a and b
   e. both a and c

17. The macroeconomic orthodoxy as it existed at the beginning of the 1970s is known as:
   a. classical economics
   b. Keynesian economics
   c. monetarism
   d. new classical economics

18. The percent of the labor force that is not employed is the:
   a. unemployment rate
   b. labor force
   c. full employment rate
   d. employment ratio

Problems and/or Essay Questions:

1. The Table on page 7 comes from the Economic Report of the President, 1997. It contains data on levels of the major spending components of GDP in each year since 1929.

   a. Pick three components of GDP and analyze for: trend, cyclical behavior, and any definable changes in trend over major subperiods.

   b. Analyze the behavior of GDP for trend, cycle, and trend changes.

   c. Some economists believe that government spending changes cause GDP changes. Use this data to see if changes in government spending are followed by trend or cyclical changes in GDP.

Table 1.—Gross Domestic Product

[Billions of dollars; quarterly data are seasonally adjusted at annual rates]

Year and quarter	GDP	Personal consumption expenditures				Gross private domestic investment							Net exports [1]			Government [2]			Final sales of domestic product	GNP	Percent change from preceding period	
		Total	Durable goods	Non-durable goods	Services	Total	Fixed investment					CBI	Net	Exports	Imports	Total	Federal	State and local			GDP	Final sales of domestic product
							Total	Nonresidential			Residential											
								Total	Structures	PDE												
1929	103.8	77.5	9.2	37.7	30.5	16.7	14.9	11.0	5.5	5.5	4.0	1.7	0.4	5.9	5.6	9.3	1.7	7.6	102.1	104.6		
1930	91.1	70.2	7.2	34.0	29.0	10.6	11.0	8.6	4.4	4.2	2.4	-.4	.3	4.4	4.1	9.9	1.8	8.1	91.4	91.8	-12.3	-10.5
1931	76.4	60.7	5.5	29.0	26.2	5.9	7.0	5.3	2.6	2.6	1.8	-1.1	0	2.9	2.9	9.8	1.8	8.0	77.6	76.9	-16.1	-15.1
1932	58.6	48.7	3.6	22.7	22.3	1.1	3.6	2.9	1.4	1.5	.8	-2.5	0	2.0	1.9	8.7	1.8	6.9	61.0	58.9	-23.4	-21.3
1933	56.2	45.9	3.5	22.3	20.2	1.7	3.1	2.5	1.1	1.4	.6	-1.5	.1	2.0	1.9	8.6	2.2	6.4	57.7	56.5	-4.0	-5.5
1934	65.9	51.4	4.2	26.7	20.5	3.7	4.3	3.3	1.2	2.1	.9	-.6	.3	2.6	2.2	10.4	3.2	7.2	66.4	66.1	17.1	15.1
1935	73.1	55.9	5.1	29.3	21.5	6.7	5.6	4.3	1.4	2.8	1.3	1.1	-.2	2.8	3.0	10.8	3.3	7.5	72.0	73.5	11.0	8.4
1936	83.6	62.2	6.3	32.9	23.0	8.7	7.5	5.8	1.9	3.9	1.7	1.2	-.2	3.0	3.2	13.0	5.5	7.5	82.4	83.9	14.3	14.5
1937	91.8	66.8	6.9	35.2	24.7	12.2	9.5	7.5	2.7	4.8	2.1	2.7	0	4.0	4.0	12.7	5.0	7.7	89.1	92.2	9.7	8.1
1938	85.9	64.2	5.7	34.0	24.6	7.1	7.7	5.5	2.1	3.4	2.1	-.6	.9	3.8	2.8	13.7	5.6	8.1	86.5	86.3	-6.4	-2.9
1939	91.9	67.2	6.7	35.1	25.4	9.3	9.1	6.1	2.2	3.9	3.0	.2	.8	3.9	3.1	14.6	5.9	8.8	91.7	92.3	7.0	6.0
1940	101.2	71.2	7.8	37.0	26.4	13.6	11.2	7.7	2.6	5.2	3.5	2.4	1.4	4.8	3.4	15.0	6.4	8.5	98.8	101.6	10.1	7.8
1941	126.7	81.0	9.7	42.9	28.5	18.2	13.8	9.7	3.3	6.4	4.1	4.4	1.0	5.4	4.4	26.5	17.9	8.5	122.2	127.2	25.2	23.7
1942	161.6	88.9	6.9	50.8	31.3	10.5	8.5	6.3	2.2	4.1	2.2	1.9	-.3	4.3	4.6	62.7	54.1	8.5	159.7	162.1	27.6	30.7
1943	198.3	99.7	6.5	58.6	34.6	6.1	6.9	5.4	1.8	3.7	1.4	-.8	-2.4	3.9	6.3	94.9	86.6	8.3	199.1	198.7	22.7	24.7
1944	219.7	108.5	6.7	64.3	37.4	7.8	8.7	7.4	2.4	5.0	1.4	-.9	-2.2	4.8	6.9	105.6	97.2	8.3	220.6	220.2	10.8	10.8
1945	223.2	119.9	8.0	71.9	40.0	10.9	12.3	10.6	3.3	7.3	1.7	-1.4	-.9	6.7	7.5	93.3	84.4	8.9	224.6	223.5	1.6	1.8
1946	222.6	144.3	15.8	82.7	45.8	31.3	25.1	17.3	7.4	9.9	7.8	6.2	7.1	14.1	7.0	39.9	29.2	10.7	216.4	223.3	-.3	-3.6
1947	244.6	162.3	20.4	90.9	51.0	35.0	35.5	23.5	8.1	15.3	12.1	-.5	10.8	18.7	7.9	36.5	22.8	13.7	245.1	245.8	9.9	13.2
1948	269.7	175.4	22.9	96.6	56.0	48.1	42.4	26.8	9.5	17.3	15.6	5.6	5.4	15.5	10.1	40.8	24.5	16.3	264.1	271.2	10.3	7.8
1949	267.8	178.9	25.0	94.9	59.0	36.7	39.6	24.9	9.2	15.7	14.6	-2.8	5.2	14.4	9.2	47.0	28.0	19.0	270.6	269.1	-.7	2.4
1950	294.6	192.7	30.8	98.2	63.7	54.2	48.3	27.8	10.0	17.8	20.5	5.9	.7	12.3	11.6	47.1	26.3	20.7	288.7	296.1	10.0	6.7
1951	339.7	208.7	29.9	109.2	69.7	60.3	50.3	31.8	12.0	19.9	18.4	10.1	2.4	17.0	14.6	68.3	45.3	23.0	329.7	341.7	15.3	14.2
1952	358.6	219.7	29.3	114.7	75.7	54.0	50.5	31.9	12.2	19.7	18.6	3.5	1.0	16.3	15.3	83.8	59.4	24.5	355.0	360.7	5.5	7.7
1953	379.7	233.5	32.7	117.8	83.0	56.3	54.5	35.1	13.6	21.5	19.4	1.8	-.8	15.2	16.0	90.7	64.5	26.2	377.9	381.7	5.9	6.4
1954	381.3	240.7	32.1	119.7	89.0	53.8	55.8	34.7	13.9	20.8	21.1	-1.9	.3	15.7	15.4	86.4	57.4	29.0	383.2	383.4	.4	1.4
1955	415.1	259.1	38.9	124.7	95.5	69.0	64.0	39.0	15.2	23.9	25.0	4.9	.4	17.6	17.2	86.7	54.9	31.7	410.2	417.7	8.9	7.0
1956	438.0	271.9	38.2	130.8	103.0	72.2	68.1	44.5	18.2	26.3	23.6	4.1	2.3	21.2	18.9	91.6	56.7	34.8	433.9	440.9	5.5	5.8
1957	461.0	286.7	39.7	137.1	109.9	70.6	69.7	47.5	19.0	28.6	22.2	.9	4.0	23.9	19.9	99.8	61.3	38.5	460.1	464.2	5.3	6.1
1958	467.3	296.3	37.2	141.7	117.4	64.5	64.9	42.5	17.6	24.9	22.3	-.4	.4	20.4	20.0	106.1	63.8	42.3	467.7	470.1	1.4	1.6
1959	507.2	318.1	42.7	148.5	127.0	78.8	74.6	46.5	18.1	28.3	28.1	4.2	-1.7	20.6	22.3	112.0	67.2	44.8	503.0	510.1	8.5	7.6
1960	526.6	332.2	43.3	152.9	136.0	78.8	75.5	49.2	19.6	29.7	26.3	3.2	2.4	25.3	22.8	113.2	65.6	47.6	523.3	529.8	3.8	4.0
1961	544.8	342.6	41.8	156.6	144.3	77.9	75.0	48.6	19.7	28.9	26.4	2.9	3.4	26.0	22.7	120.9	69.1	51.8	541.9	548.4	3.5	3.5
1962	585.2	363.4	46.9	162.8	153.7	87.9	81.8	52.8	20.8	32.1	29.0	6.1	2.4	27.4	25.0	131.4	76.5	55.0	579.1	589.4	7.4	6.9
1963	617.4	383.0	51.6	168.2	163.2	93.4	87.7	55.6	21.2	34.4	32.1	5.7	3.3	29.4	26.1	137.7	78.1	59.6	611.7	621.9	5.5	5.6
1964	663.0	411.4	56.7	178.7	176.1	101.7	96.7	62.4	23.7	38.7	34.3	5.0	5.5	33.6	28.1	144.4	79.4	65.0	658.0	668.0	7.4	7.6
1965	719.1	444.3	63.3	191.6	189.4	118.0	108.3	74.1	28.3	45.8	34.2	9.7	3.9	35.4	31.5	153.0	81.8	71.2	709.4	724.5	8.5	7.8
1966	787.8	481.9	68.3	208.8	204.8	130.4	116.7	84.4	31.3	53.0	32.3	13.8	1.9	38.9	37.1	173.6	94.1	79.5	774.0	793.0	9.5	9.1
1967	833.6	509.5	70.4	217.1	222.0	128.0	117.6	85.2	31.5	53.7	32.4	10.5	1.4	41.4	39.9	194.6	106.6	88.1	823.1	839.1	5.8	6.3
1968	910.6	559.8	80.8	235.7	243.4	139.9	130.8	92.1	33.6	58.5	38.7	9.1	-1.3	45.3	46.6	212.1	113.8	98.3	901.4	916.7	9.2	9.5
1969	982.2	604.7	85.9	253.2	265.5	155.0	145.5	102.9	37.7	65.2	42.6	9.5	-1.2	49.3	50.5	223.8	115.8	108.0	972.7	988.4	7.9	7.9
1970	1,035.6	648.1	85.0	272.0	291.1	150.2	148.1	106.7	40.3	66.4	41.4	2.2	1.2	57.0	55.8	236.1	115.9	120.2	1,033.4	1,042.0	5.4	6.2
1971	1,125.4	702.5	96.9	285.5	320.1	176.0	167.5	111.7	42.7	69.1	55.8	8.5	-3.0	59.3	62.3	249.9	117.1	132.8	1,116.9	1,133.1	8.7	8.1
1972	1,237.3	770.7	110.4	308.0	352.3	205.6	195.7	126.1	47.2	78.9	69.7	9.9	-8.0	66.2	74.2	268.9	125.1	143.8	1,227.4	1,246.0	9.9	9.9
1973	1,382.6	851.6	123.5	343.1	384.9	242.9	225.4	150.0	55.0	95.1	75.3	17.5	.6	91.8	91.2	287.6	128.2	159.4	1,365.2	1,395.4	11.7	11.2
1974	1,496.9	931.2	122.3	384.5	424.4	245.6	231.5	165.6	61.2	104.3	66.0	14.1	-3.1	124.3	127.5	323.2	139.9	183.3	1,482.8	1,512.6	8.3	8.6
1975	1,630.6	1,029.1	133.5	420.6	475.0	225.4	231.7	169.0	61.4	107.6	62.7	-6.3	13.6	136.3	122.7	362.6	154.5	208.1	1,636.9	1,643.9	8.9	10.4
1976	1,819.0	1,148.8	158.9	458.2	531.8	286.6	269.6	187.2	65.9	121.2	82.5	16.9	-2.3	148.9	151.1	385.9	162.7	223.1	1,802.0	1,836.1	11.5	10.1
1977	2,026.9	1,277.1	181.1	496.9	599.0	356.6	333.5	223.2	74.6	148.7	110.3	23.1	-23.7	158.8	182.4	416.9	178.4	238.5	2,003.8	2,047.5	11.4	11.2
1978	2,291.4	1,428.8	201.4	549.9	677.4	430.8	403.6	272.0	91.4	180.6	131.6	27.2	-26.1	186.1	212.3	457.9	194.4	263.4	2,264.2	2,313.5	13.0	13.0
1979	2,557.5	1,593.5	213.9	624.0	755.6	480.9	464.0	323.0	114.9	208.1	141.0	16.9	-24.0	228.7	252.7	507.1	215.0	292.0	2,540.6	2,590.4	11.6	12.2
1980	2,784.2	1,760.4	213.5	695.5	851.4	465.9	473.5	350.3	133.9	216.4	123.2	-7.6	-14.9	278.9	293.8	572.8	248.4	324.4	2,791.9	2,819.5	8.9	9.9
1981	3,115.9	1,941.3	230.5	758.2	952.6	556.2	528.1	405.4	164.6	240.9	122.6	28.2	-15.0	302.8	317.8	633.4	284.1	349.2	3,087.8	3,150.6	11.9	10.6
1982	3,242.1	2,076.8	239.3	786.8	1,050.7	501.1	515.6	409.9	175.0	234.9	105.7	-14.5	-20.5	282.6	303.2	684.8	313.2	371.6	3,256.6	3,273.2	4.1	5.5
1983	3,514.5	2,283.4	279.8	830.3	1,173.3	547.1	552.0	399.4	152.7	246.7	152.5	-4.9	-51.7	277.0	328.6	735.7	344.5	391.2	3,519.4	3,546.5	8.4	8.1
1984	3,902.4	2,492.3	325.1	883.6	1,283.6	715.6	648.1	468.3	176.0	292.3	179.8	67.5	-102.0	303.1	405.1	796.6	372.6	424.0	3,835.0	3,933.5	11.0	9.0
1985	4,180.7	2,704.8	361.1	927.6	1,416.1	715.1	688.9	502.0	193.3	308.7	186.9	26.2	-114.2	303.0	417.2	875.0	410.1	464.9	4,154.5	4,201.0	7.1	8.3
1986	4,422.2	2,892.7	398.7	957.2	1,536.8	722.5	712.9	494.8	175.8	319.0	218.1	9.6	-131.5	320.7	452.2	938.5	435.2	503.3	4,412.6	4,435.1	5.8	6.2
1987	4,692.3	3,094.5	416.7	1,014.0	1,663.8	747.2	722.9	495.4	172.1	323.3	227.6	24.2	-142.1	365.7	507.9	992.8	455.7	537.2	4,668.1	4,701.3	6.1	5.8
1988	5,049.6	3,349.7	451.0	1,081.1	1,817.6	773.9	763.1	530.6	181.3	349.3	232.5	10.9	-106.1	447.2	553.2	1,032.0	457.3	574.7	5,038.7	5,062.6	7.6	7.9
1989	5,438.7	3,594.8	472.8	1,163.8	1,958.1	829.2	797.5	566.2	192.3	373.9	231.3	31.7	-80.4	509.3	589.7	1,095.1	477.2	617.9	5,407.0	5,452.8	7.7	7.3
1990	5,743.8	3,839.3	476.5	1,245.3	2,117.5	799.7	791.6	575.9	200.8	375.1	215.7	8.0	-71.3	557.3	628.6	1,176.1	503.6	672.6	5,735.8	5,764.9	5.6	6.1
1991	5,916.7	3,975.1	455.2	1,277.6	2,242.3	736.2	738.5	547.3	181.7	365.6	191.2	-2.3	-20.5	601.8	622.3	1,225.9	522.6	703.4	5,919.0	5,932.4	3.0	3.2
1992	6,244.4	4,219.8	488.5	1,321.8	2,409.4	790.4	783.4	557.9	169.2	388.7	225.6	7.0	-29.5	639.4	669.0	1,263.8	528.0	735.8	6,237.4	6,255.5	5.5	5.4
1993	6,558.1	4,459.2	530.2	1,370.7	2,558.4	876.2	855.7	604.1	176.4	427.7	251.6	20.5	-60.7	658.6	719.3	1,283.4	518.3	765.0	6,537.6	6,576.8	5.0	4.8
1994	6,947.0	4,717.0	579.5	1,428.4	2,709.1	1,007.9	946.6	660.6	184.5	476.1	286.0	61.2	-90.9	721.2	812.1	1,313.0	510.2	802.8	6,885.7	6,955.2	5.9	5.3
1995	7,265.4	4,957.7	608.5	1,475.8	2,873.4	1,038.2	1,008.1	723.0	200.6	522.4	285.1	30.1	-86.0	818.4	904.5	1,355.5	509.6	846.0	7,235.3	7,270.6	4.6	5.1
1996	7,636.0	5,207.6	634.5	1,534.7	3,038.4	1,116.5	1,090.7	781.4	215.2	566.2	309.2	25.9	-94.8	870.9	965.7	1,406.7	520.0	886.7	7,610.2	7,637.7	5.1	5.2

1. Net exports of goods and services.
2. Government consumption expenditures and gross investment.
GDP Gross domestic product
CBI Change in business inventories
GNP Gross national product
PDE Producers' durable equipment

2. Explain why the relationship between unemployment and inflation in the late 1970s baffled macroeconomists.

3. Name at least six different schools of thought that have developed in macroeconomic research.

4. Explain a merchandise trade deficit. How does the fall in Asian currency values contribute to this deficit?

5. What caused the United States to evolve from being the world's largest creditor nation to the world's largest debtor nation?

6. What has happened to the federal budget deficit since the 1950s?

CHAPTER 2

MEASUREMENT OF MACROECONOMIC VARIABLES

OVERVIEW

Prior to considering macroeconomic models, the real-world counterparts to the variables that appear in such models are examined. These macroeconomic variables are defined, and values for the major ones in selected years are given.

The following variables from the national income accounts are considered, along with their interrelationships:

gross domestic product: a measure of all currently produced goods and services evaluated at market prices.

national income: the sum of all factor earnings from current production of goods and services.

personal income: the national income accounts measure of the income received by persons from all sources.

personal disposable income: when personal tax payments are subtracted from personal income, we get disposable (after-tax) personal income.

Next, the distinction between real and nominal GDP is explained. The concept of the implicit GDP deflator is developed, and the way in which the GDP deflator can be used to measure changes in the aggregate price level is illustrated (see Table 2.6). Two other price indices, the consumer price index (CPI) and the producer price index are also described. The consumer price index measures the retail prices of a fixed market basket of several thousand goods and services purchased by households. The producer price index measures the wholesale prices of approximately 3000 items.

The final topic considered is the concept of potential output. Potential output is defined as the level of real output that the economy could produce at high rates of resource utilization. In the short run, fluctuations in output and employment come primarily as variations in actual output around potential output. The cyclical variation in actual output around the level of potential output during the 1959-2000 period is examined in Figure 2.2.

Self-Tests

Multiple-Choice Questions:

1. A measure of all currently sold final goods and services evaluated at market prices is:
    a. GDP
    b. potential GDP
    c. NDP
    d. none of the above

2. A measure of net output that reflects how much of the capital stock is used up in the production process is:
   a. net investment
   b. factor income
   c. net national product
   d. capital consumption allowance

3. If final sales exceed production, inventory accumulation:
   a. is negative
   b. is positive
   c. ceases
   d. is larger than GDP

4. Personal consumption expenditures measure the production of goods destined for consumers. This usually averages about _____ percent of GDP:
   a. 2
   b. 90
   c. 50
   d. 65

5. One major component of investment is:
   a. residential construction
   b. important housing services
   c. government purchases of roads
   d. all of the above

6. The most volatile of the components of GDP is:
   a. wages and salaries
   b. consumption spending
   c. government spending
   d. investment spending

7. Included in the government sector of the national income accounts is (are):
   a. government interest payments
   b. government transfer payments
   c. government Social Security payments
   d. government spending on goods and services
   e. all of the above

8. The main difference between personal income and personal disposable (after-tax) income is:
   a. sales taxes
   b. payroll and income taxes (including transfer payments)
   c. excise taxes
   d. government spending

9. In the national income accounts, personal saving is found:
   a. by adding collections of money and financial assets
   b. by a survey of financial institutions
   c. as a residual after subtracting taxes and outlays from income
   d. none of the above

10. In any given year (except the base year), nominal and real GDP will change by the same percentage if:
    a. output is not changing
    b. prices are not changing
    c. output is falling and prices are rising
    d. output is rising and prices are falling

11. The following are the actual numbers for GDP and real GDP for 1993 and 1994:

	NGDP	RGDP
1993	6244.4	6244.4
1994	7636.0	6928.4

    The inflation rate, as measured by the GDP deflator, during 1994 was about:
    a. 1 percent
    b. 20 percent
    c. 5 percent
    d. 2 percent

12. Potential output is a measure of the level of GDP achievable:
    a. if everyone is working
    b. if capital is utilized at an 86% rate and labor at about a 94% rate
    c. at a zero inflation rate
    d. when capital usage is high enough such that net investment equals zero

13. The consumer price index (CPI):
    a. measures currently produced goods and services at market prices
    b. measures the retail prices of a fixed "market basket" of several thousand goods and services purchased by households
    c. measures the wholesale prices of approximately 300 items
    d. measures the prices of goods and services purchased by a particular household

14. We can use the implicit GDP deflator to:
    a. measure the changes in the aggregate price level
    b. measure the changes between two years
    c. both a and b
    d. none of the above

15. The direct contribution of the foreign sector to GDP is represented by:
    a. net exports
    b. net imports
    c. gross exports less capital inflows
    d. personal consumption

16. Gross exports are:
    a. purchases by domestic buyers of goods and services produced abroad
    b. currently produced goods and services sold to foreign buyers
    c. equal to imports minus net exports
    d. none of the above

17. The largest component of national income is:
    a. rental income of persons
    b. net interest
    c. compensation of employees
    d. proprietor's income
    e. corporate profits

18. Real GDP is a measure of output in terms of:
    a. current dollars
    b. constant prices from a base year
    c. average prices
    d. historical dollars

19. The sum of all factor earnings from current production of goods and services is:
    a. gross domestic product
    b. net domestic product
    c. personal income
    d. national income

20. The implicit GDP deflator is equal to:
    a. (real GDP/consumer price index) $\times$ 100
    b. (nominal GDP/real GDP) $\times$ 100
    c. (real GDP + nominal GDP) $\times$ 100
    d. (nominal GDP/producer price index) $\times$ 100
    e. none of the above

21. Assuming that profits are earned in the United States by a foreign-owned firm, then these profits:
    a. would be included in both GDP and GNP
    b. would be included in GNP but not GDP
    c. would only be included in GDP
    d. none of the above

22. Not included in the consumption component of gross domestic product are:
    a. Capital goods
    b. Consumer durable goods
    c. Nondurable consumption goods
    d. Consumer services

23. Assume that gross national product is $7500.5 billion, depreciation is $1000.8 billion, and indirect taxes are $449.2 billion. What is net national product?
    a. $6050.5 billion
    b. $6499.7 billion
    c. $7051.3 billion
    d. $8501.3 billion

24. Net national product is depicted as gross national product minus:
    a. depreciation
    b. national income
    c. personal income
    d. personal disposable income

25. Inventory investment is:
    a. never positive
    b. often negative
    c. can be positive or negative
    d. always positive

26. Business fixed investment:
    a. consists of purchases of a newly produced plant and equipment
    b. includes the building of single- and multi-family housing units
    c. is the change in business inventories
    d. is the smallest subcomponent of investment

27. The size of the underground economy in the United States is estimated to be:
    a. 2 percent of GDP
    b. more than 20 percent of GDP
    c. between 5 and 15 percent of GDP
    d. none of the above

28. Policymakers utilize GDP figures:
    a. to monitor short-run fluctuations in economic activity
    b. to observe long-run growth trends
    c. as a means to measure welfare
    d. both a and b
    e. all of the above

29. A new chain-weighted measure of real GDP:
    a. is quite different when compared to previous measures that used the base year method
    b. was introduced by the Bureau of Economic Analysis in 1995
    c. uses the average of prices in a given year and prices in the previous year instead of using prices in a base year as weights
    d. both b and c
    e. all of the above

30. In 1996, an advisory commission, appointed by the Senate Finance Committee estimated that, due to certain distortions, the CPI overstates inflation by:
   a. 1.1 percentage points per year
   b. 2.0 percentage points per year
   c. .25 percentage points per year
   d. .50 percentage points per year

Problems and/or Essay Questions:

1. Could disposable income ever be greater than national income? Explain!

2. Carefully define the term gross domestic product, and explain which transactions are/are not included in gross domestic product.

3. You are given the following information for 1997:
Sales to consumers of final goods	$100
Sales to firms of final goods	$175
Sales to the government of final goods	$ 75
Net exports (X)	$ 25
Change in business inventories	$ 10

   How much was GDP in 1997?

   If the change in business inventories had equaled <u>minus</u> 10 instead of plus 10, then how much would GDP have been in 1997?

4. Define the "inflation rate." If the values of the GDP deflator in 1986 and 1987 equaled 113.9 and 117.7, what was the inflation rate in 1987? Explain exactly what this information might mean to the average citizen. Finally, is this inflation rate a good measure of how an individual's cost of living changes?

5. Business cycles can be described in terms of the deviation of actual GDP from potential GDP. How? Use some historical examples in your explanation. What would happen to the gap between actual GDP and potential GDP if we learned that the "high employment" unemployment rate rose to 6% very recently?

6. GNP and GDP differ in the treatment of international transactions. Explain this difference.

7. One of the nation's most accurate measures of economic activity is GDP. This measure, however, is not without limitations. Describe these limitations.

8. Assume that the implicit GDP deflator rose from 55.3 in 1979 to 60.3 in 1980. Calculate the rate of inflation between those 2 years.

9. Define the "underground economy" and provide some examples.

10. Why is gross domestic product not a welfare measure? Give some examples.

11. Many economists and policymakers have argued that the CPI overstates increases in the cost of living. How does this affect the U.S. Treasury? Furthermore, explain the three major possible sources of the upward bias.

PART II: MACROECONOMIC MODELS
CHAPTER 3
CLASSICAL MACROECONOMICS (I): EQUILIBRIUM OUTPUT AND EMPLOYMENT

OVERVIEW

The chapters in Part II (Chapters 3-13) analyze the major macroeconomic models. Chapter 3 is the first of two chapters on the classical macroeconomic model and deals with the classical theory of output and employment.

After an introductory section that explains the background for the development of classical economics as an attack on the mercantilist position, the classical equilibrium model is presented. The building blocks of the classical system—the aggregate production function, the labor demand schedule, and the labor supply schedule—are derived. The production function, which is based on the technology of individual firms, is a relationship between the level of output and the levels of factor inputs. In the short run, changes in output come as the level of the labor input is varied, holding the capital stock constant. Therefore, the production function provides a relationship, which in the classical model determines output once we find the equilibrium level of employment. In the classical model, the forces of supply and demand in the labor market determine the quantity of labor employed.

The labor demand schedule shows the quantity of the labor input firms will hire for each level of the real wage, where in the aggregate, as well as for individual firms, an increase in the real wage will lower labor demand (see Figure 3.2). The labor supply schedule shows the aggregate amount of labor that individuals will supply at each level of the real wage. Under the assumptions made in the text, labor supply depends positively on the level of the real wage (see Figure 3.3). Equilibrium employment is determined at the point of intersection of the labor demand and supply curves. Equilibrium output is then determined using the production function relationships (see Figure 3.4).

With the above relationships (aggregate production functions, labor supply and demand schedules), the classical aggregate supply schedule is derived. The vertical aggregate supply schedule illustrates the supply-determined nature of output and employment in the classical system. The effects, in the labor market, of an increase in the aggregate price level are analyzed to show how the money wage must rise proportionally to restore equilibrium (see Figure 3.5). The real wage and, as a consequence, the level of employment are unchanged. Given the supply-determined nature of output in the classical system, factors, such as changes in the quantity of money, do not affect output.

Two assumptions implicit in this classical theory of output are:

(1) Perfectly flexible prices and wages; and

(2) Perfect information on the part of all market participants about market prices, in this case the relevant market price being the real wage.

We return to the discussion of these assumptions when other macroeconomic systems are discussed. We will also see in the next chapter that even within the classical system, if the money wage is not perfectly flexible, the aggregate supply schedule will not be vertical, and demand as well as supply factors will affect real output and employment. Keynesians stress demand factors as key determinants of cyclical output changes. New business cycle theorists, on the other hand, explain these output deviations by supply events, like changes in the technology or the oil shocks of the 1970s.

Techniques in Depth

1. The Classical Production Function

This function relates inputs to output. The inputs are labor (N) and capital (K). In the short run, capital is assumed fixed ($K = \bar{K}$). Assume output (Y) is related to these inputs as follows:

$$Y = 12N - N^2 + 3\bar{K}$$

where $\bar{K} = 12$ units. Therefore, in the short run, changes in output are determined by changes in the labor input:

$$Y = 12N - N^2 + 36$$

To better understand this function, consider the following table that gives values of Y for various values of N:

N	$Y = 12N - N^2 + 36$
0	36
1	47
2	56
3	63
4	68
5	71

Notice that this is <u>not</u> a linear relationship. The key to seeing this is that unitary increases in N cause ever-decreasing changes in Y. The marginal product of labor (MPN) tells how much output changes when one more unit of labor is employed:

N	MPN $= \Delta Y/(\Delta N = 1)$
0	–
1	47 – 36 = 11/1 = 11
2	56 – 47 = 9/1 = 9
3	63 – 56 = 7/1 = 7
4	68 – 63 = 5/1 = 5
5	71 – 68 = 3/1 = 3

If we graph *Y* and *MPN*, we see:

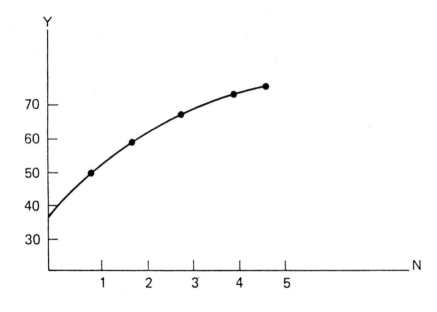

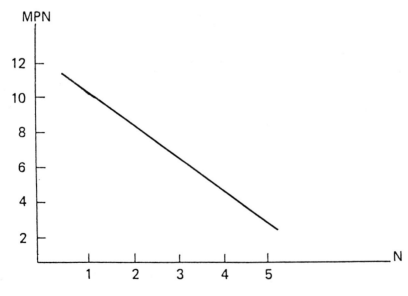

These graphs show that as more labor is used in conjunction with given technology and a given capital stock, output rises by successively less with each unit of labor input. This is commonly referred to as "diminishing returns."

2. The Classical Labor Demand Function

In the short run, the firm demands labor in order to produce output. In microeconomics, we learn that a competitive firm maximizes its profits if it hires that amount of labor that just makes the price paid per unit of labor (W) equal to the value derived from one more unit of labor. The latter equals the extra output it generates (MPN) times the price received per unit of output sold (P). Therefore, the firm maximizes profits if:

$$W = P \times MPN$$

In our example, the marginal product of labor is $(12 - 2N)$, if so, then:

$$W = P(12 - 2N)$$

Using a little algebra:

$$W/P - 12 = -2N, \text{ and finally}$$

$$N = 6 - \tfrac{1}{2}(W/P)$$

This expression for N shows that:

a. the amount of labor (N) that maximizes the firm's profits,
b. is inversely related to the wage paid (W), and
c. positively related to the price of the firm's product (P).

We can then fill in the following table:

W/P	$N = 6 - \tfrac{1}{2}(W/P)$
1.00	5½
2.00	5
3.00	4½
4.00	4
6.00	3
12.00	0

Therefore, the labor demand curve appears as on the graph. The student should reconstruct the N^d curve based on the following assumption of a more productive labor force: $MPN = 24 - 2N$.

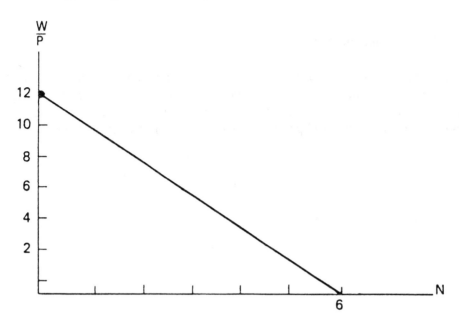

3. Exercises in Classical Output Determination

Let us take a simple, linear classical production system, given by the following equations:

$$Y = 36 + 12N$$

$$N^d = 40 - 1(W/P)$$

$$N^s = 4 + 5(W/P)$$

We can graph this system as follows:

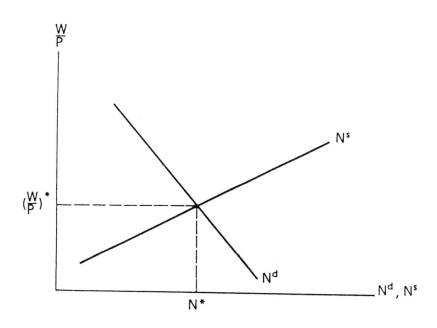

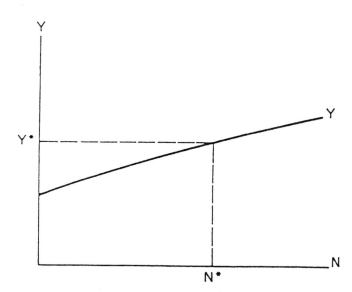

The first graph shows the values of N and W/P, which make labor demand equal to labor supply: N^*, $(W/P)^*$. The second graph of the production function translates the equilibrium amount of labor (N^*) into an amount of output, Y^*.

Mathematically, we can solve for N and Y if we know the value of W/P and we impose the equilibrium condition that $N = N^d = N^s$. Therefore,

$$N = 40 - 1(W/P) = 4 + 5(W/P)$$

Collecting the terms:

$$-1(W/P) - 5(W/P) = 4 - 40,$$

$$W/P = -36/-6 = 6$$

So, if $W/P = 6$, then

$$N^d = 40 - 1(6) = 34$$

$$N^s = 4 + 5(6) = 34, \text{ and}$$

$$N = N^d = N^s = 34$$

By the production function,

$$Y = 36 + 12N = 36 + 12(34)$$

$$= 36 + 408 = 444$$

What happens if workers' tastes change such that they prefer work over leisure (not induced by a change in wages but rather by a change in attitudes)? We can analyze this by rewriting the new "motivated" N^s function as:

$$N^s = 8 + 5(W/P)$$

Graphically, the results can be seen vividly. This change is exhibited by a parallel rightward shift in the N^s function (with a given N^d function) to $N^{s'}$:

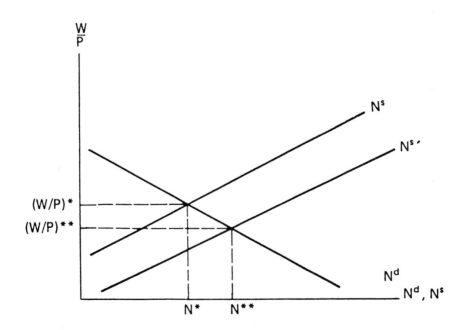

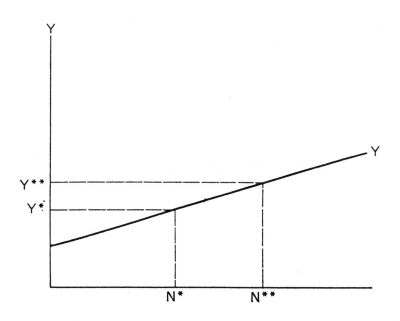

Here, we clearly see that the increased motivation of households towards work leads to lower real wages, higher equilibrium employment, and more output.

The mathematics can be used to check the solution. Trace through the same steps as above, but using the new N^s function:

$$N^d = N^s$$

$$40 - 1(W/P) = 8 + 5(W/P)$$

$$-1(W/P) - 5(W/P) = 8 - 40$$

$$W/P = -32/-6 = 5\ 1/3$$

$$N^d = 40 - 1(5\ 1/3) = 34\ 2/3$$

$$N^s = 8 + 5(5\ 1/3) = 34\ 2/3$$

$$N = N^d = N^s = 34\ 2/3$$

$$Y = 36 + 12N$$

$$= 36 + 12(34\ 2/3)$$

$$= 36 + 416 = 452$$

Classical Macroeconomics (I): Equilibrium Output and Employment   24

Self-Tests

Multiple-Choice Questions:

1. Macroeconomics is the study of forces that affect:
   a. output
   b. prices
   c. employment
   d. all of the above

2. It is a tenet of classical economics that even in short-run equilibrium:
   a. full employment must exist
   b. the interest rate equals the natural growth rate
   c. investment equals zero
   d. inflationary expectations equal zero

3. Classical economists believed:
   a. in bullionism
   b. in the need for state action to assist capitalism
   c. real factors determined the wealth of nations
   d. money determined the wealth of nations

4. Mercantilism:
   a. preceded classicism
   b. viewed money as wealth and a spur to economic activity
   c. believed state action was necessary to ensure markets existed for all goods produced
   d. both b and c
   e. all of the above

5. According to the classical labor supply function, an equiproportionate rise in wages and all product prices would:
   a. induce a substitution of labor for leisure
   b. induce a substitution of labor for goods
   c. cause the substitution effect to swamp the income effect
   d. have no effect on labor supply

6. In the classical model, the levels of output and employment are determined solely by:
   a. government deficits
   b. the money supply
   c. supply factors
   d. all of the above

7. In the classical model with the money wage on the vertical axis and employment on the horizontal axis, an increase in the price level will:
   a. shift the labor demand schedule to the left
   b. shift the labor supply schedule to the left
   c. shift both the labor supply and demand schedules to the left
   d. not cause either curve to shift

8. The classical aggregate supply curve is:
   a. vertical
   b. horizontal
   c. vertical, but only in the short run
   d. horizontal in the long run

9. In the classical model, a rise in real aggregate demand:
   a. raises real aggregate supply
   b. lowers real aggregate supply
   c. raises prices
   d. both b and c
   e. both a and c

10. The classical labor market assumes:
    a. an auction market
    b. perfectly flexible wages and prices
    c. perfect information
    d. all of the above

11. In the classical system, for a given money wage, a fall in the price level would cause the equilibrium level of:
    a. labor demand to fall
    b. labor supply to fall
    c. labor demand to rise
    d. labor supply to rise
    e. none of the above

12. The marginal product of labor (MPN) is:
    a. the increase in output per each increase in labor input
    b. the increase in labor inputs per each increase in output
    c. the relationship between the level of output and level of factor inputs
    d. the relationship of labor demand and the real wage

13. In the determination of labor supply:
    a. the firm maximizes profits
    b. the individual maximizes profits
    c. the firm maximizes utility
    d. the individual maximizes utility

14. A shift in the production function is a result of:
    a. a change in the capital stock over time
    b. technical change which alters the amount of output for given levels of input
    c. a change in the population
    d. both a and b
    e. both b and c

15. The classical model does not adequately explain:
    a. supply-side economics
    b. cyclical movements in output
    c. the labor market
    d. technological change

16. The term macroeconomics originated in (the):
    a. 1970s
    b. 1910
    c. 1930s
    d. 1950

17. The General Theory of Employment, Interest and Money was written by:
    a. Alfred Marshall
    b. John Stuart Mills
    c. A. C. Pigou
    d. John Maynard Keynes
    e. Adam Smith

18. The aggregate labor demand schedule is shown as:
    a. $N^d = f(W/P)$
    b. $N^d = f(P/W)$
    c. $N^s = g(W/P)$
    d. $N^s = g(P/W)$

19. In the classical system, the supply of labor is a function of:
    a. the marginal product of labor
    b. the money wage
    c. the money supply
    d. the real wage

20. In the classical system, labor demand:
    a. depends directly on the level of the real wage
    b. depends inversely on the level of the real wage
    c. is independent of the level of the real wage
    d. rises with an increase in the real wage

21. Classical economists:
    a. were in favor of governmental policies to ensure an adequate demand for output
    b. emphasized the role of monetary factors in determining output and employment
    c. stressed the self-adjusting tendencies of the economy
    d. none of the above

22. When plotted against employment, the marginal product of labor curve is:
    a. vertical
    b. horizontal
    c. upward sloping
    d. downward sloping

23. Factors that determine output and employment in the classical model are:
    a. the level of demand for investment goods by the business sector
    b. the quantity of money
    c. the level of government spending
    d. none of the above

24. The aggregate labor supply function is shown as:
    a. $N^d = f(P/W)$
    b. $N^s = g(W/P)$
    c. $N^s = f(P/W)$
    d. $N^d = g(W/P)$

25. According to the classical model, if there is a 5 percent decrease in both the nominal (money) wage and the price level, then the quantity of labor supplied will:
    a. also decrease by 5 percent
    b. increase by 5 percent
    c. remain the same as before the decrease
    d. decrease by less than 5 percent

26. The aggregate demand curve for labor is the:
    a. horizontal summation of the individual firms' demand curves
    b. vertical summation of the individual firms' demand curves
    c. horizontal summation of all the individual supply curves
    d. vertical summation of the individual firms' supply curves

27. According to the classical economists, the level of individual satisfaction depends:
    a. positively on real income and negatively on leisure
    b. negatively on real income and positively on leisure
    c. positively on both real income and leisure
    d. positively on real income only

28. An increase in population would:
    a. shift the labor supply curve to the right
    b. shift the labor supply curve to the left
    c. have no effect on the labor supply curve
    d. shift both the labor demand curve and the labor supply curve to the left

29. In the classical model, if a worker's money wage rose from $10 per hour to $20 per hour while all product prices doubled this worker would:
    a. supply more labor after the hourly wage increase
    b. supply less labor after the wage change
    c. supply the same amount of labor after the hourly wage increase
    d. demand less leisure

30. According to an auction market:
    a. all participants make decisions based on announced real wage rates
    b. all participants make decisions based on announced product prices
    c. labor and output are assumed to be traded in markets that are continually in equilibrium
    d. all of the above
    e. none of the above

Problems and/or Essay Questions:

1. Assume a production function is given by $Y = 14N - N^2 + 49$.
   Answer the following:
   a. What happens to *MPN* as *N* rises from zero to 7 units?
   b. No firm would ever produce in the range when *N* is greater than 7. Why?
   c. Why isn't capital more apparent in this specification?
   d. Assume production technology changes such that each unit of labor is more productive (better-educated employees for example). How would you alter the above production function? What would that do to the graphs of *MPN* and *Y*?

2. Consider a profit-maximizing firm whose *MPN* is given by: $MPN = 18 - 6N$. Assume it pays its workers $W = \$18$ per day and the price of its product is $P = \$12$:
   a. Graph this firm's labor demand function.
   b. How much labor will it employ?
   c. How much will it employ if:
      i. price falls to $10;
      ii. wage falls to $9; and
      iii. both i and ii occur simultaneously?

3. Assume that the classical labor market can be represented by the following equations:

$$Y = 20 + 8N$$

$$N^d = 5 - 4(W/P)$$

$$N^s = 4 + .5(W/P)$$

$$N^d = N^s$$

   a. Calculate values of *W/P*, N^d, N^s, and *Y* which put the labor market in equilibrium.
   b. How would this solution change if:
      i. firms rearrange their plants in such a way as to make workers doubly productive;
      ii. firms finally receive a long-awaited order of capital which doubles the size of the capital stock; and
      iii. a price freeze reduces every firm's prices by exactly 50 percent?

4. Explain the factors that determine output and employment in the classical system. What property or properties do these factors have in common? Illustrate graphically the relationship between each of these factors and the equilibrium levels of output and employment in the classical system.

5. What is a business cycle? Give three examples of events which might have caused business cycles in the 1970s and which are compatible with real business cycle models.

6. Explain the difference between endogenous and exogenous variables. Give examples from the classical model.

7. Explain the relationship between the production function and the labor demand curve.

8. How do real business cycle theorists explain cyclical movements in output?

9. John Maynard Keynes used the term classical to refer to virtually all economists who had written on macroeconomic questions prior to 1936 but more conventional modern terminology distinguishes between two periods in the development of economic theory before 1930. Name the two periods and cite some of the famous economists and their works during those periods.

10. Why is the labor supply curve positively sloped?

11. What two tenets of mercantilism did the classicists attack?

CHAPTER 4

CLASSICAL MACROECONOMICS (II): MONEY, PRICES, AND INTEREST

OVERVIEW

This chapter completes the analysis of the classical macroeconomic system. The first topic considered is the determination of the price level within the classical system. This requires a discussion of the role of money in the classical system as specified by the quantity theory of money. A classical aggregate demand schedule is derived and put together with the classical aggregate supply schedule to illustrate the determination of price and output in the classical system. According to the quantity theory of money, the level of aggregate demand is determined by the quantity of money. Changes in the quantity of money shift the aggregate demand schedule. Since the aggregate supply schedule is vertical, such shifts in the aggregate demand schedule will cause changes in the price level but will not affect the level of real output. The quantity theory of money is, therefore, a theory of how the aggregate price level is determined in the classical system.

The classical loanable funds theory of interest rate determination is presented. Within this context, the way in which the interest rate adjusts to stabilize aggregate demand when there are shocks to sectoral demands for output is illustrated. This is done by analyzing the effects of an autonomous fall in investment demand. Within the same context, the way in which this type of interest rate adjustment leads to a "crowding-out" effect when there is an increase in government spending in the classical model is illustrated. The classical economists' conclusions concerning monetary and fiscal policy can be summarized as follows. An increase (decrease) in government spending or decrease (increase) in the level of tax collections will cause the interest rate to rise (fall) with no effect on output, employment, or the aggregate price level. An increase (decrease) in the quantity of money will cause a proportionate increase (decrease) in the aggregate price level with no effects on the levels of output and employment. Any increase in government spending (or decrease in taxes) which is financed through an increased money supply, therefore, raises real aggregate demand. Furthermore, changes in tax rates are shown to affect the labor supply decision and, therefore, this type of fiscal policy shifts the aggregate supply curve and affects output and prices. A final section of the chapter summarizes the classical equilibrium system.

Techniques in Depth

1. Constructing the Classical Aggregate Demand (Y^d) Equation from the Equation of Exchange

    Recall the equation of exchange:

    $$M = kPY$$

Solve for Y and assume we are dealing only with equilibrium situations, so treat $Y^d = Y$:

$$Y^d = M/k \times 1/P.$$

For a moment assume $M = 400$, $k = ¼$. So,

$$Y^d = 400/¼ \times 1/P$$

$$Y^d = 1600 \times 1/P$$

So given $M/k = 1600$, the relationship between Y^d and P can be shown by the following:

P	Y^d
1	1600
1.5	800
3	400
8	100

M^d

We can also show it in a two-dimensional diagram.

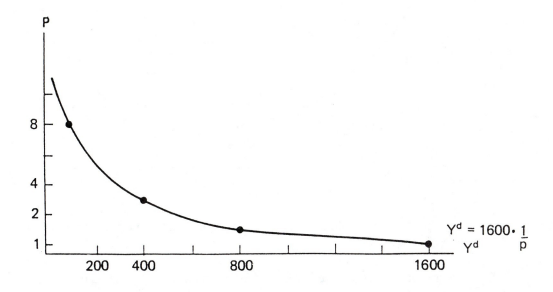

This one line is drawn assuming $k = ¼$ and $M = 400$. What if M was instead 800? Then,

$$Y^d = 800/¼ \times 1/P = 3200 \times 1/P$$

and, therefore,

P	Y^d
1	3200
2	1600
4	800
8	400

and,

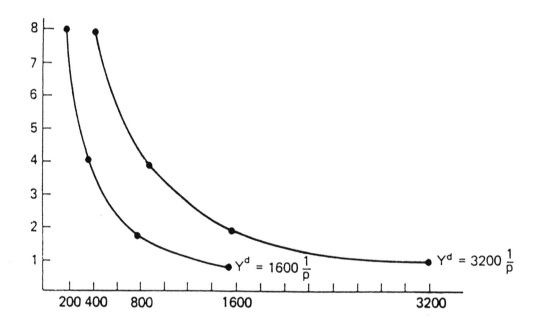

Notice how at a large value of M, the curve is further "out" (up and to the right). You should now see what happens if k changes from 1/4 to 1/8.

This curve is called an aggregate demand curve because M/kP is a measure of spending power. If M rises or k falls, one has more money than one wants to hold, so one spends it, i.e., demands more goods and services. Notice that if we superimpose the classical aggregate supply curve on the P, Y^d diagram, we see that the change in M from 400 to 800 affects only the price level. This graph is depicted on the following page.

You should now explain what happens if people start using credit cards more extensively. Assume the money supply stays equal to 400. (Hint: using credit cards should have some effect upon k.)

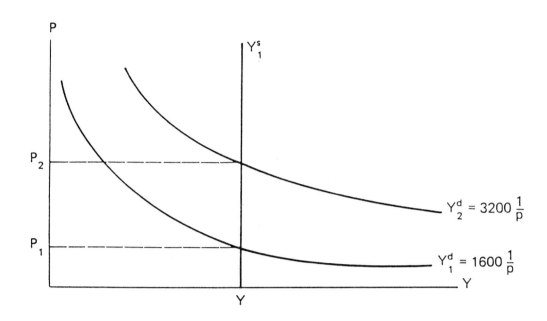

2. Interest Rates in the Classical Model

Assume that the demand for loanable funds is by: (1) the government which sells government bonds to cover its deficit $(g - t)$, and (2) firms which sell private bonds so as to buy investment goods (i).

Therefore, the total demand for loanable funds is $i + (g - t)$. Recall that investment is related inversely to interest rates (r) and positively to expected profits (R). In that case, we could write the demand for loanable funds as:

$$d = -200r + 50R + (g - t)$$

In a two-dimensional graph with d and r on the axes, this appears as:

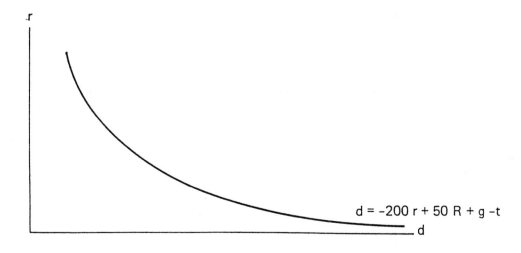

Anything which increases R or the government deficit increases d, given any interest rate, i.e.; it shifts the d curve to d'.

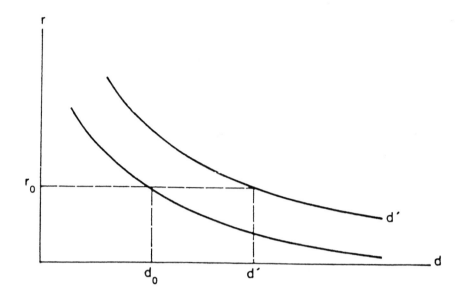

The supply of loanable funds comes from savers who will want to save more at higher interest rates. Saving also depends upon people's taste for current versus future consumption, or their frugality, f. Assume the supply of loanable funds is: $s = 300r + 50f$. This can be expressed as:

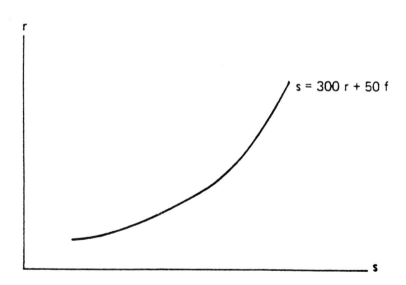

Increases in frugality yield more saving and, therefore, a larger supply of loanable funds at any interest rate (a shift to the right to s'):

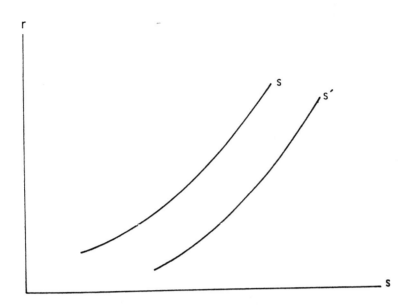

If the government attempts to spend more than it taxes, it demands more loanable funds. If households' frugality is unchanged, the model shows that the private sector must demand fewer loanable funds. Therefore, the extra government spending "crowds out" private spending. The interest rate performs this task. Let us see how. The increase in $g - t$ shifts the d curve rightward:

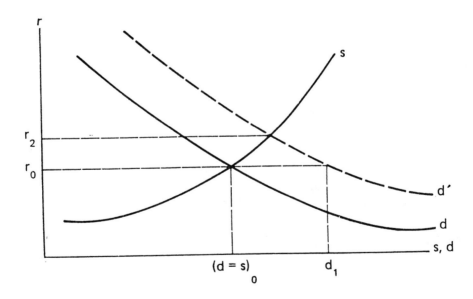

With unchanged r_0 initially, demand for loanable funds is d_1. But supply is still s_0. This excess demand ($d_1 > s_0$) forces up interest rates to r_2. This increase pushes down i and thus reduces private spending. Also, note that the rise in r to r_2 causes saving to rise. With income fixed, this means consumption demand falls. Therefore, the rise in g_t is an increase in aggregate demand that generates offsetting declines in both C and i. The end result is that the interest rate insures that aggregate demand will remain equal to the fixed aggregate supply.

The equilibrium solution shows a higher rate of supply and demand for loanable funds at a higher interest rate.

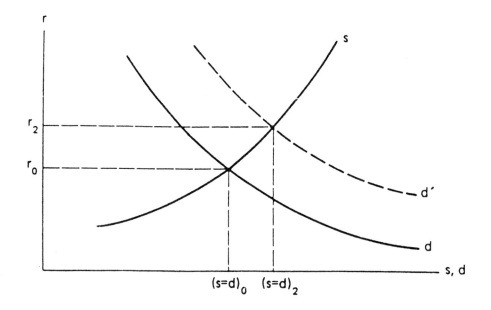

The student should now explain the effects of a reduction in expected profits upon s, i, r, and aggregate demand.

Self-Tests

Multiple-Choice Questions:

1. The starting point for the classical theory of money was the:
   a. law known as Say's Law
   b. equation of exchange
   c. loanable funds theory
   d. none of the above

2. The income velocity of money is more useful than the transactions velocity of money because:
   a. income is easier to measure than transactions
   b. we are more concerned with income than with transactions
   c. it is difficult to get a measure of the price of all goods traded
   d. all of the above

3. The equation of exchange:
   a. is a truism
   b. is a definition
   c. determines the price level
   d. all of the above

4. Velocity will increase with:
   a. longer pay periods
   b. more frequent use of charge cards
   c. prohibition of trade credit
   d. none of the above

5. Which of the following statements is true?
   a. Classicists thought output was demand determined
   b. The Cambridge equation focuses on the need for speculative money balances
   c. Income velocity is the reciprocal of the proportion of nominal income demanded to be held as money
   d. Classical economists thought that velocity was mostly determined by the money supply

6. Classical economists assume:
   a. bond demand is directly generated by investment spending
   b. bond supply rises when interest rates rise
   c. people's saving is generally devoted to bonds since money earns no return
   d. bond demand is independent of the interest rate

7. According to classical economics, an increase in government spending financed by bonds:
   a. has no effect on aggregate demand
   b. has no effect on the price level
   c. reduces consumption and investment spending
   d. all of the above

8. Classical economists stressed:
   a. the need for fiscal policy to stabilize real output
   b. the need for monetary policy to stabilize real output
   c. both a and b
   d. neither a nor b

9. An increase in the marginal income tax rates which is offset by an equal reduction in lump sum taxes should:
   a. raise aggregate demand
   b. reduce aggregate demand
   c. raise aggregate supply
   d. reduce aggregate supply

10. The Kemp-Roth bill was a supply-side program which:
    a. raised income taxes
    b. reduced business taxes
    c. called for an across-the-board income tax cut
    d. reduced taxes on saving accounts to reduce interest rates

11. During a hyperinflation:
    a. the price level reaches abnormally high rates of change
    b. the unemployment level reaches abnormally low levels
    c. the money supply reaches abnormally high rates of change
    d. a and c only
    e. all of the above

12. In the classical system, with no change in the supply of loanable funds, an increase in the demand for loanable funds will result in:
    a. no change in the interest rate
    b. a decrease in the interest rate
    c. an increase in the interest rate
    d. none of the above

13. Bond-financed government spending which pushes up the interest rate may result in:
    a. the crowding-out of private consumption
    b. the crowding-out of private investment
    c. both a and b
    d. neither a nor b

14. According to the quantity theory of money, a 5 percent increase in the money stock would lead to a 5 percent rise in the:
    a. level of nominal GDP
    b. level of real GDP
    c. price level
    d. none of the above

15. According to the classical system, saving is:
    a. a function of the price level
    b. a function of the real wage
    c. a function of the interest rate
    d. a function of income

16. According to the classical system, an increase in the money stock:
    a. shifts the aggregate supply curve to the right
    b. shifts the aggregate supply curve to the left
    c. shifts the aggregate demand curve to the left
    d. shifts the aggregate demand curve to the right

17. In the classical system, an increase in government spending can be financed:
    a. with taxes
    b. by selling bonds to the public
    c. by the creation of new money
    d. a and b only
    e. all of the above

18. In the classical system, successive increases in the money stock:
    a. raise both the price level and output
    b. raise the price level but leave output unchanged
    c. lower both the price level and output
    d. lower the price level but leave output unchanged

19. According to the classical model, a reduction in the marginal income tax rate would:
    a. only affect output
    b. only affect employment
    c. affect both output and employment
    d. neither affect output nor employment

20. The classical equilibrium system was attacked by (the):
    a. real business cycle theory
    b. Keynesian theory
    c. monetarist theory
    d. new classical theory

21. In the classical model, a reduction in the marginal income tax rate would:
    a. increase the after-tax real wage and decrease the labor supply
    b. increase the labor supply and decrease the after-tax real wage
    c. increase the after-tax real wage and leave the labor supply unchanged.
    d. decrease both the after-tax real wage and the labor supply
    e. increase both the after-tax real wage and the labor supply

22. Assuming that, over a given period, the value of transactions in current dollars were $5,000 billion and the money stock were $250 billion, then the transaction velocity of money would be:
    a. 20
    b. 15
    c. 200
    d. none of the above

23. In the classical model, a decrease in government spending shifts the
    a. supply of loanable funds to the right
    b. supply of loanable funds to the left
    c. demand for loanable funds to the right
    d. demand for loanable funds to the left

24. According to classical economists:
    a. monetary policy was not important since the quantity of money did not determine the price level
    b. stable money was a requirement for stable prices
    c. the quantity of money affected the equilibrium values of output, employment, and the interest rate
    d. none of the above

Classical Macroeconomics (II): Money, Prices, and Interest

25. According to the quantity theory, the quantity of money determines the:
   a. employment level
   b. interest rate
   c. level of real output
   d. price level
   e. none of the above

26. The Fisherian version of the quantity theory equation is:
   a. $M = kPy$
   b. $y = \underline{c} + \underline{i} + g$
   c. $MV = Py$
   d. $s = i + (g - t)$

27. In the classical system, saving:
   a. is shown as an upward-sloping function of the interest rate
   b. is plotted as a downward-sloping function of the interest rate
   c. provides the supply of loanable funds
   d. both $\underline{a}$ and $\underline{c}$

28. In the classical system, factors that determine the interest rate are:
   a. real saving
   b. the value of the government deficit
   c. real investment demand
   d. all of the above
   e. none of the above

Problems and/or Essay Questions:

1. Explain how an equation (like the equation of exchange) can be treated as an identity one minute and as an equilibrium the next.

2. If a new government policy encourages individuals to save more, the classical model predicts lower interest rates. What does it predict for consumption, investment, and aggregate demand? Assume this policy does not alter $g - t$.

3. In the classical model, the supply of money affects nominal aggregate demand but not the level or composition of real aggregate demand. Why not? Why doesn't a rise in money cause interest rates to change?

4. In classical economics, a rise in government spending may or may not raise real aggregate demand and the price level. Upon what does this depend?

5. A successful Kemp-Roth bill would have raised output and lowered prices after 1981. Why should it have those effects? Did it?

6. Fiscal policy may or may not affect output and employment (i.e., supply-side effects). Explain how a tax cut may or may not affect the supply side.

7. Explain the role of monetary policy in the classical system. Did classical economists consider monetary policy to be important? Why or why not?

8. Explain what is meant by hyperinflation.

9. In the nineteenth and early twentieth centuries the classicists did not pay much attention to the supply-side effects of changes in income tax rates. Why?

10. Classical economists stressed the self-adjusting tendencies of the economy. What are those self-stabilizing mechanisms?

CHAPTER 5

THE KEYNESIAN SYSTEM (I): THE ROLE OF AGGREGATE DEMAND

OVERVIEW

This is the first of four chapters on Keynesian macroeconomics. In this first chapter, a very simple version of the Keynesian model is analyzed. This simple model neglects money and interest rates as well as the effects of changes in the price level and the level of the money wage. Money and interest rates are introduced into the model in Chapter 6. Chapter 7 analyzes policy effects in the resulting version of the Keynesian model (the IS-LM curve model). Chapter 8 takes account of the effects of price and wage changes. There, the Keynesian theory of aggregate supply is considered.

The Keynesian model is introduced against the background of the chronic unemployment that was experienced by Great Britain beginning in the mid-1920s, and by other industrialized nations in the 1930s. Keynes' explanation for this unemployment was a deficiency of aggregate demand. This simple Keynesian model, where output is determined by aggregate demand, is then presented. A central notion of the Keynesian model is that for a level of output to be an equilibrium level requires that output be equal to aggregate demand in the simple model; this condition is expressed as:

$$Y = E = C + I + G$$

where Y is total output, E equals aggregate demand, C equals household consumption, I equals <u>desired</u> business investment expenditure, and G equals the government sector's demand for output.

Next, the determinants of aggregate demand (C, I, G) are explained. An important distinction to remember in this regard is that between <u>induced</u> expenditures, which are those which vary closely with current income, and <u>autonomous</u> expenditures, which change independently and cause equilibrium income to vary. Consumption is primarily an induced expenditure, while investment and government spending are components of autonomous expenditures. Changes in autonomous expenditures will, as they affect income, have an induced effect on consumer demand. This is the Keynesian multiplier process described in Section 5.5. Changes in the unstable investment component of autonomous expenditures will, therefore, have a destabilizing effect on consumer expenditures as well. A change in government spending or tax collections can be used by the policymaker to offset these effects of shifts in aggregate demand as illustrated by the example in Figure 5.8.

The Appendix to Chapter 5 incorporates imports and exports of goods and services into the Keynesian system. There we see why the Keynesian spending multiplier might be smaller for a country with a high import sensitivity to income. We also see that autonomous export and import changes have a multiple impact on equilibrium income.

Techniques in Depth

1. Aggregate Demand — A Numerical Example

We will write out the major components of the simple Keynesian model. On the left is the equation used in the textbook. On the right is a numerical example:

(1) $C = a + bY_D$ $C = 100 + .75\, Y_D$

(2) $I = \bar{I}$ $I = 250$

(3) $G = \bar{G}$ $G = 60$

Note: the bar over the variable means it is exogenous (or autonomous).

Here are three more equations of relevance:

(4) $E = C + I + G$ (definition)

(5) $Y_D = Y - \bar{T}$ $\bar{T} = 60$ (definition)

(6) $Y = E$ (equilibrium condition)

Let us begin with the consumption function (1) and the definition of Y_D (5). Using these together, we get:

$$C = 100 + .75(Y - 60)$$

$$C = 100 + .75Y - 45$$

$$= 55 + .75Y$$

The consumption-income relationship is:

Y	C
0	55
100	130
200	205
300	280
500	430

We can graph this as follows:

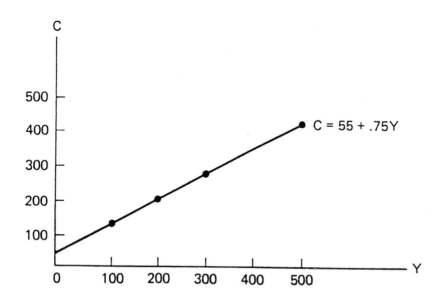

The $\bar{I}$ and $\bar{G}$ equations can be handled together. Notice that neither is related to income:

Y	$\bar{I}$	$\bar{G}$
0	250	60
100	250	60
200	250	60
300	250	60
500	250	60

We can graph these, too:

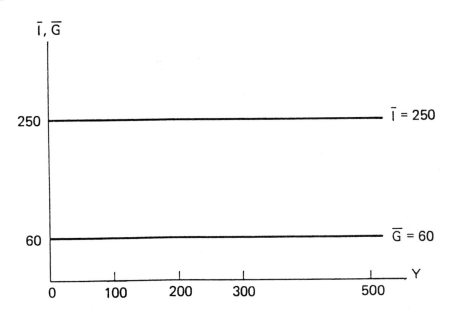

The aggregate demand equation (4) is:

$$E = C + I + G$$

If we add equations (1), (2), and (3), we get:

$$E = a + b(Y - T) + \bar{I} + \bar{G}, \text{ or}$$

$$E = 100 + .75(Y - 60) + 250 + 60$$

$$E = 100 + .75Y - 45 + 250 + 60$$

$$E = 365 + .75Y$$

The relationship between Y and E is:

Y	E
0	365
100	440
200	515
300	590
500	740

We can graph Y and E as:

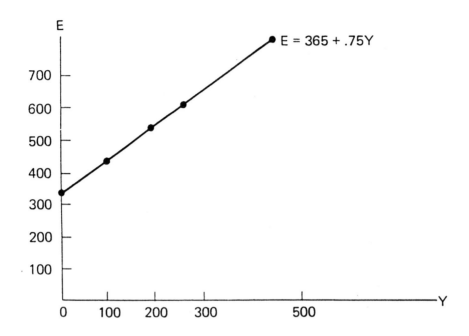

To check, we can reconstruct the C, $\bar{I}$, and $\bar{G}$ charts and simply add vertically, and we should get the same E equation.

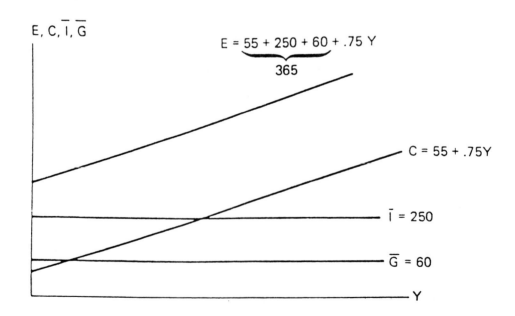

Note, on adding:

$$C = 55 + .75Y$$
$$+ I = 250 + 0Y$$
$$+ G = 60 + 0Y$$
$$\overline{}$$
$$E = 365 + .75Y$$

2. Solving for Equilibrium Output

We just showed that:

$$E = (a - bT) + \bar{I} + \bar{G} + bY$$

or numerically,

$$E = 365 + .75Y$$

Equilibrium occurs when $E = Y$, so at equilibrium:

$$Y = 365 + .75Y$$

Gather terms:

$$Y - .75Y = 365$$

now solve,

$$Y = 365/.25 = 1460$$

This says that the only income level that provides equilibrium is $Y = 1460$.

Suppose $Y = 1460$, then:

$$C = 55 + .75Y$$
$$= 55 + .75(1460)$$
$$= 55 + 1095$$
$$= 1150$$

Recall also:

$$\bar{I} = 250$$
$$\bar{G} = 60$$

So, if $Y = 1460$, then

$$E = 1150 + 250 + 60$$
$$= 1460$$

So, $Y = E$, if $Y = 1460$.

What if $Y = 1500$? Then:

$$C = 55 + .75Y$$
$$= 55 + 1125$$
$$= 1180$$

So,

$$E = 1180 + 250 + 60$$
$$= 1490$$

We see here that if $Y = 1500$, then $E = 1490$. This means $Y = 1500$ is <u>not</u> an equilibrium level of output. In this case, we would have less demand than output; that is, $10 worth of goods produced would not be sold. In this case, unintended inventory accumulation is $10. Therefore, $I_r = 260$, even though $I = 250$.

The student should see that for given values of the autonomous variables (in this case $\bar{I} = 250$, $\bar{G} = 60$, $T = 60$, and $a = 100$) and for a given MPC ($b = 75$), the simple model produces only one equilibrium level.

Let us see this point using the graphs. Recall from our example that $E = C + I + G = 365 + .75Y$.

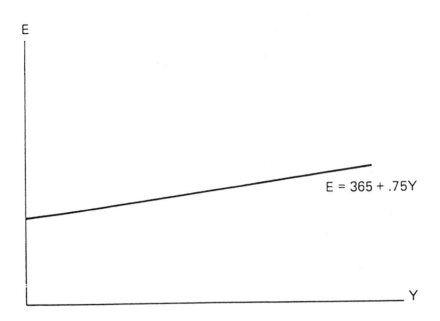

To find the place where $E = Y$ on this diagram, we must measure both Y <u>and</u> E on the vertical axis. To exaggerate this point, consider what line would have to fit in this space if it measures Y on the <u>vertical and horizontal</u> axes:

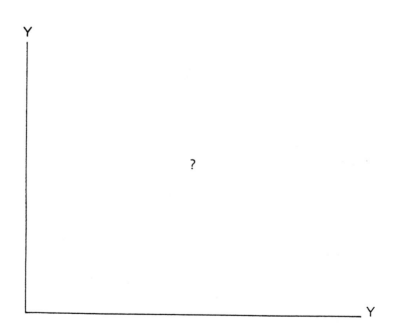

It must be the line: $Y = Y$. It looks silly, but one way of seeing what this line looks like is to rewrite this as: $Y = 0 + 1Y$. That is, the intercept is 0 and the slope is 1.0. It turns out this is a line with a 45 degree angle:

The Keynesian System (I): The Role of Aggregate Demand 50

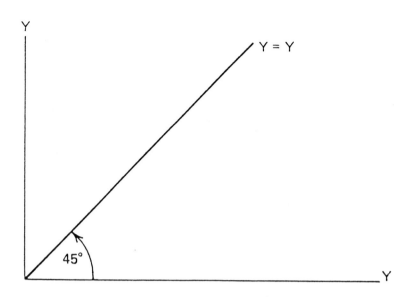

Now put both E and Y on the vertical axis:

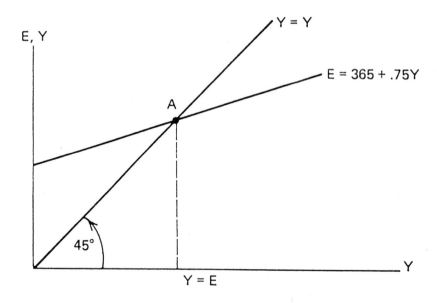

The only place where $Y = E$ is at the point marked A. Thus, there is only a single level of Y which equilibrates the model.

What if $Y = \hat{Y}$, at a level above $Y = E$?

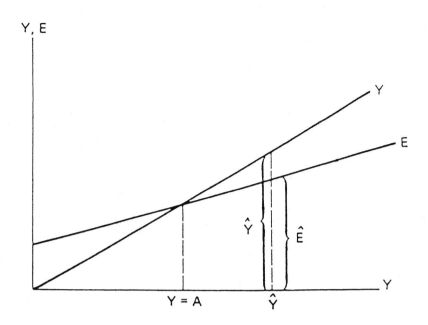

Notice at $\hat{Y}$ that the value of E evaluated at $\hat{Y}$ is $\hat{E}$. We see that $\hat{E} < \hat{Y}$. Therefore, demand is less than supply—this is <u>not</u> an equilibrium point.

3. Changes in Equilibrium Income

We need to backtrack some now. Using the same example, let us review several points.

In equilibrium:

$$Y = E$$

$$Y = C + I + G$$

$$Y = 365 + .75Y$$

$$Y = a - b\bar{T} + \bar{I} + \bar{G} + bY$$

Clearing terms:

$$Y - bY = a - b\bar{T} + \bar{I} + \bar{G}$$

$$Y(1-b) = a - b\bar{T} + \bar{I} + \bar{G}$$

$$Y = \frac{a - b\bar{T} + \bar{I} + \bar{G}}{1-b}$$

Putting in the numbers we used above:

$$Y = Y = \frac{100 - 45 + 250 + 60}{1 - .75}$$

$$Y = 365/.25 = 1460$$

We can easily see what might cause equilibrium output to change. Suppose firms grow pessimistic about future sales prospects and alter their investment plans. If $I = 250$ and they lower it to 200, then $\Delta I = -50$. Since

$$Y = (a - b\bar{T} + \bar{I} + \bar{G})/(1 - b)$$

the calculation is now:

$$Y = (100 - 45 + 100 + 60)/.25$$

$$Y = 315/.25 = 1260$$

The $\Delta I = -50$ has caused equilibrium Y to fall from 1460 to 1260. Therefore, $\Delta Y = 1260 - 1460 = -200$. A fall in planned I of 50 produced a fall in Y of 200. The spending multiplier is defined as:

$$\Delta Y/\Delta I = -200/-50 = 4.0$$

To consider this more simply, remember that equilibrium output is given by:

$$Y = \frac{1}{1-b}(a - b\bar{T} + \bar{I} + \bar{G})$$

If $b = .75$, then:

$$\frac{1}{1-b} = \frac{1}{1-.75} = \frac{1}{.25} = 4$$

$$Y = 4(a - b\bar{T} + \bar{I} + \bar{G}), \text{ or,}$$

$$\Delta Y = 4(\Delta a - \Delta b\bar{T} + \Delta \bar{I} + \Delta \bar{G})$$

The student should see that changes in a, $\bar{T}$, $\bar{I}$, or $\bar{G}$ will have multiple impacts on equilibrium Y. For example, a rise in a, I or G of \$100, increases Y by \$400. A fall in T of 100, however, increases Y by only \$300. This is because the change in T is always premultiplied by b before it is multiplied by $1/(1-b)$.

The Keynesian System (I): The Role of Aggregate Demand

Self-Tests

Multiple-Choice Questions:

1. According to Keynes, the high unemployment in Britain during the 1920s and 1930s was due to:
   a. high wages
   b. high unemployment benefits
   c. deficient demand
   d. insufficient supply-side incentives, especially high corporate tax rates

2. Keynes believed that classical economics provided neither the explanation nor the solution for the massive unemployment of the 1930s. He believed the fatal flaw of this theory was:
   a. its neglect of wages
   b. its neglect of aggregate demand
   c. its emphasis on money demand
   d. its emphasis on short-run output determination

3. Which of the following expressions of the simple Keynesian model is the equilibrium condition?
   a. $Y = C + I + G$
   b. $Y = C + S + T$
   c. $E + C + I + G$
   d. $Y = C + I_r + G$

4. Which of the following expressions of the simple Keynesian model is <u>not</u> an equilibrium condition?
   a. $Y = C + I + G$
   b. $I_r = I$
   c. $S + T = I + G$
   d. none of the above

5. Whenever unintended inventory accumulation exists:
   a. I plus G is greater than S plus T
   b. I is less than I_r
   c. I_r is less than I
   d. there is an excess demand for output

6. A researcher finds that the typical household, when given an extra $150, usually spends about $105 of it. If the consumption function is in the form of $C = a + bY_D$, then the researcher has found that:
   a. the average propensity to consume is .7
   b. the marginal propensity to consume is .7
   c. the average propensity to save is .3
   d. none of the above

7. An "autonomous" variable in the Keynesian model is one that:
   a. is primarily determined by income
   b. primarily determines the level of income
   c. hardly ever fluctuates
   d. all of the above

8. Keynes believed that investment spending:
   a. was highly unstable
   b. was heavily influenced by expectations
   c. was heavily influenced by interest rates
   d. makes income behavior subject to "fits and starts"
   e. none of the above

9. The Keynesian spending multiplier:
   a. would be higher for countries that save more at the margin than most countries
   b. would be lower for countries that save more at the margin
   c. would be lower for countries that consume more at the margin
   d. measures the multiple impact of an induced change in spending upon equilibrium output

10. If the MPC is 0.9, then an increase in taxes of 10 units will cause equilibrium income to fall by:
    a. 10 units
    b. 9 units
    c. 90 units
    d. 100 units

11. If government spending and taxes both rise by 50 units, then equilibrium income will:
    a. remain the same
    b. rise by 50 units
    c. rise by 200 units
    d. fall by 150 units

12. If the marginal propensity to consume (b) is exactly equal to the marginal propensity to import, then the Keynesian spending multiplier is:
    a. zero
    b. one
    c. infinity
    d. undefined

13. In the circular flow chart of income and output, saving is:
    a. an injection
    b. a leakage
    c. a flow
    d. both b and c

14. In the open-economy simple Keynesian model, the equilibrium condition is:
    a. $Y = C + I + G$
    b. $Y = C + I + G + X$
    c. $Y = C + I + G - Z$
    d. $Y = C + I + G + X - Z$

15. Assuming the consumption function is $25 + 0.9Y_D$, then the saving function will be:
    a. $25 + 0.1Y_D$
    b. $-25 + 0.9Y_D$
    c. $-25 + 0.1Y_D$
    d. none of the above

16. If a consumer's consumption function is shown as $C = 25 + .8Y$, where C is the level of consumption and Y is the level of his/her income, then at what point will his/her spending be equal to his/her income?
    a. 25
    b. 50
    c. 75
    d. 125

17. Assuming the saving function is $-25 + 0.2Y_D$, then the consumption function will be:
    a. $25 + 0.8Y_D$
    b. $25 + 0.2Y_D$
    c. $25 - 0.8Y_D$
    d. $25 - 0.2Y_D$

18. The slope of the Keynesian consumption function is equal to:
    a. the marginal propensity to consume
    b. the marginal propensity to save
    c. average propensity to consume
    b. average propensity to save

19. Assuming an *MPC* of 0.6, then if government spending increases by 30 and investment decreases by 15, by how much will equilibrium income increase?
    a. 18
    b. 15
    c. 37.5
    d. 75

20. Within the simple Keynesian model, if the *MPC* (*b*) were 0.75 then the tax multiplier ($\Delta Y/\Delta T$) would be:
    a. -3
    b. -1
    c. -4
    d. -5

21. The slope of the Keynesian saving function is equal to the:
    a. marginal propensity to consume
    b. marginal propensity to save
    c. marginal tax rate
    d. average propensity to save

22. The General Theory of Employment, Interest and Money was written by:
    a. Alfred Marshall
    b. A. C. Pigou
    c. James Tobin
    d. Milton Friedman
    e. John Maynard Keynes

24. In the simple Keynesian model with no government sector and no foreign trade sector, saving:
    a. must equal desired investment
    b. must equal realized investment
    c. must equal household consumption
    d. will always exceed actual investment

25. The equation for the balanced budget multiplier is shown as:
    a. $(1/1 - b) + (- b/1 - b)$
    b. $(1/1 - b) - (b/1 - b)$
    c. $(1/1 + b) + (- b/1 - b)$
    d. $(1/1 + b) - (b/1 + b)$
    e. none of the above

26. A decrease in taxes:
    a. shifts the consumption schedule upward
    b. shifts the consumption schedule downward
    c. decreases the level of disposable income
    d. does not shift the consumption schedule

27. According to Keynesian theory, which of the following is not a component of aggregate demand?
    a. Net exports
    b. Household consumption
    c. Personal saving
    d. Desired business investment demand
    e. Government purchases of goods and services

28. If the government wants to increase its spending on goods and services by $75 billion without increasing the overall level of aggregate demand, it should:
    a. increase taxes by $75 billion
    b. decrease taxes by $75 billion
    c. increase taxes by more than $75 billion
    d. increase taxes, but by less than $75 billion
    e. leave tax receipts unchanged

29. An increase in the demand for our exports will:
    a. have a contractionary effect on equilibrium income
    b. have an expansionary effect on equilibrium income
    c. not affect equilibrium income
    d. will always decrease domestic employment

Problems and/or Essay Questions:

1. Assume the following:

   $C = a + bY$ $a = 200$ $b = .09$
   $I = \bar{I}$ $\bar{I} = 100$
   $G = \bar{G}$ $\bar{G} = 300$
   $Y = E$
   $T = \bar{T}$ $\bar{T} = 300$

   a. Describe the relationship between income and:
      i. C,
      ii. I,
      iii. G, and
      iv. T.
   b. Which variables are exogenous?
   c. Which variables are endogenous?
   d. Which variables are policy variables?
   e. How much is the *MPC*?
   f. How much is the *APC*, if $Y = 400$? How much is the *APC*, if $Y = 1000$?
   g. Derive, and then graph the *E* function. Then show how it would differ if:
      i. $G = 400$, or
      ii. $b = .5$.
   h. What is the numerical difference between the slope of the *C* equation and the slope of the *E* equation? Explain your answer.
   i. What is the numerical difference between the intercept of the *C* equation and the intercept of the *E* equation? Explain your answer.
   j. What level of income equilibrates this model? What happens if $Y = 3500$?
   k. What is the value of the spending multiplier? What would be the value of the multiplier if $b = .5$ instead of .9?
   l. What happens to the equilibrium level of income if $\bar{G}$ rises by 100? Why does *Y* rise so much more than *G*?
   m. What happens to the equilibrium level of income if both $\bar{G}$ and $\bar{T}$ simultaneously rise by 100? Compare this result to the one found for l. If a rise in *G* raises spending, and a rise in *T* lowers it, why does this solution show a rise in *Y*?

2. What is the value of the simple Keynesian spending multiplier when:
   a. $MPS = .3$
   b. $MPC = .8$
   c. $\Delta C/\Delta Y = .6$
   d. $APC = .9$

The Keynesian System (I): The Role of Aggregate Demand   58

3. The following table describes the relationship between C and Y. What C equation underlies these numbers? Graph the equation.

Y	C
0	85
100	175
500	535
700	715
1400	1345

4. The simple Keynesian model assumes that if $Y \neq E$, then forces will automatically be set in motion which will make $Y = E$. Describe these forces. For example, suppose we know that equilibrium output equals $500, but today actual Y is $650. What is it that lowers actual Y to $500 eventually? Describe the process.

5. One criticism of the classical model is that it neglected a theory of how aggregate demand influences output. How has Keynes solved that problem?

6. Cite one or more historic examples about the effect of aggregate demand policy on the U.S. economy.

7. In the open-economy simple Keynesian model, what are the effects of an increase in exports and conversely, an increase in imports on equilibrium income?

8. Assume that $b = 0.75$ and autonomous investment increases by $100 billion. By how much will equilibrium income increase?

9. In the Keynesian consumption function, $C = a + bY_D$, what is represented by a and b?

10. Did Keynes' analysis differ from the classical view with respect to the relationship between investment and the interest rate?

11. Assume that $b = 0.8$, show the tax multiplier and the governmental expenditure multiplier. Next, Is there a relationship between the absolute value of tax and government expenditure multipliers? What are the effects of an increase in spending accompanied by an equal increase in taxes?

CHAPTER 6

THE KEYNESIAN SYSTEM (II): MONEY, INTEREST, AND INCOME

OVERVIEW

In the first part of this chapter, the role of money in the Keynesian framework is explained. Fundamental to Keynes' theory of money was his view that money affected income primarily via an effect on the interest rate. An increase in the money stock, for example, would lower the interest rate, which, in turn, would increase the level of aggregate demand and income. Therefore, to analyze the role of money, two linkages are considered: that connecting the interest rate to aggregate demand and that connecting money and the interest rate. To explain the latter, Keynes' theory of money demand must be considered in this part of the chapter. The most important feature of Keynes' theory of money demand was that, in addition to the transactions demand for money, he considered the demand for money as an asset—what he termed the speculative demand for money. This led Keynes to view the interest rate, which is the return to holding bonds (the alternative to holding money as an asset), as a determinant of money demand. Therefore, in contrast to the classical theory where money demand depends only on income, the Keynesian money demand function contains both the levels of income and the interest rate as arguments.

The second part of the chapter develops the Keynesian IS-LM model to illustrate the determination of equilibrium values of income and the interest rate for both the money and product markets. The LM schedule is upward sloping and shows the combination of income and the interest rate that clears the money market. The IS schedule is the downward sloping product market equilibrium schedule. After deriving these two schedules, the factors that determine whether each schedule is relatively steep or flat are considered. The factors that will shift the curves are also discussed.

For the case of the LM schedule, the discussion focuses on the relationship between the slope of the schedule and the value of the interest elasticity of money demand, as well as the manner in which the schedule shifts with changes in the money supply or shifts in the money demand function. The relationship between the interest elasticity of investment and the slope of the IS schedule is examined. Shifts in the IS schedule with changes in government spending, taxes, and autonomous investments are considered.

Techniques in Depth

1. The LM Equation

The LM equation is one way of showing, with graphical techniques, the equilibrium in the money market. That condition is stated algebraically as:

$$M_0^s = C_0 + C_1 Y + C_2 r$$

Let us give the following values to the parameters:

$$C_1 = .50$$

$$C_2 = -25.00$$

$$C_0 = 100.00$$

Therefore, $M_0^s = 100 + .50Y - 25r$. What we want to do is graph the money market in the following diagram:

To see clearly how to graph the LM curve, solve the money market equilibrium equation (MMEE) for r:

$$r = (1/C_2)M_0^s - (C_0/C_2) - (C_1/C_2)Y, \text{ or,}$$

$$r = (-M_0^s/25) + 4 + .02Y$$

This is the equation for a straight-line equation with intercept $[4 - (M_0^s/25)]$ and slope $(+.02)$. If $M_0^s = 400$, then the intercept would be $4 - (400/25) = 4 - 16 = -12$. Therefore, we would draw the LM equation with an intercept of -12 and slope of $.02$.

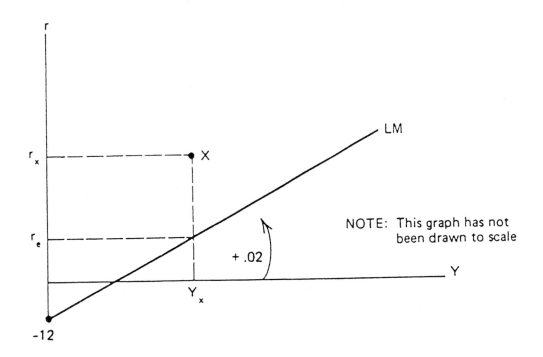

Since all points <u>on</u> the LM curve satisfy the MMEE, they are all the combinations of r and Y that produce money market equilibrium. But what about point X?

Obviously, this is not a point of equilibrium. But what do we know if the LM is as shown above, but the economy is producing Y_x and r_x? If Y_x was the right Y for equilibrium, then r_e would be the right r for equilibrium. But $r_x > r_e$! Chapter 6 explains that a <u>high</u> r produces <u>low</u> money demand. Therefore, we can conclude at point X there is an excess supply of money. We can conclude that the LM curve tells us that all combinations of r and Y above it are excess supplies; all combinations below it are excess demands:

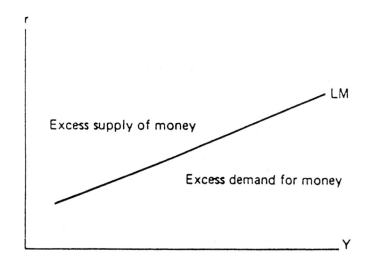

The LM equation may be very flat or very steep or somewhere in between. Recall the slope is given by $-(C_1/C_2)$, (also recall that C_2 is negative). Therefore, if C_1 is very large or C_2 is very small absolutely, then $-(C_1/C_2)$ is also a large number. Thus, the LM curve would have a large slope in that case. A large slope means that a relatively small change in Y entails a rather large change in r to maintain money market equilibrium.

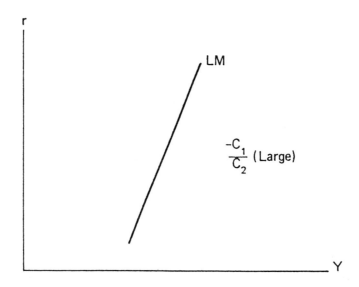

This LM curve is very steep if:

C_1, the <u>income</u> elasticity of money demand, is large, or
C_2, the <u>interest</u> elasticity of money demand, is absolutely small.

What is often called the "liquidity trap" occurs when C_2 is infinitely large in absolute value. Therefore, the liquidity trap results in:

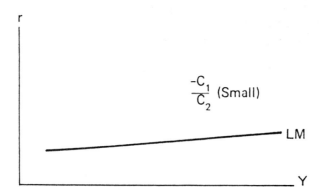

We can see why and how the LM curve <u>shifts</u> by focusing on the intercept term: $(-C_0/C_2) + (M_s/C_2)$. In our graph, the values of C_0, C_2, and M^s were 100, −25, and 420, respectively. Therefore, the intercept equals $(-100/-25) + (420/-25) = 4 - 16 = -12$. If the money supply rises to 500, then the intercept becomes:

$$(-100/-25) + (500/-25) = 4 - 20 = -16$$

Therefore, a rise in the money supply is shown as:

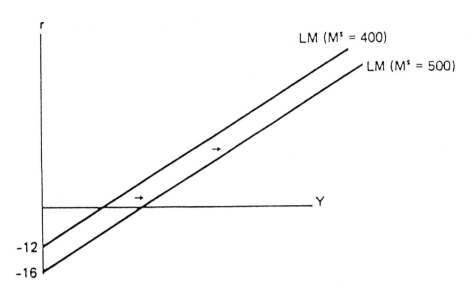

This is a parallel shift, since the rise in M_0^s has no effect on the slope of LM.

Reconsider the meaning of the term C_0. It embodies all things that affect M^d which are unrelated to Y or r. For example, the movement to a cashless society might lower M^d. We can model this event by showing it as a reduction in C_0. For example, if C_0 falls from 100 to 75, then the intercept is:

$$(-75/-25) + (400/-25) = 3 - 16 = -13$$

So, we can show this kind of exogenous <u>drop</u> in money demand as:

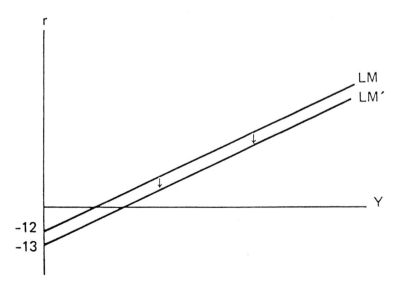

The Keynesian System (II): Money, Interest, and Income 64

2. The IS Equation

The IS equation is the goods market equilibrium. Below are the equations we used in Chapter 5 to describe the workings of the goods market.

(1) $C = a + bY_D$ $C = 100 + .75Y_D$

(2) $I = \bar{I}$ $\bar{I} = 250$

(3) $G = \bar{G}$ $\bar{G} = 60$

(4) $E = C + I + G$

(5) $Y_D = Y - \bar{T}$ $\bar{T} = 60$

(6) $Y = E$

Now, we will generalize the model a little by specifying the role of interest rates in affecting investment spending. We will replace equation (2) with

(2') $I = \bar{I} - dr$ $I = 350 - 10r$

The parameter d (which corresponds to i_0 in the Appendix to Chapter 6) describes how much a rise in interest rates reduces I. In this case, a rise in r by 1 percentage point reduces I by $10.

Using algebra to add $C + I + G$ and setting this equal to Y:

$$Y = 100 + .75(Y - 60) + 350 - 10r + 60$$

$$Y = 100 - 45 + 350 + 60 + .75Y - 10r$$

$$Y - .75Y = 465 - 10r$$

$$Y = [465/(1 - .75)] - [10/(1 - .75)]r$$

and finally,

$$Y = 1860 - 40r$$

So that we don't lose track of the variables, in the terms of our model:

$$Y = \frac{a - b\bar{T} + \bar{I} + \bar{G}}{1 - b} - \left(\frac{d}{1 - b}\right)r$$

The student should see that these two versions are equivalent and are both forms of the goods equilibrium equation. Now, if we want to plot this IS curve on the same diagram as the LM curve, let us use the algebra to solve for r in terms of Y:

$$r = \frac{a - b\bar{T} + \bar{I} + \bar{G}}{d} - \left(\frac{1-b}{d}\right)Y$$

and using our numerical example, this is:

$$r = 465/10 - (.25/10)Y, \text{ or}$$

$$r = 46.5 - .025Y$$

This is in the form of a linear equation with intercept of $(a - b\bar{T} + \bar{I} + \bar{G})/d = 46.5$ and slope $[(1-b)/d] = -.025$. The IS curve appears as:

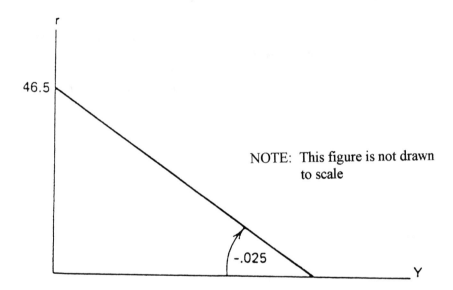

NOTE: This figure is not drawn to scale

It is clear that the parameters b and d determine the degree of the negative slope. If the MPC (b) is large or if the interest sensitivity of I (d) is large, then $[(1 - b)/d]$ is absolutely small and the IS curve is very flat.

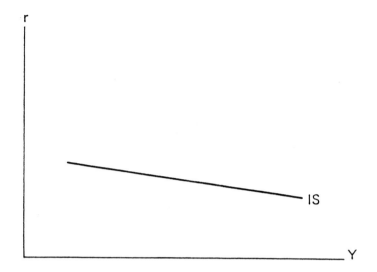

In this case, it takes a very large change in Y, given a change in r, to restore goods market equilibrium. Of course, the IS curve would be very steep if b and/or d is small absolutely.

The point X on the next diagram is a market outcome with r_x and Y_x assumed to be the current values or r and Y:

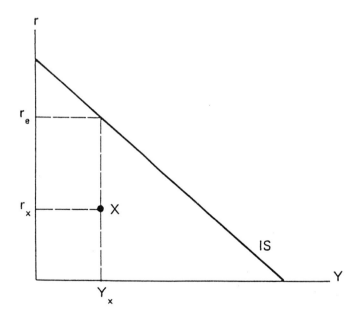

What is the state of the goods market at X? We can determine this by following the same steps we used in a similar exercise with the LM equation. Assume Y_x is the equilibrium value of Y. For the goods market to be in equilibrium, then the interest rate would be r_e. Since $r_x < r_e$, the interest rate today is too <u>low</u> to provide a goods market equilibrium. If r is too low, then according to equation (2'), I is too <u>high</u>. So, there must be more demand for goods than supply. This is called an excess demand for goods. We can now label the quadrant accordingly:

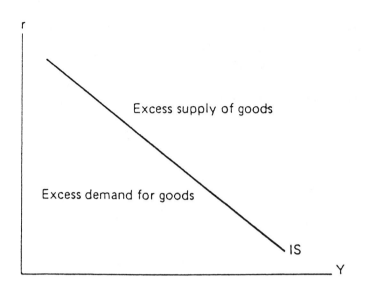

The IS curve will shift in a parallel fashion (with one exception) if the intercept changes. Recall the intercept for the model:

$$(a - b\bar{T} + \bar{I} + \bar{G})/d$$

If a, $\bar{I}$, or $\bar{G}$ rises or if $\bar{T}$ falls, the intercept rises and the IS curve shifts rightward:

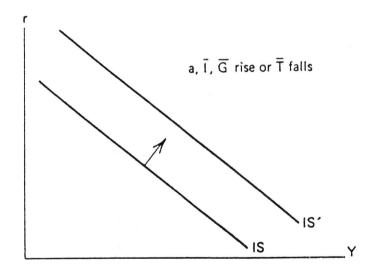

This is a parallel shift, since the slope $-[(1 - b)/d]$ is not changing. For example, if $\bar{T}$ falls from $60 to $40, then the intercept equals:

$$[100 - .75(40) + 350 + 60]/d = 48.0$$

Therefore, the reduction in $\bar{T}$ has raised the intercept from 46.5 to 48.0 in the manner shown above.

3. Model Stability

If we are willing to assume that the real economy is stable, then a useful working model of the economy should, when not in equilibrium, move towards equilibrium automatically. Here, we consider how the simple Keynesian IS-LM model behaves in disequilibrium.

Recall how the IS and LM curves sliced the r, Y quadrant into disequilibrium levels:

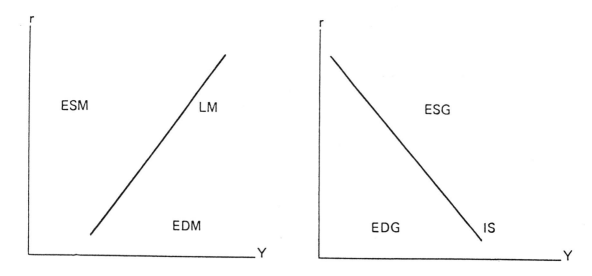

Putting these two curves together, we get four quadrants:

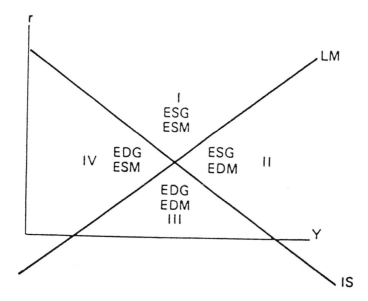

In each of the four quadrants we have different disequilibrium situations:

I: Dual excess supplies
II: ESG and EDM
III: Dual excess demands
IV: EDG and ESM

The Keynesian System (II): Money, Interest, and Income

To see how the economy responds in each of these quadrants, we make two reasonable assumptions:

(1) An EDG always causes firms to produce more, i.e., EDG → $Y\uparrow$ and conversely, ESG → $Y\downarrow$.

(2) An EDM causes people to sell bonds, and this puts pressure on interest rates to rise, i.e., EDM → $r\uparrow$ and conversely, ESM → $r\downarrow$.

Using these assumptions, we can now superimpose arrows of change in each of the four quadrants. An arrow going right (→) or left (←) implies output will either rise or fall. An arrow going up (↑) or down (↓) implies a tendency for interest rates to rise or fall.

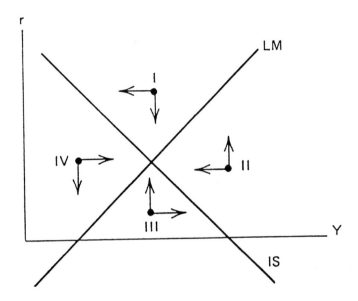

We can replace these two-way arrows with rough directionals. The student should view these as forces pushing r and Y towards the intersection of IS and LM in a counterclockwise direction:

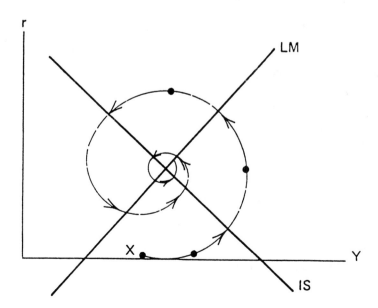

If r and Y start at point X, the "gravitational" tendencies of the model (shown in the previous diagram) reveal the automatic forces working on r and Y as they are pulled towards the values that simultaneously equilibrate the two markets. [Note that this works as long as the IS curve is fairly vertical (d is relatively small) and the LM curve is fairly horizontal (C_2 is large). Assuming the opposite leads to an unstable model in which the path moves away from the equilibrium point.]

Self-Tests

Multiple-Choice Questions:

1. According to Keynes, money affects income:
   a. because it shifts the IS curve
   b. because it causes people to feel wealthier and, therefore, they spend more
   c. because money earns a high rate of return
   d. via an effect on interest rates

2. In reality, interest rates affect which of these categories of spending?
   a. Housing and construction
   b. Plant and equipment
   c. Government spending
   d. All of the above

3. According to Keynes, if an individual had an excess supply of money, it also meant he or she:
   a. had an excess demand for goods
   b. had an excess demand for bonds
   c. had an excess demand for labor
   d. all of the above

4. For holders of outstanding perpetuities, a rise in market interest rates implies a commensurate:
   a. fall in bond prices and a capital loss
   b. fall in bond prices and a capital gain
   c. rise in bond prices and a capital gain
   d. rise in bond prices and a capital loss

5. A rise in the level of the money supply generates:
   a. an excess supply of money
   b. a larger demand for bonds
   c. a higher market price for bonds
   d. a lower market interest rate
   e. all of the above

6. A simultaneous rise in interest rates and income implies:
   a. a movement along a given LM curve
   b. a rightward shift of the LM curve
   c. a leftward shift of the LM curve
   d. a rise in the money supply, ceteris paribus

7. The IS curve shifts to the right if:
   a. taxes rise
   b. government spending falls
   c. the money supply rises
   d. investment spending increases exogenously

8. If the economy temporarily has an excess demand for money:
   a. the LM curve will shift to equilibrate the market
   b. the IS curve will shift to equilibrate the market
   c. there is a tendency for r to rise
   d. there is a tendency for Y to rise

9. We know the equilibrium values of r and Y have been obtained if:
   a. these values lie on a given IS curve
   b. these values lie on a given LM curve
   c. there is no tendency for r and Y to change
   d. the values of all exogenous variables are momentarily fixed
   e. all of the above

10. A cut in taxes would cause:
    a. a shift to the right in the LM schedule
    b. a shift to the left in the LM schedule
    c. a shift to the right in the IS schedule
    d. a shift to the left in the IS schedule

11. If the value of the MPC (b) were .8, then an increase in government spending of 10 units would cause the IS schedule to shift to the right by:
    a. 5 units
    b. 9 units
    c. 10 units
    d. 50 units
    e. 100 units

12. Which of the following statements is most true about money, especially M1?
    a. Its market interest rate is zero
    b. Its market interest rate is not zero but is fixed
    c. Its market interest rate is not fixed but changes less than the bond return
    d. None of the above are true

13. If the money demand function is given by

    $$Md = 100 + .05Y - 25r$$

    then an increase in the money supply of 5 units will shift the LM curve:
    a. to the right by 5 units
    b. to the left by 5 units
    c. to the right by 25 units
    d. to the left by 100 units
    e. to the right by 100 units

14. According to Keynes, one of the reasons people hold money is to be ready in case of unexpected expenditures. This is called:
    a. speculative demand
    b. transactions demand
    c. precautionary demand
    d. money demand

15. In the case that the interest elasticity of money demand is very large, people would hold any increase in money balances with only a small decrease in the interest rate. Keynes called this:
    a. liquidity preference
    b. liquidity constraint
    c. liquidity shift
    d. liquidity trap

16. At any point on the LM curve:
    a. product market equilibrium exists
    b. labor market equilibrium exists
    c. money market equilibrium exists
    d. both the goods market and the money market are needed in order to achieve equilibrium

17. According to Keynes, the precautionary demand for money:
    a. varies positively with income
    b. varies negatively with income
    c. varies positively with the interest rate
    d. none of the above

18. In the Keynesian system, total money demand is shown as:
    a. $Md = Y(L + r)$
    b. $Md = L(Y - r)$
    c. $Md = L(Y, r)$
    d. $Md = L(Y \times r)$

19. According to Keynes, all financial assets could be divided into:
    a. liquid and near-liquid assets
    b. durable goods and nondurable goods
    c. corporate equities and bonds
    d. money and all nonmoney assets

20. If the value of the MPC were 0.6, then a fall in taxes of 50 units would cause the IS schedule to shift to the left by:
    a. 50 units
    b. 75 units
    c. 100 units
    d. 125 units

21. Assuming that money demand is highly interest elastic, then the money demand schedule is:
    a. relatively steep
    b. relatively flat
    c. always negatively sloped
    d. positively sloped

22. A fall in the interest rate will shift the:
    a. IS curve to the right
    b. IS curve to the left
    c. LM curve to the right
    d. none of the above

23. If the consumption function is $C = 100 + 0.75Y_D$, then an increase in taxes of 25 units will shift the IS schedule to the left by:
    a. 75 units
    b. 50 units
    c. 100 units
    d. 25 units

24. The IS curve is the:
    a. money market equilibrium schedule
    b. labor market equilibrium schedule
    c. product market equilibrium schedule
    d. stock market equilibrium schedule

25. Assuming that money demand is completely interest insensitive, then the
    a. IS schedule will be vertical
    b. IS schedule will be horizontal
    c. LM schedule will be horizontal
    d. LM schedule will be vertical

26. A shift in the money demand function that decreases the amount of money demanded at given levels of income and the interest rate shifts the:
    a. LM curve downward and to the left
    b. LM curve upward and to the right
    c. IS curve to the left
    d. IS curve to the right

27. Points to the left of the LM schedule show that:
    a. the amount of money demanded exceeds the amount of money supplied
    b. the amount of money supplied exceeds the amount of money demanded
    c. saving plus taxes will exceed investment plus government purchases
    d. investment plus government purchases will exceed saving plus taxes

28. The condition for product market equilibrium can be shown as:
    a. $Y = C + I + G$
    b. $I + G = S - T$
    c. $I(r) + G = S(Y - T) + T$
    d. both a and c
    e. all of the above

29. In the equation $M^d = c_0 + c_1 Y - c_2 r$, the parameter c_1 is the:
    a. increase in money demand per unit increase in income
    b. decrease in money demand per unit increase in income
    c. amount by which money demand declines per unit increase in the interest rate
    d. amount by which money demand increases per unit decrease in the interest rate

30. According to the Keynesian theory, an exogenous fall in the money supply is most likely to:
    a. raise interest rates, investment, and aggregate demand
    b. lower interest rates, investment, and aggregate demand
    c. raise interest rates and lower investment and aggregate demand
    d. lower interest rates and raise investment and aggregate demand

Problems and/or Essay Questions:

1. The LM equation is given by

$$Ms = C_0 + C_1 Y + C_2 r$$

   where

$$C_0 = 900$$

$$C_1 = 3.5$$

$$C_2 = -100$$

   Assume that M_0^s originally is 600. Assume also that the following values of Y occur during the next 5 years: 100, 200, 300, 400, 500.

   a. What interest rate equilibrates the money market in each of those years?
   b. If the money supply rises to 900 in year 2, then what interest rate will generate money market equilibrium in year 2?
   c. Describe what happens to the above LM curve (given $M_0^s = 400$) if
      i. people decide to hold larger amounts of money, regardless of Y and r.
      ii. the demand for money grows more sensitive to changes in the interest rate.
      iii. the demand for money grows more sensitive to changes in Y.

2. Derive the LM equation mathematically, and explain what causes it to shift. What causes it to be steep or flat?

3. Suppose the market price of a bond is $120. If you are promised $6 per year in interest, what is the market return on the bond? If instead you buy the bond today for $60, what is the market interest rate? If you firmly believe the market return on this will be 3% next year, will you buy this bond today at $60? If you believe the market return will rise to 15%, will you buy it today at $60 or at $100? Explain your answers.

4. Assume the following equations characterize the goods market:

    $C = 250 + .90YD$

    $I = 100 - 5r$

    $\bar{G} = 300$

    $\bar{T} = 300$

    a. Derive the IS curve. Plot it.
    b. If equilibrium r equals 10, how much is equilibrium Y?
    c. Describe what happens to the IS cur$\underline{ve}$ if:
        i. firms get more bullish and raise I to $\underline{250}$.
        ii. households get more squeamish, and C falls to 150.
        iii. firms are more sensitive to interest rates, and d rises absolutely to 20.

5. Explain in words why the IS curve slopes downward to the right.

6. Describe the state if disequilibrium that exists at each point noted with an X below.

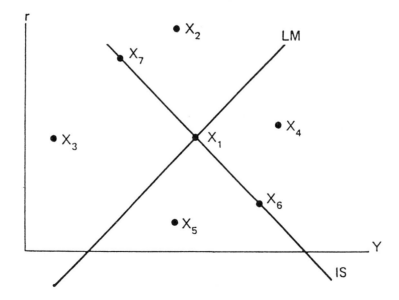

Then, describe the movement in both r and Y that should occur from each point.

7. Define M1. Economists have found that the demand for M1 is slightly less responsive to changes in interest rates since 1980. Explain why.

8. Explain the case in which the Keynesian demand function is similar to the classical money demand function.

9. Explain Keynes' precautionary demand for money. Give some examples.

10. Explain Keynes' liquidity preference.

11. What possible influence does the interest rate have on residential construction investment?

CHAPTER 7

THE KEYNESIAN SYSTEM (III): POLICY EFFECTS IN THE IS-LM MODEL

OVERVIEW

In Chapter 6, the IS-LM curve model was developed. The factors that will shift each of the curves were examined, and the determinants of the slopes of the two curves were considered. In this chapter, the IS-LM curve model is used to analyze the effects of various policy actions on the equilibrium levels of income and the interest rate.

In the first section of the chapter, the way in which changes in the money stock and shifts in the money demand function affect the LM schedule, income and the interest rate is illustrated. In this section, the following results are derived:

(1) An increase (decrease) in the money stock will cause the rate of interest to decline (rise) and the level of income to rise (fall).

(2) An upward (a downward) shift in the money demand function, which is an increase (decrease) in the amount of money demanded for given levels of income and the interest rate, will cause the interest rate to rise (fall) and income to fall (rise).

(3) An increase (decrease) in the level of government spending will cause both the levels of income and the interest rate to rise (fall).

(4) An increase (decrease) in taxes will cause both income and the interest rate to fall (rise).

These results are summarized in Table 7.1. One important point to note concerning fiscal policy effects is that the change in income for a given change in either G or T is smaller in the IS-LM curve model than in the simple Keynesian model presented in Chapter 5. To see why, consider the effects of an increase in government spending. As income starts to rise due to this increase in aggregate demand, the interest rate must rise to maintain equilibrium in the money market (as the IS schedule shifts upward along the LM schedule). This increase in the interest rate causes a decline in investment that offsets part of the expansionary effect of the rise in government spending. It is because of this "crowding out" of investment that the fiscal-policy-induced rise in income will be less in the IS-LM curve model than in the simple Keynesian model of Chapter 5.

The second section of the chapter examines the relationship between monetary and fiscal policy effectiveness and the slopes of the IS and LM curves. By effectiveness is meant the size of the effect on income of a given change in the policy variable. Fiscal policy is shown to be more effective the steeper the IS schedule and the flatter the LM schedule. Monetary policy is shown to be most effective where the LM schedule is steep and the IS schedule is flat. Extreme cases, such as the vertical IS curve case, where monetary policy is completely ineffective, are also analyzed. The results from this section are summarized in Table 7.2. Our conclusion drawn is that the monetary-fiscal policy mix matters, especially for investment spending. Since easy money leads to lower interest rates and more investment spending, while fiscal policies. These policies appear to have benefited the economy in the early 1960s; Keynesians have criticized Reagan's programs for doing the opposite.

Techniques in Depth

1. Solving the IS-LM Model: Fiscal Effects

Chapter 7 shows how changes in numerous autonomous variables will disrupt an existing equilibrium and produce changes in output and interest rates in the IS-LM model. In Chapter 6, we showed that the IS curve represents the equilibrium in the commodity market and it can be expressed as:

$$r = \frac{a - b\bar{T} + \bar{I} + \bar{G}}{d} - \frac{(1-b)}{d}Y$$

The LM equation, the money market equilibrium statement, is expressed as:

$$r = (1/C_2)M_0^s - (C_0/C_2) - (C_1/C_2)Y$$

We showed in Chapter 6 that:

(1) increases in a, $\bar{I}$, $\bar{G}$ and decreases in $\bar{T}$ shift the IS curve rightward;

(2) increases in M_0^s and decreases in C_0 shift the LM curve rightward;

(3) a large value of b or a large value of d makes for a flatter IS curve; and

(4) a small value of C_1 or a large value of C_2 makes for a flatter LM curve.

Let us see how a solution emerges in this model.

First, consider normal values of C_1, C_2, b and d, and trace the effects of an increase in G on r and Y. We begin with full equilibrium:

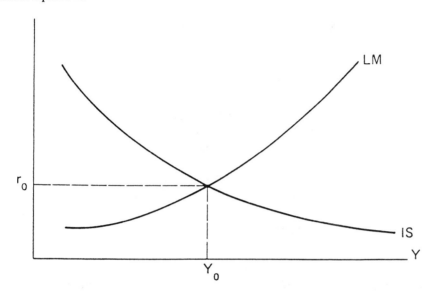

The rise in G shifts the IS rightward:

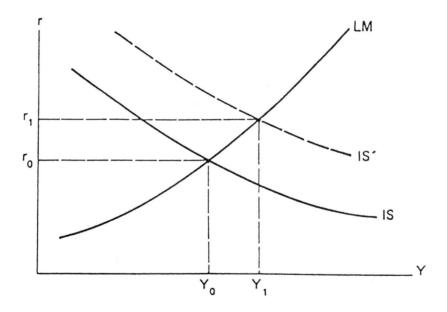

It is easy to see that the new equilibrium position has a higher Y and r. To see why, let us trace the steps:

(1) The rise in G means that firms produce Y_0; there is an immediate excess demand for goods (EDG).

(2) Firms will respond by producing more:

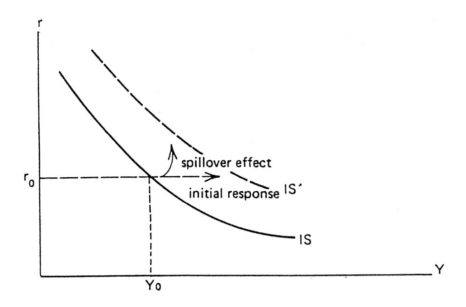

(3) But as Y rises, there is a spillover effect into the money market, as individuals and firms demand more transactions balances. Since M_0^s is unchanged, the rising Y causes an excess demand for money (EDM).

(4) This puts pressure on r to rise:

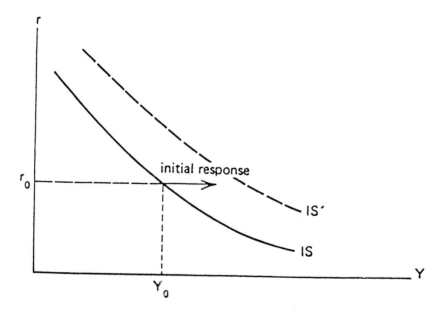

The previous diagram shows why there is pressure leading to higher Y and r. But this is not the end!

(5) The rise in r has a feedback effect back into the goods market, since a rise in r leads to less I. The fall in I produces a smaller EDG and offsets or reduces the pressure for Y to rise:

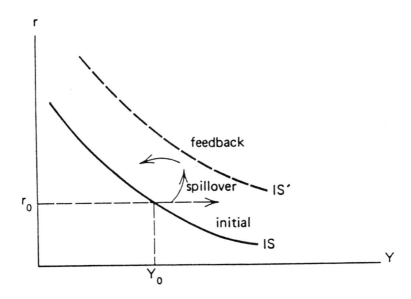

(6) The reduction in Y then relieves the extent of EDM and puts downward pressure on r. The full experiment can be pictured as:

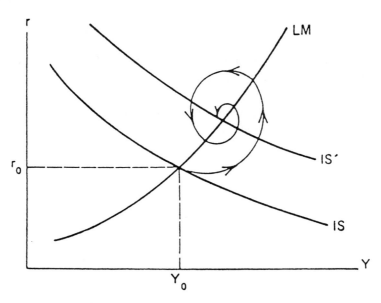

In what case would the "bang for buck" from a rise in $\bar{G}$ be especially small? According to the logic of the model, this would occur if:

(1) A rise in Y produces a large rise in money demand. In this case, C_1 is large (LM is steep).

(2) An EDM takes a very large change in r to produce money market equilibrium. This is true if C_2 is very small (LM is steep).

(3) A rise in r produces a large reduction in I. This is true if d is large (IS is flat).

Therefore, the logic of the model shows that the conditions that lead to the smallest effect of $\bar{G}$ on Y are a steep LM curve and a flat IS curve. Notice how the graph reinforces the logic:

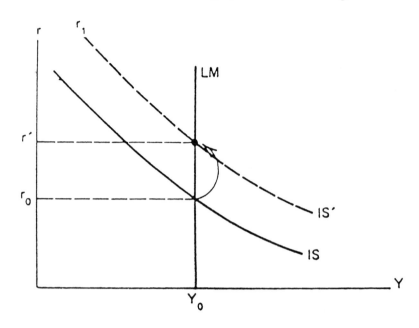

Here, we see that if the LM curve is vertical, a rise in G produces no effect on Y. It raises r only and leads to I being "crowded out" to the exact amount of the rise in G.

Similar logic shows that the best case for the big effect of $\bar{G}$ on Y consists of the opposite conditions: small d, small C_1, and large C_2. These conditions imply a very steep IS and a flat LM.

2. Solving the Model: Monetary Effects

Now we discuss the effect of increasing the money supply, assuming normal model elasticities. A rise in M_0^s will shift the LM curve rightward, providing a higher equilibrium value of Y with a lower r:

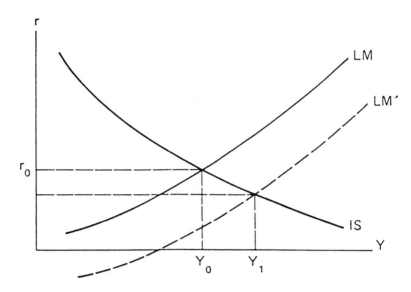

Let us trace the steps involved in this conclusion:

(1) The rise in M_0^s creates an excess supply of money (ESM).

(2) Individuals demand bonds with the extra money, and this forces $r \downarrow$.

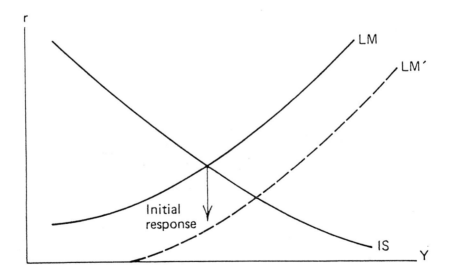

(3) As *r* falls, it encourages more *I*. This generates an EDG and puts pressure on *Y* to rise. This is the spillover effect:

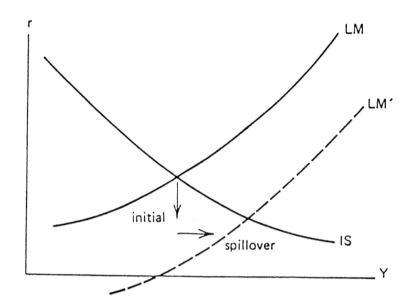

(4) Now the rise in *Y* increases the transactions demand for money. This offsets the original ESM and reduces pressure on interest rates to fall; this is a feedback effect:

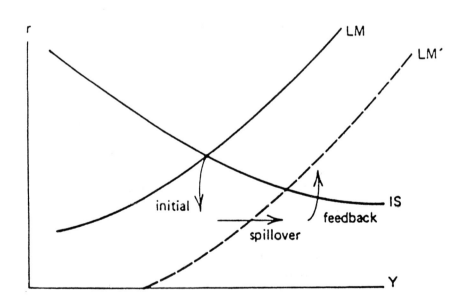

(5) The rise in r now offsets the increase in I and reduces the EDG and lets Y rise less. We can summarize all these effects of the initial increase in M_0^s as:

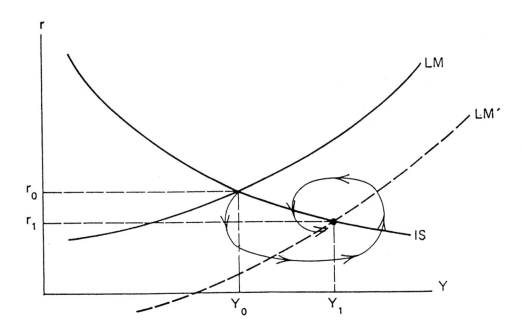

The model produces the largest changes in Y if:

(1) the excess supply of money leads to a large initial fall in r. This happens if C_2 is small (steep LM).

(2) the reduction in r leads to a large rise in I. This is true if d is large (flat IS).

(3) the rise in Y leads to a small EDM. This arises if C_1 is large (steep LM).

Notice that money has a large effect on Y if a rise in money produces a sizeable drop in interest rates that causes I to rise. This works especially well if the rise in Y does not lead to subsequently large interest rate increases. It is especially interesting that the case of <u>large monetary</u> effects on Y does not lead to subsequently large interest rate increases. It is especially interesting that the case of <u>large monetary</u> effects on Y (small C_2 or large C_1 and d) are exactly the conditions which lead to <u>small fiscal</u> effects on Y.

Self-Tests

Multiple-Choice Questions:

1. According to the IS-LM model, a change in the size of the government budget, holding the deficit constant, will cause income:
    a. to change in the same direction as the change in the size of the budget
    b. to change in the opposite direction from the change in the size of the budget
    c. to be unaffected
    d. none of the above

The Keynesian System (III): Policy Effects in the IS-LM Model

2. Monetary policy is more likely to be highly effective:
   a. if investment demand is highly interest elastic
   b. if money demand is not highly interest elastic
   c. if the IS curve is nearly horizontal
   d. all of the above

3. Fiscal policy has more "bang-for-the-buck" if:
   a. investment demand is highly interest elastic
   b. money demand is not highly interest elastic
   c. the LM curve is flat
   d. all of the above

4. At low interest rates, one would expect:
   a. high anticipated inflation
   b. high interest elasticity of investment demand
   c. high interest elasticity of money demand
   d. low interest elasticity of money demand

5. In the IS-LM model, an autonomous reduction in money demand should:
   a. lower interest rates and output
   b. raise interest rates and output
   c. lower interest rates and raise output
   d. raise interest rates and lower output

6. An increase in taxes in the IS-LM model is shown by a:
   a. leftward shift in the LM curve
   b. rightward shift in the LM curve
   c. leftward shift in the IS curve
   d. rightward shift in the IS curve

7. A rise in government spending accompanied by an autonomous increase in the public's demand to hold money balances would:
   a. raise interest rates and output
   b. lower interest rates and output
   c. raise output but affect interest rates ambiguously
   d. raise interest rates but affect output ambiguously

8. Given income is held constant, then an increase in the money supply causes:
   a. a shift of the LM curve
   b. a fall in the interest rate
   c. an excess demand for bonds
   d. all of the above

9. Given the money supply is held constant, a rise in income causes:
   a. a movement along a given LM curve
   b. a rise in interest rates
   c. an excess supply of bonds
   d. all of the above

10. In both the IS-LM and classical models, it is generally true that:
    a. the government spending multiplier is greater than the tax multiplier
    b. complete crowding-out occurs
    c. saving is primarily affected by interest rates
    d. none of the above

11. Within the Keynesian framework, there is a preference for a policy mix of:
    a. tight fiscal and monetary policy
    b. easy fiscal policy and tight monetary policy
    c. easy fiscal and monetary policy
    d. tight fiscal policy and easy monetary policy

12. A tax cut accompanied by an increase in the quantity of money will:
    a. increase income, but the effect on the interest rate is uncertain
    b. increase both income and the interest rate
    c. increase income and lower the interest rate
    d. lower the interest rate, but the effect on income is uncertain

13. An autonomous decline in investment demand:
    a. shifts the IS schedule to the left
    b. shifts the IS schedule to the right
    c. shifts the LM schedule to the left
    d. shifts the LM schedule to the right

14. With a vertical LM curve, an increase in the money stock:
    a. will increase the interest rate
    b. will decrease investment demand
    c. will not change equilibrium income
    d. will increase equilibrium income

15. In general, a steep IS curve and a flat LM curve result in:
    a. effective fiscal policy and effective monetary policy
    b. ineffective fiscal policy and ineffective monetary policy
    c. effective fiscal policy and ineffective monetary policy
    d. ineffective fiscal policy and effective monetary policy

16. Fiscal policy action is most effective when the IS curve is:
    a. flat
    b. relatively flat
    c. relatively steep
    d. vertical

17. The lower the interest elasticity of money demand:
    a. the steeper the LM curve
    b. the flatter the LM curve
    c. the steeper the IS curve
    d. the flatter the IS curve

18. Monetary policy is least effective when:
    a. the IS curve is vertical
    b. the LM curve is vertical
    c. the LM curve is relatively steep
    d. the LM curve is relatively flat

19. The difference between the simple Keynesian model and the IS-LM curve model is that the IS-LM curve model:
    a. excludes a commodity market
    b. includes a commodity market
    c. excludes a money market
    d. includes a money market

20. In the IS-LM model, an increase in taxes:
    a. decreases income and increases the interest rate
    b. increases income but decreases the interest rate
    c. decreases both income and the interest rate
    d. increases both income and the interest rate

21. In the IS-LM model, an increase in the level of government spending will increase
    a. both income and the interest rate
    b. income, but leave the interest rate unchanged
    c. income, but decrease the interest rate
    d. the interest rate only

22. In the liquidity trap case where the LM schedule is nearly horizontal:
    a. fiscal policy is ineffective and monetary policy is effective
    b. monetary policy is ineffective and fiscal policy is effective
    c. both monetary policy and fiscal policy are highly effective
    d. both monetary and fiscal policies are ineffective most of the time

Figure 7.1

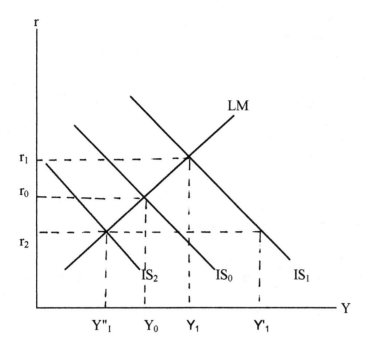

23. According to Figure 7.1, an increase in government spending:
    a. shifts the IS schedule to the left by $\Delta G(-b/1-b)$
    b. shifts the IS schedule to the right by $\Delta G(1-b/1-b)$
    c. shifts the IS schedule to the right by $\Delta G(1/1-b)$
    d. shifts the IS schedule to the left by $\Delta G(1/1-b)$

24. According to Figure 7.1, an increase in taxes:
    a. shifts the IS schedule to IS_1
    b. shifts the IS schedule to IS_2
    c. leaves the IS schedule at IS_0
    d. shifts neither the IS schedule nor the LM schedule

25. According to Figure 7.1, an autonomous decline in investment demand results in:
    a. a rise in income from Y_0 to Y_1 and a rise in the interest rate from r_0 to r_1
    b. a fall in income from Y_0 to Y''_1 and a fall in the interest rate from r_0 to r_2
    c. no change in either income or the interest rate
    d. none of the above

26. The expression for the slope of the LM curve can be shown as:

    a. $\Delta r/\Delta Y \big|_{LM} = c_1/c_2$

    b. $\Delta r/\Delta Y \big|_{LM} = c_1 \times c_2$

    c. $\Delta Y/\Delta r \big|_{LM} = c_2/c_1$

    d. $\Delta r/\Delta Y \big|_{LM} = c_2 + c_1$

27. According to the modern Keynesian view:
    a. only fiscal policy is effective in controlling income
    b. only monetary policy can affect income
    c. both fiscal and monetary policies are effective in controlling income
    d. none of the above

28. An autonomous decline in investment:
    a. shifts the saving function to the right
    b. shifts the investment schedule to the right
    c. shifts the investment schedule to the left
    d. leaves the investment schedule unchanged

29. In the simple Keynesian model, government spending changes:
    a. have a greater per dollar effect on income than do tax changes
    b. have a smaller per dollar effect on income than do tax changes
    c. have an equal per dollar effect on income, as do tax changes
    d. can have either a greater or lesser per dollar effect on income than do tax changes

30. The slope of the LM curve depends most crucially on the interest elasticity of:
    a. consumption
    b. saving
    c. investment
    d. money demand

Problems and/or Essay Questions:

1. It is often said that the government's fiscal policy has direct effects upon output, while the Federal Reserve's monetary policy only indirectly affects output. Comment on the following:
   a. Monetary policy's impact is direct, since it depends on "interest rate effects."
   b. Monetary policy works best when the LM equation is flat and the IS equation is steep.
   c. Fiscal policy works best when the interest elasticity of money demand is absolutely small.
   d. A reduction in taxes has no effect on equilibrium output if the LM curve is vertical.

2. Describe the logic involved in the reduction in interest rates generated by an autonomous reduction in money demand. Be sure to describe how all aspects of the economic system interact in your discussion.

3. Why is there a connection between changes in the money supply and changes in interest rates? Begin your answer by recalling what we assume people will do if they have money balances.

4. Describe fully what determines the position and slopes of the IS and LM equations.

5. Explain why James Tobin remarked that President Reagan's policy mix was like pointing the engine of a train to Boston while heading the caboose to New York. What would President Reagan say to Mr. Tobin?

6. The difference between the simple Keynesian model and the IS-LM curve model is that the IS-LM curve model includes a money market. Explain how this affects the results of the simple Keynesian model (for instance, an increase in government spending).

7. In the Keynesian model, there is a preference for a policy mix for "tight" fiscal policy and "easy" monetary policy. Explain this preference.

8. If fiscal policy is used to expand the economy, how do the Keynesians suggest monetary policy should be implemented?

9. The slope of the LM curve is shown as $\Delta r/\Delta Y \big|_{LM} = c_1/c_2$. What is the crucial parameter and what does it determine? Explain.

10. Graphically show and analyze the effects of an increase in the quantity of money.

11. According to the Keynesian view, either monetary or fiscal policy can affect income. Are the effects of each policy on the interest rate, and, therefore, on investment similar or different? Explain how they differ/are similar in the case of an expansionary monetary policy action and an expansionary fiscal policy action.

CHAPTER 8

THE KEYNESIAN SYSTEM (IV): AGGREGATE SUPPLY AND DEMAND

OVERVIEW

To this point in the discussion of the Keynesian model, both the price level and the money wage have been assumed to be fixed. With these assumptions, output is determined solely by aggregate demand. This chapter considers the Keynesian theory of aggregate supply and shows that when prices and wages are not assumed to be constant, both supply and demand factors are important determinants of output in the Keynesian system.

The first relationship derived is the Keynesian aggregate demand curve that shows the level of output demanded for each value of the aggregate price level. This aggregate demand curve is then put together with the classical aggregate supply curve to illustrate that, regardless of the theory of aggregate demand, as long as classical assumptions are made about the labor market, output will remain supply-determined. Alternative Keynesian aggregate supply schedules are then derived, first assuming that the price level varies but the money wage is fixed, then for the case where both the price level and the level of the money wage are variable. In both models, the changes in aggregate demand (shifts in the aggregate demand schedule) are seen to affect both price and output. These models remain Keynesian in nature. It is true, however, that the effect on output of a given change in aggregate demand is smaller here than in the IS-LM model where the price level and level of the money wage were taken as given. The remaining sections of the chapter examine the independent effects of supply factors on output, employment, and the aggregate price level. The final section of the chapter compares the classical and Keynesian theories and policy conclusions. To do this, the classical and Keynesian aggregate supply and demand schedules are contrasted.

On the supply side, the classical aggregate supply schedule is vertical, reflecting the supply-determined nature of real output within the classical system. The Keynesian supply schedule slopes upward to the right; both supply and demand factors affect real output in the Keynesian model. On the demand side, the position of the classical aggregate demand schedule depends only on the quantity of money (for a fixed level of the velocity of money). The classical theory of aggregate demand was a completely monetary one, where the role of demand was to determine the aggregate price level. The position of the Keynesian aggregate demand curve depends on the quantity of money and on other variables such as the level of government spending, the level of tax collections, and the level of autonomous investment expenditures.

On policy issues, the classical economists are non-interventionists, stressing the self-adjusting properties of the economy. The Keynesian position is a more activist one. Keynesians believe that private sector aggregate demand, particularly investment demand, is unstable and that there is a need for government stabilization policies.

Techniques in Depth

1. Introducing the Price Level into the IS and LM Equations

Purchasing power refers to the quantity of goods a given amount of money commands. For example, in a monetary economy we can measure goods in nominal terms or in purchasing power or real terms. The IS-LM model is cast in real terms. To emphasize that it is in real terms, the nominal values (I, G, T, and Y) are put into (deflated) real terms (i, g, t, y) by dividing the nominal value by the price level. For example, $i = I/P$.

The model assumes that economic decisions are made in real terms. For example, firms decide to buy 20,0000 units at a price of $100. If the price doubles to $200, the model assumes the decision is unchanged. Therefore, a rise in P to $200 entails nominal spending of $I = \$4,000,000$ to leave $i = 20,000$ intact.

This assumption applies to consumption, government spending, taxes, and to money demand. The exception, however, is that we assume the nominal money supply is not automatically increased with changes in P. Therefore, we cannot assume that the real money supply is unaffected by changes in P, and we must write it as M_0^s/P. This implies that the IS-LM model is written explicitly in real terms as:

$$y = c + i + g$$

$$M_0^s/P = M^d(y, r)$$

2. The Aggregate Demand Equation (Y^d)

As its name implies, the Y^d function involves the elements that constitute the demand-side effects in the macroeconomic model of the economy. As such, it embodies elements from the goods market (IS equation). Elements like a, i, t and g obviously affect Y^d. Autonomous elements from the money market, C_0 and M_0^s, indirectly affect Y^d by first affecting interest rates. The price level also affects Y^d because of its role in the money market. A rise in P, given the nominal money stock M_0^s, reduces the purchasing power of the stock of money and creates an excess demand for money which raises interest rates and lowers Y^d.

Therefore, the autonomous variables that affect the level of Yd are: a, g, i, t, and i_0. Additionally, the nominal variable, M_0^s, and the price level, P, affect Y^d. We can always deduce <u>how</u> each of these variables affects Y^d by recalling the logic of the IS-LM model. For example, consider the effects of a reduction in real taxes. This autonomously increases real disposable income and real consumption spending. Recalling the IS-LM apparatus, we show this as a rightward shift of the IS curve:

The Keynesian System (IV): Aggregate Supply and Demand   94

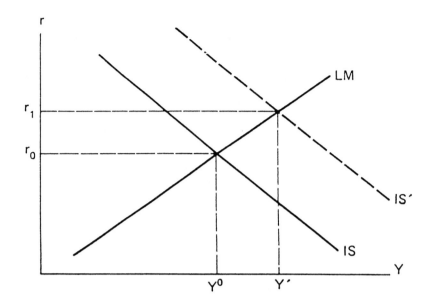

The model suggests that, once the adjustment of the interest rate and the interactions between markets are accounted for, the level of demand has increased from Y^0 to Y'.

By applying similar logic, we can show that <u>increases</u> a, i, g, M_0^s and <u>decreases</u> in C_0, t, and P all raise real aggregate demand.

How do we show these changes on the following two-dimensional diagram?

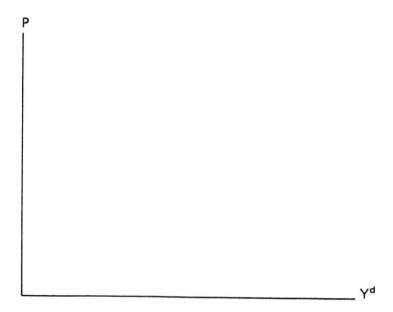

We exhibit the inverse relationship between P and Y^d with a negative slope:

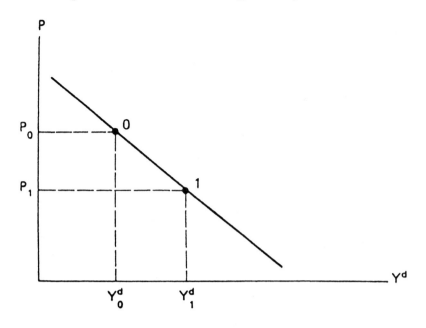

Consider what is happening as we move from point 0 to point 1. As prices fall, this raises the purchasing power of the money supply. This excess supply of money pushes r down, and this increases i. Therefore, we associate a <u>lower</u> price level with a higher level of Y^d. We show this as a movement along a given Y^d curve.

How do we show the effects of changes in i, a, g, t, and M_0^s? These are the factors that will shift the Y^d curve. For example, a reduction in real taxes which raises Y^d shifts the function to the right:

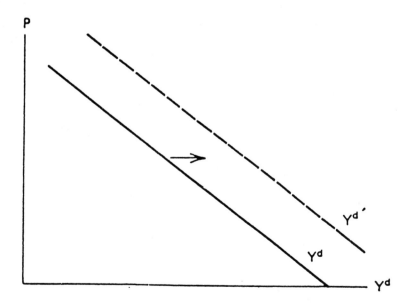

A reduction in M_0^s that reduces Y^d shifts the Y^d curve leftward:

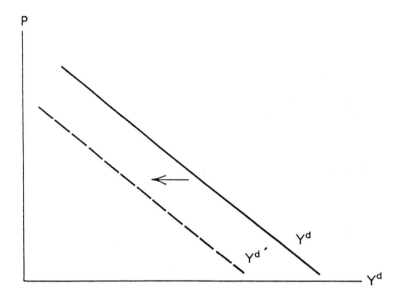

3. Interactions of Price and Output in the Y^s and Y^d Model

The aggregate demand (Y^d) and aggregate supply (Y^s) curves embody elements from all the markets of the economy. Together they form a powerful tool with which we can understand the behavior of the economy. Here we will practice working with the model.

The contract model assumes that wages are fixed. In the Keynesian model, they are sluggish. Therefore, when prices rise (or fall), wages rise (or fall) less, and it is profitable for firms to expand (reduce) production. The Y^s curve, which relates P and Y^s, therefore, in either model, is upward sloping:

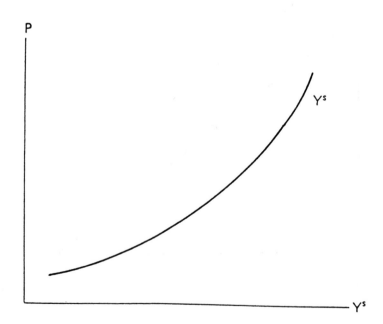

Other things besides price affect output supplied; changes in these variables shift the Y^s curve. For example, if firms purchase a larger capital stock, if workers become more productive, or if the cost of the energy input falls, profit-maximizing firms would:

(a) raise Y^s with given P,
(b) lower P with given Y^s,
(c) some combination of (a) and (b).

These amount to a rightward shift in Y^s. In effect, anything that directly affects the cost of producing a unit of output (evaluated at a given level of output) will shift the Y^s curve. Increases in unit costs shift it left; decreases shift it right.

Factors that shift the line:

Y^d curve	Y^s curve
autonomous consumption spending	wages (for a given level of N)
autonomous investment spending	price expectations
autonomous government spending	technology
autonomous tax changes	energy prices
autonomous money demand	capital prices
autonomous money supply	

The above is just a partial list, but it is suggestive of all the things we can analyze using the Y^s and Y^d model.

Let us take a couple of simple examples first. Any experiment must begin with a change in an autonomous variable. We begin with the assumption that all markets are in equilibrium. For there to be changes occurring to the endogenous variable (Y, P, r, etc.), the existing equilibrium must be disturbed by an external shock—a change in one of the exogenous variables. This shifts one or more of the curves. Then we need to explain how the new solution develops.

For example, assume g rises. This shifts the Y^d curve rightward:

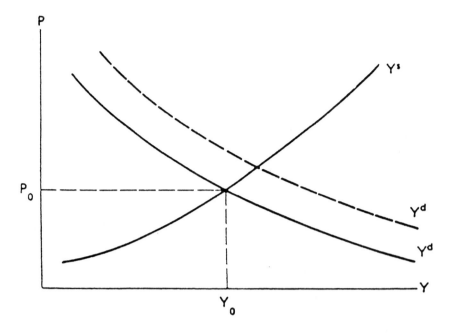

Starting from Y_0, P_0, let us analyze what happens after such a change.

"As the curtain opens," firms are producing Y_0. However, if firms and households purchase their previous amount of $c + i$, but the government now demands more goods, there will exist an excess demand for goods (EDG) at the original price, P_0:

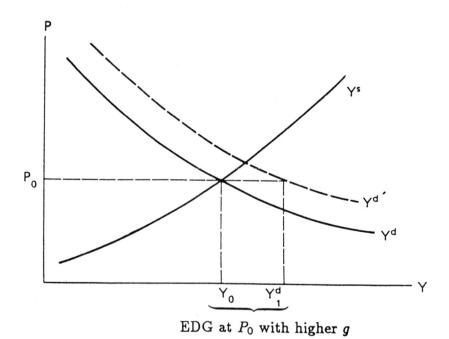

EDG at P_0 with higher g

This EDG puts pressure on prices to rise. This increase in prices affects both suppliers and demanders. The rise in P with M_0^s held constant creates an excess demand for money (EDM), raises r, and reduces i. Therefore, we move <u>along</u> <u>the new</u> Y^d to a lower quantity of demand. At the same time, the higher price is inducing firms to hire more workers to produce more. This effect of P on Y^s is shown as a movement <u>along the Y^s curve</u>.

Notice: with the EDG, there are automatic forces going into effect erasing the EDG. The arrows below show the movement toward the new equilibrium with higher P and Y:

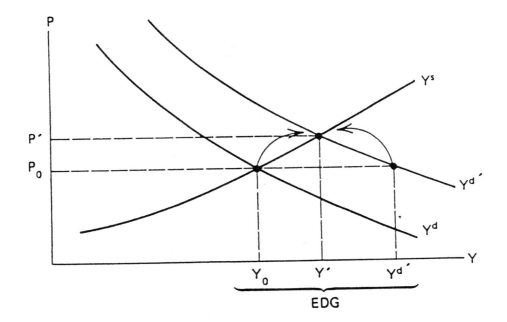

Note: The Keynesian model predicts that increases in autonomous demand will cause <u>both</u> output and prices to change in the same direction as the demand impulse.

Now consider the effects of a supply event. Assume that workers begin to firmly believe that inflation will subside in the coming year. This automatically reduces wages, lowers unit costs, increases the demand for labor, and shifts the Y^s curve rightward:

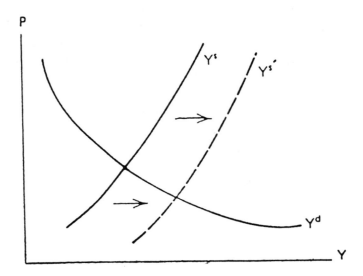

If market prices do not adjust immediately, the increased desire of firms to produce more causes an excess supply of goods (ESG) at price P_0:

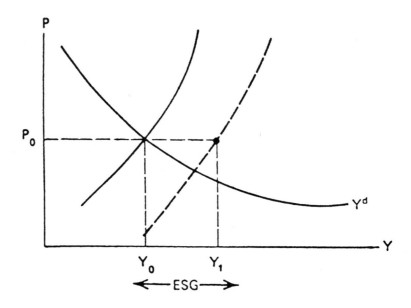

This ESG puts pressure on prices to fall. The fall in prices creates an excess supply of money, a fall in r, a rise in i and, therefore, we move along the Y^d curve to a higher quantity of aggregate demand. At the same time, the lower price diminishes the desires of firms to produce so much more, and they cut back on their hiring and output plans. Thus, we see that the fall in P is reducing the ESG. The arrows show the directions of adjustment:

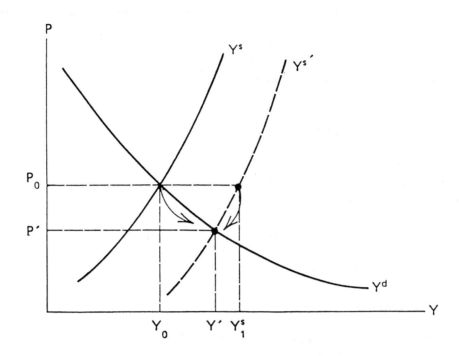

The end result of this reduction in price expectations that autonomously increased Y^s is a rise in Y^s and a fall in P. Notice: A supply shock always pushes Y and P in opposite directions.

Self-Tests

Multiple-Choice Questions:

1. According to the classical supply assumptions, the aggregate supply curve is drawn as a vertical line, because a change in the price level does not shift:
   a. the labor demand curve
   b. the labor supply curve
   c. the production function
   d. all of the above

2. With the classical assumptions about aggregate supply, there is no role for:
   a. aggregate demand in determining output
   b. interest rates in determining demand
   c. prices to determine demand
   d. monetary policy to determine output
   e. both a and d

3. Compared to the case where the price level is fixed, if prices can vary,
   a. M_0^s affects output more, g affects it less
   b. g affects output more; M_0^s affects it less
   c. both M_0^s and g affect output more
   d. both M_0^s and g affect output less

4. Even if wages were perfectly flexible, the Keynesian aggregate supply equation would still be upward sloping if:
   a. workers supply labor according to the expected price
   b. firms hire labor according to the expected price
   c. price expectations are based on currently observed prices
   d. information is free

5. In the Keynesian model, supply factors:
   a. have no effect upon output
   b. generate a vertical supply curve
   c. play an independent role in output determination
   d. have no effect upon prices

6. A rise in workers' expectation of the price level has the effect of:
   a. shifting the Y^s curve rightward
   b. shifting the Y^s curve leftward
   c. shifting the Y^d curve leftward
   d. shifting the Y^d curve rightward

7. Autonomous increases in the price of raw material tend to:
   a. have direct cost-push effects
   b. have indirect effects on aggregate supply by affecting price expectations
   c. shift the aggregate supply curves
   d. all of the above

8. The classical and Keynesian aggregate demand curves are alike in one respect, since:
   a. a rise in price raises Y^d in both models
   b. a rise in g raises Y^d in both models
   c. a fall in t raises Y^d in both models
   d. a rise in M^s raises Y^d in both models

9. Keynesians believe that:
   a. Y^d is inherently stable
   b. active policies are necessary to keep the economy stable
   c. fiscal policy is always less effective than monetary policy
   d. all of the above
   e. none of the above

10. What major international event focused attention on the importance of supply shocks?
    a. The oil price shock of 1973-74
    b. The Watergate incident
    c. Nixon's wage and price controls
    d. The end of the Bretton Woods system

11. Compared with the fixed-wage Keynesian model, when the money wage is variable, an increase in government spending will cause:
    a. output to rise by less and price to rise by more
    b. output and price to rise by less
    c. output to rise by more and price to rise by less
    d. output and price to rise by more

12. Which of the following events occurred in 1990 that had an effect on the supply-side of the economy?
    a. There was a favorable supply shock as oil prices fell
    b. There was an increase in oil prices as Iraq invaded Kuwait
    c. There was an increase in the supply of defense weapons as Iraq invaded Kuwait
    d. There was a decrease in energy prices because of a technological breakthrough

13. The equilibrium condition along the IS curve can be shown as:
    a. $g + i(r) = t - s(y)$
    b. $i(r) - g = s(y) - t$
    c. $i(r) + g = s(y) + t$
    d. $i(r) - g = s(y) + t$

14. The Keynesian labor supply function can be shown as:
    a. $N^s = t(W/P^e)$
    b. $N^s = t(P^e/W)$
    c. $N^s = f(W/P)$
    d. $N^s = f(P/W)$

15. According to the Keynesians, the economy is unstable because of the instability of aggregate demand. The component of aggregate demand primarily responsible for this instability is:
    a. consumption
    b. net exports
    c. government spending
    d. private investment

16. A decrease in the money stock:
    a. shifts the LM curve to the left
    b. shifts the LM curve to the right
    c. shifts the aggregate demand schedule to the right
    d. shifts neither the LM curve nor the aggregate demand schedule

17. An autonomous increase in the price of energy input:
    a. causes output to rise and the price level to fall
    b. causes output to fall and the price level to rise
    c. induces a fall in both output and the price level
    d. induces a rise in both output and the price level

18. Assuming a vertical supply curve, output will:
    a. decrease
    b. increase
    c. be unchanged
    d. none of the above

19. According to the Keynesian model with a fixed money wage and a flexible price level, an increase in taxes will lower:
    a. output, the price level, and the interest rate
    b. output and the price level, but leave the interest rate unchanged
    c. output and the interest rate, but leave the price level unchanged
    d. output and the price level, but increase the interest rate

20. In the 1970s, the United States and other industrialized countries experienced:
    a. hyperinflation
    b. stagflation
    c. stagnation
    d. a depression

21. An increase in the price level shifts:
    a. the LM curve to the right
    b. the LM curve to the left
    c. the IS curve to the right
    d. neither the IS nor the LM curves

22. The crucial assumption in the classical model is a money wage that is:
    a. always equal to the real wage
    b. rigid in an upward direction
    c. rigid in a downward direction
    d. perfectly flexible

23. According to the classical theory of labor demand, the profit-maximizing firm demands labor up to the point at which:
    a. labor and capital costs are the same
    b. the real wage is equal to the marginal productivity of labor
    c. the money wage paid to labor is just equal to the money value of the marginal product of labor
    d. either b or c
    e. none of the above

24. If one compares the effects of an increase in government spending, in the case where the price level varies while the money wage is fixed, with the case where both the price level and money wage are variable, one finds that where both vary:
    a. output rises by more and the price level rises by less
    b. output rises by less and the price level rises by more
    c. output rises by the same amount but the price level rises by more
    d. both output and the price level rise by the same amount

25. Keynesians believe that contractual arrangements are:
    a. central to an understanding of how modern labor markets function
    b. unimportant for modern labor markets
    c. necessary in order to insure perfect wage flexibility
    d. none of the above

26. Which of the following variables will shift the classical aggregate demand curve?
    a. An increase in autonomous investment expenditures
    b. An increase in government spending
    c. A decrease in taxes
    d. All of the above
    e. None of the above

27. According to the Keynesian theory of labor supply, price expectations are based:
    a. on the present behavior of the price level
    b. on the past behavior of the price level
    c. on the future behavior of the price level
    d. on the past, present, and future behavior of the price level

Problems and/or Essay Questions:

1. What is the law of diminishing returns? What relevance does it have for the demand for labor of a perfectly competitive firm?

2. Explain in words, and also show on a graph, what would happen to the demand for labor if:
    a. wages rise, ceteris paribus.
    b. prices rise, ceteris paribus.
    c. firms buy new capital goods which make the existing labor force more productive, ceteris paribus.

   Explain in words what would happen in each of these cases if there were no diminishing returns to labor (if instead there were constant returns).

3. Explain and graph a labor supply function. Explain in words what would happen if:
    a. wages rise, ceteris paribus.
    b. prices rise, ceteris paribus.
    c. the Protestant ethic runs its course and people begin to think work is not such a great idea; that is, the marginal disutility of work rises.

4. Draw a Keynesian aggregate supply function, and explain why it looks the way it does. Why is it sloped the way it is? What causes it to shift? What does it tell you about the ability of an economy to translate demand increases into output increases when:
    a. we are near to potential output?
    b. we are far from potential output?

5. a. Explain why the aggregate demand curve slopes down.
   b. What happens to interest rates as we move down along this schedule, and why?
   c. What happens to the real money stock as we move down along the aggregate demand curve?

6. What would be the effect on the aggregate demand curve of a cut in transfer payments? A rise in government spending? A sales tax increase?

7. Is it true that, in the short run, expansionary fiscal or monetary policy can increase output only by also raising prices? Explain!

8. Suppose investors suddenly become more optimistic than in the past and decide to invest more at given levels of income and interest rates. Trace the effects of such a shift through the IS and LM curves to see its effect on equilibrium income as derived with the aggregate supply and demand curves. Explain the effects of the change in optimism on interest rates, prices, and income.

9. In the early 1980s, we found U.S. output rising with falling inflation. Is that outcome compatible with major demand shocks or supply shocks? If policymakers used "tight money" to make the inflation fall even faster, how would that affect output in the short run? In the long run?

10. Graph a Keynesian aggregate supply curve with a fixed and variable money wage. Explain the difference between the two curves.

11. Explain the difference or differences between the Keynesian and classical aggregate demand schedules?

12. Compare the Keynesian effects on price and output from a given change in aggregate demand when the money wage is variable with the effects for the case in which the money wage is fixed. Is there a predictable quantitative difference? What is the reason for these results?

CHAPTER 9

THE MONETARIST COUNTERREVOLUTION

OVERVIEW

Chapter 9 is the first of two chapters that examine the monetarist model. To begin with, several characteristic monetarist propositions are listed:

(1) The supply of money is the dominant influence on nominal income.

(2) In the long run, the influence of money is primarily on the price level and other nominal magnitudes. In the long run, real variables, such as real output and employment, are determined by real, not monetary factors.

(3) In the short run, the supply of money does influence real variables. Money is the dominant factor causing cyclical movements in output and employment.

(4) The private sector of the economy is inherently stable. Instability in the economy is primarily the result of government policies.

Two policy corollaries to these propositions are:

(1) Stability in the growth of the money stock is crucial for stability in the economy. Such stability is best achieved by setting a constant growth rate for the money stock.

(2) Fiscal policy, by itself, has little systematic effect on either real or nominal income. Fiscal policy is not an effective stabilization tool.

The two chapters on monetarism explain the theoretical basis for the above propositions and the relationship between these propositions and the monetarist policy conclusions. First, in Chapter 9, the reason why the monetarists believe money is so important is considered. Chapter 10 considers the basis for the second proposition, the theory of the natural rate of unemployment.

The analysis begins with a brief look at the Great Depression and the roots of the controversy between monetarists and Keynesians. Monetarists believe the depression was largely caused by money, while Keynesians offer more eclectic explanations. The analysis continues by considering the origins of monetarism in the early 1950s with Milton Friedman's reformulation of the quantity theory of money. The development of what are called the weak and strong forms of the modern quantity theory of money is described. It is the strong form of the quantity theory of money that provides the basis for the monetarist view that money is the dominant influence on nominal income.

Next, the policy conclusions of the monetarists and Keynesians are compared. The monetarists do not believe that fiscal policy actions will have sustained systematic effects on the level of economic activity. The Keynesians view fiscal policy as an effective tool for aggregate demand management policy. Both the monetarists and Keynesians believe that monetary policy actions will have substantial and sustained effects on the level of economic activity. The monetarists believe that the best use of monetary policy to stabilize the economy would be to keep the money stock growing at a stable (constant) growth rate. The Keynesians favor a more activist or discretionary monetary policy. The final section of the chapter examines the recent behavior of the money-income relationship.

Techniques in Depth

1. Features of Monetarism — Short-Run Effects on Y^d

There are numerous features of a monetarist model, and we present some of them here and examine their implications for monetary and fiscal policies. The thrust of this chapter concerns the effect of these policies on nominal aggregate demand. An extreme form of monetarism argues that only money has important systematic effects on nominal aggregate demand. This implies that fiscal policy alone can have little effect upon Y^d. Let us examine what monetarist innovations are necessary in order to arrive at these conclusions.

(i) The demand for money is largely unaffected by the interest rate. In this case, the LM equation is very steep:

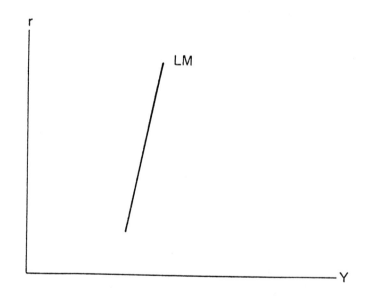

(ii) Changes in autonomous spending elements present in the IS curve are generally stable, producing shifts, but temporary ones.

Putting together (i) and (ii) suggests that output changes will be temporary and any given IS shift produces a small change in Y:

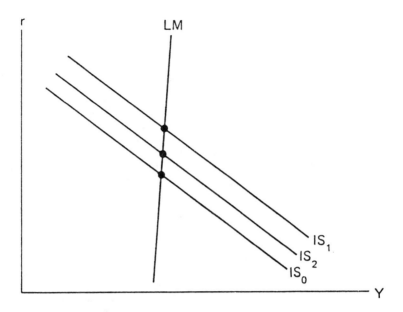

The above diagram shows that shifts in the IS curve to IS_1 will be followed by shifts back toward the original IS curve (IS_0). The nearly vertical LM curve means the small effects upon Y.

The student should recall the connection between the IS-LM apparatus and the Y^d curve. The above analysis can be restated by saying that autonomous variables in the IS curve should generate very small and temporary shifts in the Y^d curve. Fiscal policy actions, which affect the IS curve, will cause small shifts in the Y^d curve:

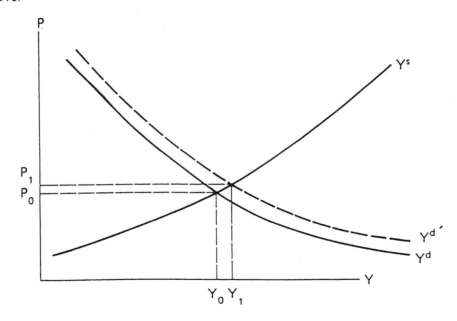

Thus, fiscal policy generates small changes in output or prices. Monetary policy principally causes shifts in the LM curve, causing large shifts in the Y^d curve.

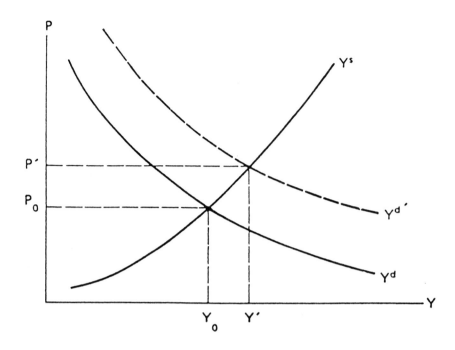

Thus, monetary policy generates larger changes in output and prices in the short run.

2. Features of Monetarism — Uncertainty and Policy

Given the analysis above, it is sometimes surprising to students when they learn that monetarists do <u>not</u> favor an active monetary stabilization policy. For example, Milton Friedman advocates setting money growth at some constant growth rate, say 3 percent, and holding it at that rate regardless of the performance of the economy. If monetary actions are believed to be so much stronger than fiscal ones, why are monetarists so reluctant to use this potent weapon?

The answer concerns uncertainty. We discuss and portray two different types of uncertainty that would lead one to understand the monetarist's reluctance to use any form of active demand management policy.

(i) Uncertainty over the timing of the impact of monetary policy

Assume that policymakers find the economy is in equilibrium at Y_0 but wish to move to Y^*. They know the economy will eventually move to Y^* automatically, but they want to hurry things, since there are too many people out of work:

The Monetarist Counterrevolution 111

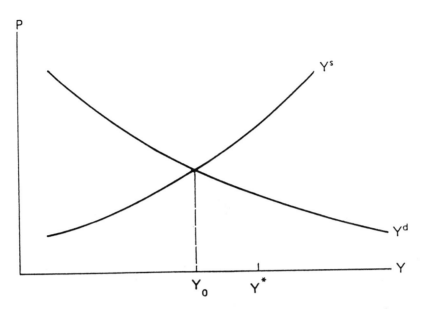

Our model explains that by raising the money supply, policymakers can shift the Y^d curve to Y^{d*} and, therefore, move the economy to Y^*:

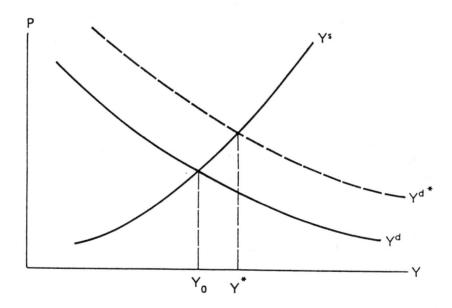

The trouble is that we do not know with certainty <u>how long</u> it takes for the Y^d curve to shift all the way to Y^{d*} after the money supply has been increased. Friedman's studies have shown that the timing of the effects of money is highly variable, ranging from a few months to a few years. Consider what damage can be done if the effect of money on Y^d comes late—after the Y^d curve has already shifted back on its own (to Y_1^d):

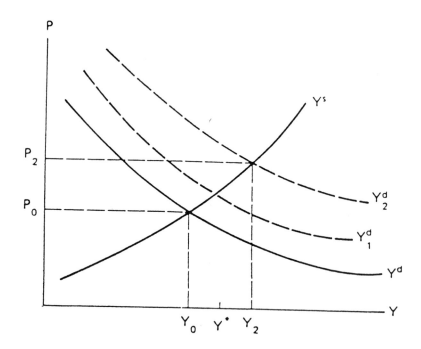

This example shows that the risk from monetary stimulus is that demand rises by too much, output rises more than desired and this raises prices too much. This can be a problem for reductions in money or if money affects things too quickly. For example, policymakers may worry that inflation will flare up in six months. Knowing that money takes time to work, they reduce M^s today. The tight money, if it works too quickly, would reduce demand too early and cause a recession.

(ii) Uncertainty about shifts in the autonomous components of the IS and LM curves

In the real world, the IS and LM curves are continuously shifting. If we can predict the direction and magnitude of these shifts, then policy can be geared to either accommodate or offset them. Unfortunately, some of the largest shifts are highly unpredictable. Even if our policies always worked with perfect timing, the lack of predictability of private sector demands for goods, money, and other financial assets makes control difficult.

Next, we picture a case where the best guess for where the future Y^d curve will lie is Y_0^d. Y_L^d and Y_h^d reflect how low or high the curve might be:

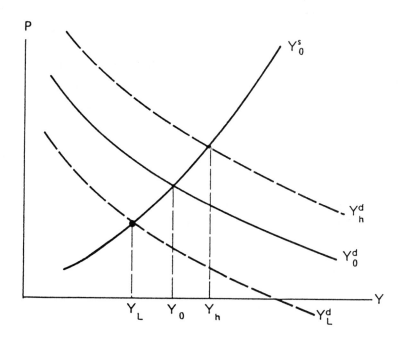

If the Y^s curve is expected to be positioned as shown by Y_0^s, then the economy would move toward any output level between Y_L and Y_h, depending upon which Y^d curve actually occurs. Monetarists believe that trying to guess about unpredictable shifts can cause output to vary too much. In other words, if we use demand management policy, the Y^d curve may swing even wider.

Monetarists would opt instead for announcing a policy of holding the money supply (or its rate of growth) constant. They believe this reduces the swings in Y^d, since, under that policy, only the private sector would be causing the shifts. They also believe that if the people believe that money will be held constant, this could also reduce the amplitude of the unpredictable shifts.

Self-Tests

Multiple-Choice Questions:

1. An important distinction between a modern quantity theorist and a modern Keynesian concerns:
   a. the flexibility of money wages
   b. the controllability of interest rates
   c. the variability or fixity of velocity
   d. all of the above

2. The "strong form" of the quantity theory argues that:
   a. interest rates negligibly affect money demand
   b. money holdings as a proportion of nominal income are relatively constant
   c. money is the dominant cause of changes in nominal income
   d. all of the above

3. Milton Friedman, a leading monetarist, espouses the view that:
   a. the government's budget alone has large effects on output
   b. the government's budget could have large effects on output, if deficits are financed by money creation
   c. the government's budget deficit, if financed by a sale of bonds, has a large effect on output
   d. if a budget deficit is accompanied by increased money, then output surely will fall

4. Monetarists believe:
   a. the IS curve is steep
   b. the LM curve is flat
   c. government spending causes small shifts in the Y^d curve
   d. all of the above

5. Monetarists believe, unlike modern Keynesians, that there are direct short–run crowding-out effects because:
   a. wealth affects money demand in the short run
   b. government bonds are an important determinant of short-run changes in wealth
   c. aggregate demand is highly affected by short-run interest rate changes
   d. all of the above

6. Monetarists believe that:
   a. the money supply should be allowed to change periodically to offset undesirable income changes
   b. fiscal policy should be used to offset undesirable income changes
   c. the money supply should not be allowed to fluctuate greatly
   d. fiscal policy should be used to stabilize interest rates

7. Milton Friedman believes that money should not be used to "fine tune" the economy because:
   a. money has a minor effect
   b. money has too large an effect
   c. we just don't know enough about the economy to correctly time policy changes
   d. the money supply is not controllable, since money demand is so unstable

8. The most likely slopes for the IS and LM schedules for the monetarist case are:
   a. LM flat, IS steep
   b. LM flat, IS flat
   c. LM steep, IS flat
   d. LM steep, IS steep

9. In the monetarist model, an increase in the level of government spending financed by selling bonds to the public would be certain to:
   a. increase output significantly
   b. increase velocity significantly
   c. increase the interest rate significantly
   d. increase the price level significantly

10. The early (circa 1945-1950) Keynesian economists believed that:
    a. the IS schedule was quite steep and the LM schedule was quite flat
    b. the IS schedule was quite flat and the LM schedule was quite steep
    c. the IS and LM schedules were both quite flat
    d. the IS and LM schedules were both quite steep

11. One distinguishing characteristic of monetarism is emphasizing a large direct impact of government deficits upon:
    a. prices
    b. interest rates
    c. output
    d. all of the above

12. In the monetarist model, the money-to-income ratio
    a. depends positively on the level of the interest rate
    b. depends positively on the level of income
    c. is highly unstable
    d. is very stable

13. Early Keynesians "pegged" interest rates:
    a. to achieve low and stable rates of interest
    b. which decreases the monetary authority's control over the quantity of money
    c. caused instability in financial markets
    d. a and b only

14. The monetarists and the Keynesians agree that the experience of the 1930s contradicted the classical view of:
    a. aggregate demand
    b. output
    c. the labor market
    d. sticky prices and wages

15. Assuming the monetary authority wants to prevent interest rate movements, then the LM curve is:
    a. downward sloping
    b. upward sloping
    c. horizontal
    d. vertical

16. Assuming the monetary authority wants to peg the interest rate, then:
    a. it has full control of the quantity of money
    b. it must stand ready to adjust the interest rate on demand
    c. it must exchange money for bonds on demand
    d. none of the above

17. According to Keynes' theory of money demand, the role of money:
    a. served as an asset only
    b. was stressed for transactions only
    c. was stressed as an asset in addition to its role in transactions
    d. was not very significant
    e. none of the above

18. Keynesians argue that the interest elasticity of the demand for money is:
    a. relatively high, while monetarists argue it is low
    b. unimportant with respect to economic activity, while monetarists disagree
    c. low, while monetarists argue it is high
    d. none of the above

19. According to Keynes, the money demand function:
    a. was predictable
    b. was unpredictable
    c. was important in determining the level of economic activity
    d. shifted with changes in the public confidence in the economy

20. According to the early Keynesians:
    a. velocity was a constant
    b. money was the dominant variable in determining GDP
    c. the price level was proportional to the quantity of money
    d. monetary policy was ineffective

21. Monetarists stress the importance of:
    a. fiscal policy for determining GDP
    b. tax cuts to control the inflation rate
    c. money in determining nominal GDP
    d. none of the above

22. According to the monetarist theory, an increase in government spending would have:
    a. a weak effect on output but a strong effect on the price level
    b. only weak effects on both output and the price level
    c. a weak effect on the price level but a strong effect on output
    d. strong effects on both the price level and output

23. Friedman, in his theory of money demand:
    a. utilized only bonds and money
    b. regarded all non-monetary assets as one category
    c. divided non-monetary assets according to bonds, equities, and durable goods
    d. none of the above

24. According to the monetarists:
    a. the LM schedule is quite flat; reflecting a high interest elasticity of money demand
    b. the IS schedule is almost vertical; reflecting a very low interest elasticity of money demand
    c. the IS schedule is quite flat; reflecting a high interest elasticity of aggregate demand
    d. the IS schedule is quite steep; reflecting a high interest elasticity of aggregate demand

25. The difference between the monetarist and Keynesian views on monetary policy is that the monetarists:
    a. believe monetary policy is effective and the Keynesians do not
    b. believe monetary policy is ineffective while the Keynesians believe it is effective
    c. favor "fine tuning" the economy with monetary policy while the Keynesians do not
    d. the monetarists favor a constant money growth rule while the Keynesians oppose such a rule

26. Friedman and others view the instability of velocity in the 1980s:
    a. as the result of stagflation
    b. as the result of disinflation
    c. as the result of hyperinflation
    d. resulting from inflation

27. In the monetarist model, crowding out:
    a. may or may not take place depending on the amount of increase in government spending
    b. occurs almost dollar for dollar with an increase in government spending
    c. does occur but it is very small with an increase in government spending
    d. none of the above

28. With respect to monetarism, events since 1980:
    a. reduced its influence
    b. revived its influence
    c. have made it clear that monetarism is a thing of the past
    d. none of the above

29. If the monetary authority wants to prevent movements in the interest rate, then the LM curve is:
    a. horizontal
    b. vertical
    c. upward sloping
    d. downward sloping

Problems and/or Essay Questions:

1. What are the crucial differences between Keynes' and Friedman's theories of money demand? Is it possible that modern Keynesians could subscribe to Friedman's view of the quantity theory of money? If so, explain what they might agree upon.

2. Explain the meaning of the following statement: "the strong quantity theory position extends the quantity theory from a theory of money demand to a theory of nominal income." Why is the strong quantity theory position so important an element of monetarism? Why isn't the weak position strong enough? (Hint: Use of the IS and LM or Y^s and Y^d curves could help you make this latter point rigorously.)

3. Use the Y^d and Y^s model to show under what conditions:
   a. money affects output in the short run.
   b. money affects prices in the short run.
   c. money affects prices only in the short run.
   d. fiscal policy affects neither output nor prices in the short run.

4. Describe in detail why monetarists generally believe that monetary policy should not be used to fine-tune the economy. How would a modern Keynesian react to this analysis?

5. How would you get from St. Paul to New Orleans? By tub or car? Explain the relevance of this seemingly ludicrous question.

6. What does empirical evidence have to say about the debate between Keynesians and monetarists? Describe some of the evidence and conclusions drawn.

7. Describe and compare the "money hypothesis" and the "spending hypothesis" of the Great Depression.

8. Explain how Milton Friedman and others perceive the instability of velocity in the 1980s.

9. Describe what occurs when the monetary authority pegs the interest rate according to the early Keynesians.

10. Compare the monetarist explanation of the Great Depression with that of the Keynesians. Do they differ? Why or why not?

CHAPTER 10

OUTPUT, INFLATION, AND UNEMPLOYMENT: MONETARIST AND KEYNESIAN VIEWS

OVERVIEW

Here, the discussion of monetarism which began in Chapter 9 is completed. The central focus of the chapter is on the second of the monetarist propositions listed in Chapter 9—In the long run, the influence of money is primarily on the price level and other nominal magnitudes. In the long run, real variables, such as real output and employment, are determined by real, not monetary, factors—The basis for this proposition is Milton Friedman's theory of the *natural rates of unemployment and output.*

The first two sections of this chapter develop the theory of the natural rate of unemployment within the context of the Phillips curve graph. Friedman's analysis of both the short-run and long-run effects of an increase in the rate of growth in the money stock is explained. The Phillips curve, within the monetarist view, is seen to be downward sloping in the short run but vertical in the long run. The difference between the short run and the long run, in this context, is that in the long run, the labor suppliers' expected inflation rate would converge to the actual inflation rate.

The third section of the chapter considers the Keynesian view of the Phillips curve. Again, there is seen to be a trade-off between inflation and unemployment in the short run but not in the long run. The quite different policy conclusions drawn by the monetarists and Keynesians, on the basis of this Phillips curve analysis, are considered. The areas of agreement between the monetarists and Keynesians on the nature of the long-run Phillips curve relationship are explained. Keynesian doubts about the concept of natural rates of output and employment are, however, also considered.

Techniques in Depth

1. Development of the Short-Run Phillips Curve

The Phillips curve is an interesting and simple embodiment of some highly policy-relevant aspects of the macroeconomic model already developed in the text. It is a useful construct for evaluating policy choices, but, in order to do this, one must be able to understand how it relates to the model.

Begin with equilibrium in the goods and labor markets:

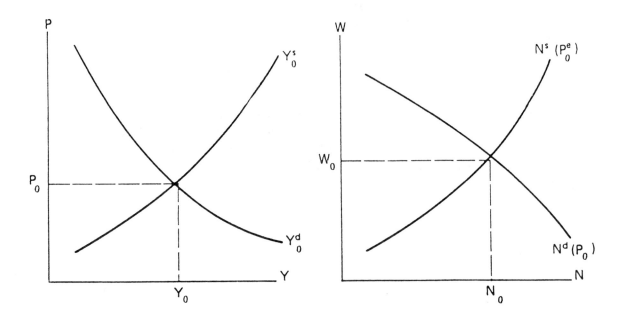

To reemphasize the problem of workers acquiring price information in the short run, we write the N^s function as $N^s(P_0^e)$ and the N^d functions as $N^d(P_0)$. This accentuates that firms have better information about the price level than households—who must form a perception of it when engaging in labor market activity. The Phillips curve helps us to portray the equilibrium (Y_0, P_0, W_0, and N_0) in other terms. For example, subtract N_0 from the size of the labor force N, and you get the number of unemployed workers. Then, divide this number by N, and this yields the short-run equilibrium unemployment rate (u_0). Furthermore, if we know today's price level (P_0) and last period's (P_{-1}), then the inflation rate ($\hat{P}$) is found by taking the percentage change [$\hat{P} = (P_0 - P_{-1})/P_{-1}$]. The point is that we can readily convert the current information P_0, N_0 to other useful information, u_0, $\hat{P}_0$. Anything that affects P and N will obviously affect u and $\hat{P}$. So, we have an option to portray the model with the above two diagrams or equivalently with the following Phillips diagram:

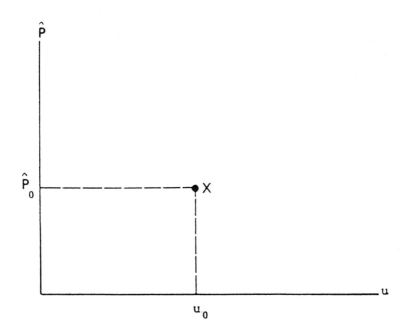

The dot marked "X" is the equilibrium found above (Y_0, P_0, N_0, W_0). If we want to know more about the behavior of u and $\hat{P}$, let us do an experiment and see how equilibrium values change. Let the money supply suddenly grow at a faster rate. The supply and demand model shows that $Y, P, N,$ and W all will rise. Further more, we also know that W/P falls since P rises by a greater amount than W:

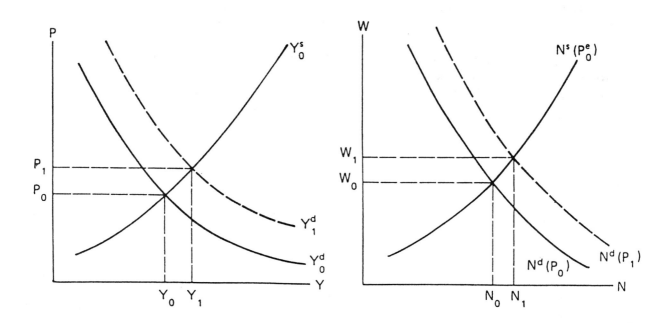

Faster money growth raises Y^d to Y_1^d and increases Y and P. Given we started from a position of stable prices, this implies that $\hat{P}$ (at least for the current period) is higher. The higher price level fools workers, and they supply the extra labor that firms demand at the higher price level. Therefore, N rises. If N is fixed, u falls. We can show the new equilibrium at point Z (Y_1, P_1, N_1, W_1) as u_1, $\hat{P}_1$:

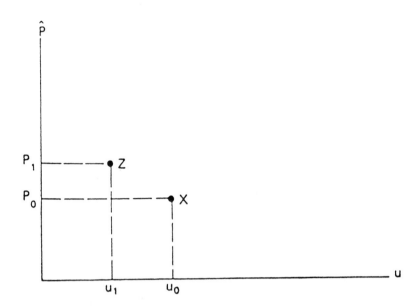

This is the theoretical basis for the Phillips curve trade-off. Note that the policymaker has traded off some inflation to gain a reduction in u by raising the rate of growth of money unexpectedly. (We will get to this in the next chapter, but the student might consider how different the result might have been if workers knew the prices were going to rise in P_1 and quickly used that information in wage contracts.)

If money growth is reduced, the model predicts the lower inflation and higher unemployment. Therefore, we can think of the negatively sloped Phillips curve as tracing out the numerous possible positions of model equilibrium. Which particular point the economy rests at depends on the growth of money and the values of the other exogenous variables of the model.

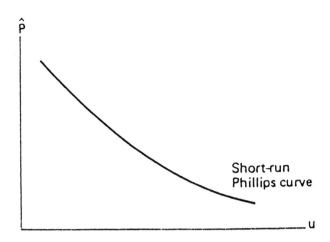

2. The Long-Run Phillips Curve

The Phillips curve described above was drawn with the assumption that price expectations of workers were fixed. But we have learned that workers will realize that their expectations were incorrect. As they learn of their errors, say $P_1 > P_0^e$, they make adjustments. If prices turn out higher than expected, they will push for higher wages:

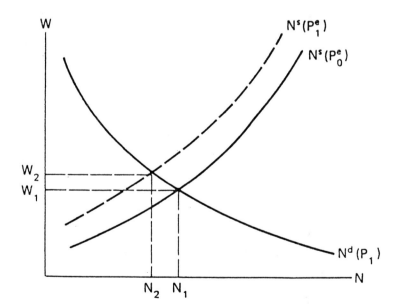

With the now-revised price expectations ($P_1^e > P_0^e$), the N^s curve shifts back; wages rise and employment falls. In the output market, the higher real wage means less output supplied at any price:

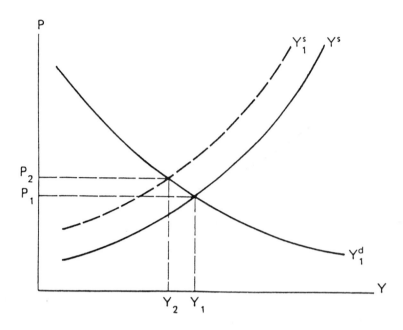

This results in even higher prices and lower output. Thus, inflation rises another notch to $\hat{P}_2$ but unemployment rises too, to u_2. This phenomenon of simultaneously rising $\hat{P}$ and u is <u>not</u> a movement along the existing Phillips curve—it is portrayed by a shift:

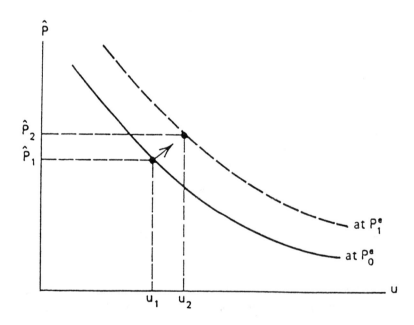

Thus, we say that the Phillips curve shifts in the long run as workers' expectations adjust.

The overall experiment can be expressed with movements along, and then a shift of, the Phillips curve (from X to Z to W):

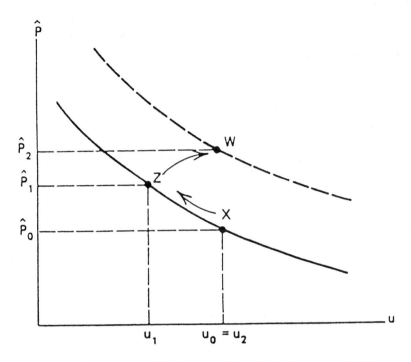

If we ignore the transient or short-run equilibrium position, Z, the long-run Phillips curve traces all those points where price expectations are correct and unchanging. Therefore, it connects points like X and W. Therefore, the long-run Phillips curve is a vertical line:

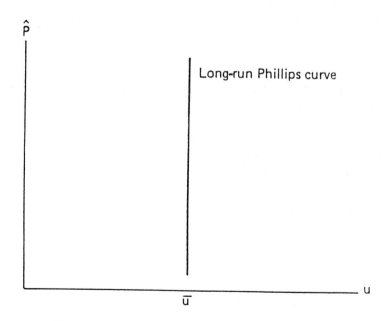

The unemployment rate, $\bar{u}$, is the natural rate of unemployment. Notice that this theory does not say that $u = \bar{u}$ all the time. It says that $\bar{u}$ is some average rate around which the unemployment rate tends to oscillate.

Self-Tests

Multiple-Choice Questions:

1. According to the theory of the "natural" rate of unemployment, there exists an equilibrium level of unemployment that is determined by:
   a. the money supply and the government deficit
   b. interest rates and inflation
   c. factor supply, technology, and institutions
   d. wage and price controls

2. Milton Friedman believes there is a trade-off between inflation and unemployment:
   a. in the short run
   b. in the long run
   c. both a and b
   d. neither a nor b

3. According to the Phillips curve theory, an unanticipated increase in the growth rate of the money supply will:
   a. cause a movement along the curve
   b. cause the curve to shift its position in the long run
   c. both a and b
   d. neither a nor b

4. According to the monetarist view, money could be used to keep the unemployment rate below the natural rate of unemployment for some time, if:
   a. monetary and fiscal policies are coordinated
   b. the rate of growth of money accelerates more than expected each period
   c. workers never have illusions about the price level
   d. all of the above

5. If money has been rising too quickly for years, the resulting inflation can be brought under control by slowing money growth. This will:
   a. quickly reduce inflation with no side effects
   b. quickly reduce inflation with higher unemployment
   c. slowly reduce inflation with no side effects
   d. slowly reduce inflation with higher unemployment

6. The theory of the natural rate of unemployment implies that policymakers can:
   a. temporarily reduce unemployment below its natural rate
   b. permanently reduce unemployment below its natural rate
   c. both a and b
   d. neither a nor b

7. Keynesians and monetarists would agree that:
   a. in the short run, the Phillips curve is vertical
   b. in the short run, the Phillips curve is downward sloping
   c. in the long run, the Phillips curve is fixed
   d. in the long run, the Phillips curve is downward sloping

8. Keynesians are interventionists, because they believe:
   a. the short-run Phillips curve is downward sloping
   b. the long-run Phillips curve is vertical
   c. private sector aggregate demand is stable
   d. all of the above

9. Keynesians are interventionists, because they:
   a. minimize the importance of uncertainty as it relates to policy
   b. believe they understand how to offset undesirable changes in the economy
   c. both a and b
   d. neither a nor b

10. Which of the following will cause the Phillips curve to shift upwards in the short run?
    a. Slower money growth
    b. Faster money growth
    c. Higher inflationary expectations
    d. Higher interest rates

11. The theory of the natural rate of unemployment implies:
    a. policymakers can permanently affect output and employment
    b. policymakers face a trade-off of inflation and unemployment in the long run
    c. policymakers cannot "peg" the unemployment rate at some arbitrarily-determined target rate
    d. a and b only

12. The natural rate theory is compatible with the monetarist view of:
    a. noninterventionist policies
    b. the constant money growth rate policy
    c. interventionist policies being responsible for increased inflation rates
    d. a and b only
    e. all of the above

13. One of the main differences between the Keynesians' and the monetarists' stabilization policies is that:
    a. the Keynesians believe policy can be used to offset short-run fluctuations
    b. the monetarists believe policy can be used to offset long-run fluctuations
    c. the Keynesians do not believe in a vertical long-run Phillips curve
    d. a and b only

14. Keynesians believe output and employment levels:
    a. are naturally convergent to equilibrium
    b. have a natural rate
    c. show persistence
    d. a and b only

15. The trade-off between inflation and unemployment is shown:
    a. by the Phillips curve
    b. by the average propensity to consume
    c. by the consumption function
    d. by the multiplier

16. According to the monetarists, the long-run Phillips curve is:
    a. horizontal
    b. vertical
    c. downward sloping but steeper than the short-run Phillips curve
    d. downward sloping but flatter than the short-run Phillips curve

17. The natural rate of unemployment:
    a. never changes
    b. is a short-term phenomenon
    c. is the same as the full employment rate of unemployment
    d. is that unemployment rate to which the economy tends to move in the long run

18. According to the monetarists:
    a. stable money stock growth is not necessary for a stable economy
    b. stable money stock growth is a requirement for economic stability
    c. fiscal stabilization policies are needed
    d. private sector aggregate demand is unstable and caused mostly by the instability of investment demand

19. Monetarists assume that suppliers of labor:
    a. have perfect information about the real wage
    b. may or may not know the real wage
    c. do not have perfect information about the real wage
    d. none of the above

20. According to the monetarists, a fall in the expected rate of inflation:
    a. will shift the short-run Phillips curve downward
    b. will shift the short-run Phillips curve upward
    c. will not affect the short-run Phillips curve
    d. none of the above

21. According to the monetarists, a bond-financed increase in government spending would have a strong effect on real output:
    a. in the long run but not the short run
    b. in the short run but not the long run
    c. in both the short run and the long run
    d. none of the above

22. In the Keynesian view:
    a. the short-run Phillips curve is vertical but the long-run Phillips curve is downward sloping
    b. the short-run Phillips curve is downward sloping but the long-run Phillips curve is vertical
    c. both the short-run and long-run Phillips curves are downward sloping
    d. both the short-run and long-run Phillips curves are vertical

23. According to Friedman's natural rate theory, expansionary monetary policies:
    a. can move output above the natural rate but leave unemployment at the natural rate
    b. can move both output and employment below the natural rate
    c. can move output above the natural rate but move the unemployment rate below the natural rate for a short time
    d. leave output at its natural rate but move unemployment below its natural rate

24. According to the monetarists:
    a. expansionary monetary policy has no effect on the natural rate of unemployment
    b. expansionary monetary policy can only temporarily move the unemployment rate below the natural rate
    c. there is a trade-off between unemployment and inflation in the short run
    d. either b or c
    e. none of the above

25. Both the Keynesians and monetarists agree that:
    a. an increase in aggregate demand will increase both output and price in the short run
    b. there is a trade-off between inflation and unemployment in the short run
    c. in the long run, when the expected price level also has time to adjust, output will not be affected by changes in aggregate demand
    d. all of the above

26. The theory of the natural rates of unemployment and output was developed by:
    a. Milton Friedman
    b. John Maynard Keynes
    c. Robert Solow
    d. Joseph Stiglitz

27. Which of the following statements is correct?
    a. Both the monetarists and the classicists agree that output is determined by demand side factors in the short run
    b. Both the monetarists and classicists agree that output is completely supply determined, even in the short run
    c. The monetarists do not agree with the classical position that output is completely supply determined, even in the short run
    d. none of the above

28. In the Keynesian model, an increase in the money stock growth rate will cause shifts in the aggregate demand schedule to the right:
    a. where the short-run effect is an increase in output only
    b. where the short-run effect is a rise in both the price level and the unemployment level
    c. with short-run increases in output, the price level, and the employment level
    d. none of the above

29. In the Keynesian model, a decline in autonomous investment will shift the:
    a. aggregate demand schedule to the right and increase output in the short run
    b. aggregate demand schedule to the left and decrease output in the short run
    c. aggregate supply schedule to the right and lower output in the short run
    d. aggregate supply schedule to the left and increase output in the short run

Problems and/or Essay Questions:

1. Below is a table of unemployment rates and inflation rates for the U.S. from 1962-97. Plot this data on a diagram with the inflation rate on the vertical axis and the unemployment rate on the horizontal axis. Then write a short essay describing the Phillips curve for the United States. How does the picture you drew correspond to the theory of the Phillips curve? Does the data provide an indication of whether there is a natural rate of unemployment?

Year	Unemployment Rate	Inflation Rate
62	5.5	1.2
63	5.7	1.6
64	5.2	1.2
65	4.5	1.9
66	3.8	3.4
67	3.8	3.0
68	3.6	4.7
69	3.5	6.1
70	4.9	5.5
71	5.9	3.4
72	5.6	3.4
73	4.9	8.8
74	5.6	12.2
75	8.5	7.0
76	7.7	4.8
77	7.0	6.8
78	6.0	9.0
79	5.8	13.3
80	7.1	12.4
81	7.6	8.9
82	9.7	3.9
83	9.6	3.8
84	7.5	4.0
85	7.2	3.8
86	7.0	1.1
87	6.2	4.4
88	5.5	4.4
89	5.3	4.6
90	5.5	6.1
91	6.7	3.1
92	7.4	2.9
93	6.8	2.7
94	6.1	2.7
95	5.6	2.8
96	5.4	3.0
97	4.9	1.7

2. Begin with a situation whereby the growth rate of money had been accelerating for years. The inflation rate has also been increasing, and policymakers decide to reduce the growth rate of money to stop inflation. Using the Phillips curve (or the Keynesian model), describe how inflation and unemployment might be affected under two very different policies:

   a. Abruptly reduce the growth rate of the money supply to zero percent, and hold it there for one or two years.
   b. Announce a policy that would gradually bring the growth rate of money down to 4 percent over a period of three to four years.

3. Go directly to the heart of the issue separating the policy beliefs of monetarists and Keynesians. Write two well-constructed paragraphs explaining why they can't agree to be either interventionists or noninterventionists. What does the natural rate of unemployment have to do with this debate?

4. The Phillips curve is more than a line connecting data dots. It is also an expression of a complex theory about the economy. Explain what is happening to output, wages, interest rates, and price expectations as we move from point A to point B to point C below? Start out by explaining what might have caused such a movement. Then, explain the behavior of the economy as it moves between these points.

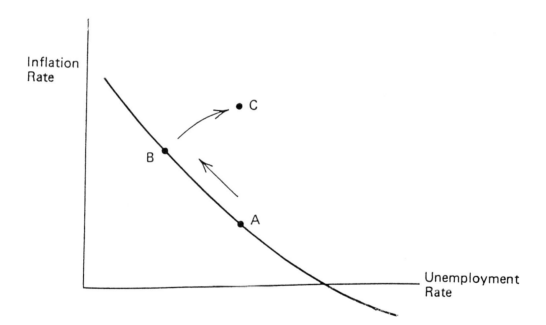

5. Define the unemployment rate. Distinguish the overall unemployment rate from the natural unemployment rate. Describe briefly how these rates have changed since World War II.

6. Explain why Friedman's natural rate hypothesis is not compatible with the classical model.

7. Describe why the Keynesians have doubts about the natural rate hypothesis. What properties do the Keynesians believe the economy's output and employment level possess?

8. What is meant by "hysteresis?"

9. Explain the Keynesian effects of a decline in autonomous investment.

10. What has the divergent behavior of unemployment in the United States and Europe in the 1990s been attributed to?

CHAPTER 11

NEW CLASSICAL ECONOMICS

OVERVIEW

The new classical model is the next major modern macroeconomic theory we consider. The new classical economics is a challenge to the Keynesian position on a very fundamental level. The new classical economists criticize the basic theoretical structure of the Keynesian model and the policy conclusions reached by Keynesians.

The structure of the chapter is as follows. The first section explains the new classical economists' concept of <u>rational expectations</u> and the policy-ineffectiveness proposition that follows from that concept. According to the hypothesis of rational expectations, expectations are formed on the basis of all the available relevant information concerning the variable being predicted. Furthermore, the rational expectations hypothesis maintains that individuals use available information intelligently; that is, they understand the way in which the variables they observe will affect the variable they are trying to predict. The central new classical policy conclusion is that the values of real variables such as output and employment are insensitive to <u>systematic</u> changes in aggregate demand in both the short and long run. The way in which unanticipated changes in aggregate demand <u>do</u> affect output and employment in the short run is also illustrated. Next, we take a broader look at the new classical economics, emphasizing the classical roots of the new classical view. The two assumptions that the new classical economists feel are necessary for fruitful macroeconomic models are explained, namely,

(1) agents act in a optimal fashion; that is; they act in their own self-interest, and

(2) markets clear.

The third section of the chapter considers the modern Keynesians' response to the argument put forward by the new classical economists. The modern Keynesians argue that:

(1) the new classical economists do not provide a plausible explanation for the persistence of deviations from full employment;

(2) the informational assumption embodied in the rational expectations concept is unrealistic in the short run; and

(3) the labor market is a more contractual market than the auction market characterization in the new classical theory.

Techniques in Depth

1. The Rational Expectations Assumption

The rational expectations assumption maintains that individuals use available relevant information intelligently to form price forecasts. In the macroeconomic model, recall that the things that actually determine the price level are all the autonomous components of Y^d and Y^s. Therefore, assume the following is a simplified quantitative description of how these variables actually affect the price level:

$$P_t = \alpha_0 + \alpha_1 M_t + \alpha_2(g_0 - t_0)_t + \alpha_3 \bar{i}_t + \varepsilon_t$$

The α's are meant to be parameters which relate changes in P_t to changes in M_t, $(g_0 - t_0)_t$, and $\bar{i}_t$. The last variable, ε_t, is a proxy for all the unpredictable other things which affect P_t. We assume the average value for ε_t over a fairly long period of time is zero.

If people are rational in the same sense as defined above, they might use the above equation to forecast prices. However, what they would use is:

$$P_t^e = \alpha_0 + \alpha_1 M_t^e + \alpha_2(g_0 - t_0)_t^e + \alpha_3 \bar{i}_t^e$$

That is, they would first make guesses about M_t, $g_0 - t_0)_t$, i_t, and ε_t. The best guess of ε_t is zero, its mean value. Then they use these guesses to forecast P^e according to the way the theory (the equation) says they should.

The implications for forecasting accuracy under rational expectations are interesting. The forecast error is defined as: $P_t - P_t^e$. Subtracting the equation for P_t^e from the one for P_t yields:

$$P_t - P_t^e = \alpha_1(M_t - M_t^e) + \alpha_2[(g_0 - t_0)_t - (g_0 - t_0)_t^e] + \alpha_3(\bar{i}_t - \bar{i}_t^e) + \varepsilon_t$$

This shows that in any <u>one</u> period, forecasting errors are possible, even with rational expectations if:

(1) agents forecast M_t, $(g_0 - t_0)_t$, or $\bar{i}_t$ poorly, or if

(2) the unpredictable catchall term turns out to be nonzero.

2. Output Changes and Rational Expectations

If we were to form a simple mathematical expression for output, Y_t, in the basic macroeconomic model, we would have to accentuate the fact that output rises (falls) only when prices rise more (less) than workers expected. This is the way aggregate demand changes cause output to change. Let us write such an output equation:

$$Y_t = Y_{t-1} + B_1(P_t - P_t^e) + V_t$$

$$B_1 > 0$$

This says that output will equal exactly what it was last year (Y_{t-1}), unless something unusual happens. That is, if something causes a forecast error ($P_t \neq P_t^e$), this will cause output to change by B_1 (the output elasticity) times the forecast error. The term V_t is meant to be an unpredictable supply event—such as an oil crisis, crop failure, etc. It, like ε_t, is assumed to have a mean value of zero.

New Classical Economics   136

Now recall from above that we developed an equation for forecast errors, $P_t - P_t^e$. Let us substitute that equation into the output equation:

$$Y_t = Y_{t-1} + B_1\alpha_1(M_t - M_t^e) + B_1\alpha_2[(g_0 - t_0)_t - (g_0 - t_0)_t^e] + B_1\alpha_3(\bar{i}_t - \bar{i}_t^e) + B_t\varepsilon_t + V_t$$

This shows that it is <u>forecast errors</u> that cause output to change from Y_{t-1}. For example, since α_1 and B_1 are not zero, if the money stock rises faster than expected, prices rise more than expected (workers are fooled), and output rises. Of course, unpredictable demand (ε_t) or supply (V_t) events will also cause output to change in the short run.

Notice what happens to output if the money stock rises but it was fully anticipated. In that case, $M_t = M_t^e$ and $M_t - M_t^e = 0$. Therefore, there is no effect of anticipated money stock on output!

Self-Tests

Multiple-Choice Questions:

1. The focal point of the new classical economists' criticism of both Keynesian and monetarist models is:
   a. assumptions about the interest elasticity of money demand
   b. assumptions about the interest elasticity of investment demand
   c. assumptions about the formation of price expectations
   d. assumptions about the behavior of the velocity of money

2. The new classical economists believe that:
   a. economic agents always forecast prices correctly
   b. economic agents know aggregate demand with certainty
   c. economic agents do not make systematic forecast errors
   d. economic agents are irrational

3. Rational expectations means that:
   a. expectations are formed using all relevant information
   b. workers use only past price information to forecast prices
   c. workers know all things that affect prices in the macro model
   d. all of the above

4. In the new classical model, the expected price level and, therefore, the labor supply and output supply functions depend upon:
   a. expected levels of the money stock
   b. expected level of government spending
   c. expected tax collections
   d. expected levels of autonomous investment spending
   e. all of the above

5. An anticipated increase in the money supply, according to the new classical model,
   a. has no effect on prices in the short run
   b. has no effect on output in the short run
   c. only affects output in the long run
   d. all of the above

6. In the new classical model, an unanticipated increase in the money supply:
   a. has no effect on output in the short run
   b. has an effect on output in the short run, but not in the long run
   c. has an effect on output in the long run and short run
   d. is impossible

7. New classical economists believe aggregate demand management policy should not be used, because:
   a. policy never affects output if people are rational
   b. anticipated monetary policy has large and destabilizing effects
   c. only unanticipated events affect output, and these are not policies
   d. all real problems are aggregate supply problems

8. Many new classical economists would look favorably upon a policy of:
   a. active stabilization with monetary policy
   b. active stabilization with government deficits and surpluses
   c. constant growth rate for the money stock
   d. lower taxation

9. A criticism of the new classical model is that it does not have an adequate explanation for:
   a. rising prices and output
   b. short-run effects of monetary policy on output
   c. persistently high unemployment rates
   d. all of the above

10. The major disagreement between Keynesians and new classical economists concerns expectation formation. If policymakers always have more and better data than private sector agents, then:
    a. the new classical economists are right, and policymakers should not actively stabilize the economy
    b. the Keynesians are right, and policymakers should actively stabilize the economy
    c. policymakers would be better off by just making better information available to private agents
    d. b or c, but not a

11. In the new classical view, the labor market is typified by:
    a. long-term contracts
    b. the invisible handshake
    c. worker reluctance to accept wage reductions
    d. auction market behavior

12. In the new classical model, an anticipated increase in government spending would cause:
    a. output and price to rise
    b. output to rise, but price would stay the same
    c. price to rise, but output would stay the same
    d. no change in price or output

13. The expectations assumed in the Keynesian model are:
    a. rational
    b. forward-looking
    c. backward-looking
    d. transitional

14. In the new classical model, an unanticipated decline in investment demand has what short-run effects?
    a. It decreases output
    b. It decreases the price level
    c. It decreases employment
    d. all of the above
    e. none of the above

15. If the above autonomous decline in investment was anticipated:
    a. the answer to question 14, would remain the same
    b. the expected level of autonomous investment would fall
    c. output and employment would remain unchanged
    d. all of the above
    e. none of the above

16. According to the rational expectations model, a demand shock:
    a. can shift the aggregate demand curve to the left or to the right
    b. is an anticipated shift in the aggregate demand curve
    c. is an unanticipated shift in the aggregate demand curve
    d. none of the above

17. According to new classical economics, systematic monetary and fiscal policy actions that change aggregate demand:
    a. affect output and employment in the short run only
    b. affect output and employment in the long run only
    c. affect output and employment in both the short run and the long run
    d. none of the above

18. In the new classical model, an unanticipated decline in investment demand:
    a. will cause output to fall with no effect on the price level
    b. will cause the price level to fall with no effect on output
    c. will neither change the price level nor output
    d. will cause both the price level and output to fall

19. In the early 1980s, the U.S. economy:
    a. experienced a costly disinflation
    b. experienced stagflation
    c. experienced hyperinflation
    d. experienced high rates of inflation

20. With respect to fiscal policy, the new classical economists:
    a. try to avoid erratic government deficit spending
    b. try to avoid excessive and inflationary stimuli
    c. favor stability
    d. all of the above

21. The similarity between the new classical economists and the monetarists is that:
    a. both believe that monetary policy has much stronger employment effects than does fiscal policy
    b. both are policy activists
    c. both believe that the interest elasticity of money demand is very high
    d. both are noninterventionists in their views on macroeconomic policy

22. According to the new classical model, an unanticipated increase in the money stock would:
    a. raise the price level and the level of real output
    b. raise the price level with no effect on real output
    c. raise real output with no effect on the price level
    d. neither change the price level nor the level of real output

23. According to new classical economists:
    a. both output and employment are sensitive to systematic aggregate demand management policies in the short run and long run
    b. both output and employment are insensitive to systematic aggregate demand management policies in the short run and long run
    c. both output and employment are only affected in the short run by systematic monetary and fiscal policy actions that change aggregate demand
    d. both output and employment are only affected in the long run by systematic monetary and fiscal policy actions that change aggregate demand

24. In the new classical model, economic agents are assumed to be rational:
    a. and possess perfect information
    b. and make no mistakes about price level predictions
    c. but they do not have perfect information
    d. and, therefore, make only long-term decisions

25. In the new classical model, the aggregate supply function:
    a. is horizontal
    b. is vertical
    c. depends on the expected values of policy variables
    d. none of the above

26. The classical and new classical models differ in that:
    a. classical economists assumed that the money wage was flexible while the new classicists assumed it was fixed
    b. classical economists are noninterventionists on policy questions while the new classicists are policy activists
    c. classical economists assumed that labor suppliers knew the real wage, while the new classicists assumed they form a rational expectation of the real wage
    d. none of the above

27. In the Keynesian model, a decline in private sector demand:
    a. should always be offset by an expansionary monetary policy action in order to stabilize aggregate demand, output, and employment
    b. should never be offset by an expansionary fiscal policy action to stabilize aggregate demand, output, and employment
    c. should be offset by either an expansionary monetary or fiscal policy action so that aggregate demand, output, and employment could be stabilized
    d. none of the above

28. In the new classical model:
    a. unforeseen declines in aggregate demand would put output and employment below the full-employment levels
    b. unforeseen declines in aggregate demand would only put employment below the full-employment level
    c. anticipated declines in aggregate demand would move output and employment below the full-employment levels
    d. announced declines in aggregate demand do not change output and employment below the full-employment levels

29. According to the new classical theory, a monetary surprise:
    a. will shift the labor supply curve to the right in the short run
    b. will shift the labor supply curve to the left in the short run
    c. will shift the aggregate supply curve to the left in the short run
    d. will not shift the labor supply curve in the short run

30. In which model are economic agents assumed to have perfect information?
    a. The Keynesian model
    b. The classical model
    c. The monetarist model
    d. The new classical model

Problems and/or Essay Questions:

1. Define rational expectations. Very specifically describe how one might form a rational expectation.

2. Following are two sets of price expectations (P_1^e and P_2^e) and the actual price level (P). Determine which price expectation is more likely to be rational. Defend your choice.

P	P_1^e	P_2^e
110	105	109
115	120	114
120	115	119
130	135	129
160	160	159

3. Use the model developed in the text to describe what happens to P, P^e, and Y in the short run when (assume rational expectations):
   a. government spending rises <u>less</u> than expected.
   b. money rises exactly as expected.
   c. investment spending does not increase, but people thought it would.

4. Again, assuming rational expectations, determine what would happen to P, P^e, and Y if the Federal Reserve System began hiding monetary data so that it took six months before people could measure the money supply. What would be the effect of an increase in the money supply directly after this practice started? What might people start doing in a year or so?

5. In the new classical view, what is the primary cause of fairly long periods of time where the unemployment rate remains high? For example, what do the new classical economists say about the Great Depression in the United States?

6. A new area of dispute between new classical economists and Keynesians concerns policy credibility. Why is this so important, and what happened in the early 1980s to make this issue emerge?

7. Compare the backward-looking nature of expectations in the Keynesian model with the forward-looking nature of rational expectations.

8. How would you explain the difference between the auction market view and the contractual view of the labor market?

9. Explain the new classical policy ineffectiveness postulate.

CHAPTER 12

REAL BUSINESS CYCLES AND NEW KEYNESIAN ECONOMICS

OVERVIEW

This chapter explores recent developments in macroeconomic research, which have resulted from the ongoing controversy between Keynesian and new classical economists.

The first section of this chapter introduces and discusses a recent development in classical thought—the real business cycle theory. Consistent with the new classical economics, the two key features of real business cycle theory are its assumptions of (1) agents who optimize and (2) markets that clear. In particular, real business cycle theorists believe that the labor market clears and that observed unemployment is essentially voluntary. Real business cycle theorists, however, disagree with other new classical economists about the source of fluctuations in employment and output. New classical economists believe that unpredicted shifts in aggregate demand are the primary cause of employment and output fluctuations. Real business cycle theorists, on the other hand, argue that aggregate supply shocks, largely through changes in technology, are the primary contributing sources of changes in employment and output.

A simple real business cycle model is developed to demonstrate the response of optimizing economic agents to aggregate supply shocks. Since these responses are the main source of macroeconomic fluctuations and result from optimizing agents, it is concluded that it would be suboptimal, in this model, to eliminate business cycles. The optimal use of macroeconomic policy, according to the real business cycle doctrine, is a mix of monetary and fiscal policy that will minimize total costs from inflation and tax distortion. This section ends with a critical evaluation of the real business cycle theory.

The second section of this chapter introduces new Keynesian models—models that have been developed as the result of the desire of modern Keynesians to improve the microeconomic foundations of the Keynesian theory. In order to make these improvements; modern Keynesians have attempted to prove that wage and price rigidities are compatible with the behavior of optimizing agents. As a result, several models have been developed, including sticky price (menu cost) models, efficiency wage models, and insider-outsider models. Although each new model represents a different approach to the Keynesian theory, they do share some common elements. For example, some form of imperfect competition is assumed for the product markets in each model. Thus, product price rigidity is a new consideration in addition to the traditional Keynesian focus on money wage rigidity. Moreover, the new Keynesian models introduce real rigidities in addition to these nominal ones.

The first of the new Keynesian models that are presented in the chapter is the sticky price (menu cost) model. A key element explaining sticky prices in this model is imperfect competition. Alternative explanations of rigidity in this model include menu costs that arise as prices are changed. This includes the literal menu cost of printing a new menu as well as such costs as loss of good will and costs associated with price wars that might ensue. The second of the new Keynesian models is the efficiency wage model.

The key idea in these models is that the efficiency of the workers depends positively on the real wage they receive. Examples of this model include the shirking model, turnover cost models, and gift exchange models. A key implication of the efficiency wage model is that real wages are set above the market-clearing level, resulting in involuntary unemployment.

The last of the new Keynesian models presented in this chapter is the insider-outsider model. This model was developed to explain the high persistent unemployment rates of the European countries after 1980. A company with a labor union is used as an example of an insider-outsider model in which the union members are insiders and nonunion members are outsiders. The insiders use bargaining power to push the real wages above the market-clearing level, resulting in unemployment for the outsiders. Cyclical unemployment of insiders, nevertheless, may also exist, causing some workers to leave the union. Thus, past unemployment turns into future unemployment, as insiders transform into outsiders. This phenomenon is termed hysteresis and creates what the new Keynesians have termed the unemployment trap.

Techniques in Depth

The following table is designed to help the student recognize the different characteristics of each model presented in this chapter.

	School of Thought	Micro-Foundations	Nature of Markets	Nature of Unemployment	Nature of Prices
Real Business Cycle Model	Classical	Yes	Markets Clear	Voluntary	Flexible
Sticky Price Model	Keynesian	Yes	Markets Do Not Clear	Involuntary	Rigid
Efficiency Wage Model	Keynesian	Yes	Markets Do Not Clear	Involuntary	Rigid
Insider-Outsider Model	Keynesian	Yes	Markets Do Not Clear	Involuntary and Cyclical	Rigid

Self-Tests

Multiple-Choice Questions:

1. The real business cycle model was developed from which of the following schools of thought?
    a. Keynesian
    b. Classical
    c. Modern Keynesian
    d. Monetarist

2. Real business cycle models and new classical models have which of the following characteristics in common?
   a. Theorists of both models believe that the cause of fluctuations in output and employment is from monetary surprises
   b. Markets clear
   c. Agents optimize
   d. B and c only
   e. All of the above

3. Unemployment is explained as being involuntary in:
   a. the sticky price (menu cost) model
   b. the efficiency wage model
   c. the insider-outsider model
   d. all of the above

4. Real business cycle theorists believe that fluctuations in output and employment are caused by:
   a. technology shocks
   b. variations in environmental conditions
   c. changes in tax rates
   d. all of the above

5. In the real business cycle model, a temporary positive technology shock:
   a. decreases labor input
   b. increases the capital stock
   c. decreases saving
   d. increases the money supply

6. In the real business cycle model, monetary policy is used to:
   a. stabilize output
   b. minimize inflation
   c. reduce unemployment
   d. all of the above

7. The new Keynesian models:
   a. have imperfect competition in product markets
   b. stress product price rigidity
   c. stress real rigidities
   d. all of the above

8. The incentive for firms to hold product prices constant even if demand falls is called:
   a. opportunity costs
   b. excess profit
   c. menu costs
   d. economic profit

9. In the efficiency wage model, the aggregate production function is given by:

$$y = F[\bar{K}, e(w/P)N]$$

The firm's goal is thus to:
a. set the real wage so that the cost of an efficiency unit of labor is minimized
b. hire labor up to the point where the cost of an efficiency unit of labor is minimized
c. increase the real wage to the point where the elasticity of the efficiency index with respect to the real wage is equal to one
d. both a and c

10. Rationales for the efficiency wage models that apply to all parts of the labor market include:
a. shirking models
b. turnover cost models
c. gift exchange models
d. all of the above
e. none of the above

11. Efficiency wage models explain:
a. money-wage rigidity
b. product price rigidity
c. real wage rigidity
d. resource price rigidity

12. According to the new Keynesian theory, the way changes in aggregate demand affect output and employment, and, thus involuntary unemployment can be explained by:
a. nominal rigidity
b. menu costs
c. real wage rigidity
d. all of the above

13. Both voluntary and cyclical unemployment exist in:
a. the real business cycle model
b. the inside-outsider model
c. the efficiency wage model
d. the sticky price (menu cost) model

14. The unemployment trap is caused by:
a. too high of an efficiency wage
b. fixed money wage contracts
c. hysteresis
d. backward-looking price expectations

15. The major criticism of the new Keynesian models is:
a. the empirical importance of models
b. the effectiveness of the efficiency wage
c. their explanation of business cycles
d. their ability to incorporate microfoundations

16. Real business cycle theory is a modern version of:
    a. supply-side economics
    b. monetarism
    c. classical economics
    d. Keynesian economics

17. The aggregate production function for real business cycle models is:
    a. $Y_t = z_t/(K_t, N_t)$
    b. $Y_t = z_t F(K_t, N_t)$
    c. $Y_t = z_t F(K_t, N_t)$
    d. $Y_t = F(K_t, N_t)$

18. Real business cycle research began:
    a. in the 1980s
    b. in the early 1970s
    c. in the late 1950s
    d. in the early 1990s

19. An important factor in new Keynesian sticky price models is:
    a. the firm must not be a perfect competitor
    b. the firm is a natural monopolist
    c. the firm must be a perfect competitor
    d. none of the above

20. In the real business cycle model, a positive technology shock:
    a. has no effect on the production function
    b. is a movement along the production function
    c. shifts the production functions down
    d. shifts the production function up

21. According to the new Keynesian economists:
    a. very little unemployment is voluntary
    b. no unemployment is involuntary
    c. a great deal of unemployment is voluntary
    d. most unemployment is involuntary

22. In real business cycle theory, a negative supply shock:
    a. results in a decline in employment but not in output
    b. results in a decline in output but not in employment
    c. would cause a decline in both output and employment
    d. would neither change output nor employment

23. In terms of unemployment, hysteresis models attempt to explain why:
    a. structural unemployment cannot be eliminated
    b. frictional unemployment is the cause of hysteresis
    c. cyclical unemployment is always present
    d. high unemployment persists even after its initial cause is long past

24. The models that explain why high unemployment has persisted in some European countries for such long periods, periods too long to be the result of fixed money-wage contracts or backward-looking price expectations, are known as:
    a. IS-LM models
    b. sticky price models
    c. insider-outsider models
    d. efficiency wage models

25. Real business cycle theorists:
    a. favor a constant money growth rate rule for the money stock
    b. reach noninterventionist policy conclusions
    c. reach policy interventionist conclusions
    d. none of the above

26. The models that view changes in real supply-side factors as determinants of short-run fluctuations in output and employment are:
    a. real business cycle models
    b. new classical models
    c. political business cycle models
    d. Keynesian models

27. According to efficiency wage models, the efficiency of workers depends:
    a. positively on the money wage they are paid
    b. positively on the real wage they are paid
    c. positively on the unemployment rate
    d. none of the above

28. According to the real business cycle model, the optimum use of monetary and fiscal policy is to combine them so that total costs from inflation and tax distortions are:
    a. equalized
    b. eliminated
    c. maximized
    d. minimized

29. Shocks most often emphasized in real business cycle theory are:
    a. changes in tax rates
    b. changes in the real (relative) prices of imported raw materials
    c. shocks to technology
    d. variations in environmental conditions

30. In the real business cycle, the capital stock :
    a. is shown as K
    b. is taken as given for each period
    c. is chosen for each period
    d. both a and b
    e. both a and c

Problems and/or Essay Questions:

1. Explain the key Keynesian criticism of the new classical model and how the real business cycle model corrects for this.

2. Explain why real business cycle theorists disagree with the new classical explanation of the cause of short-run fluctuations in output, yet have so many other similar characteristics.

3. What are two major criticisms of the real business cycle theory?

4. Using empirical evidence of labor market flows, elaborate on the second criticism in the previous question.

5. Why is it important in the sticky price models that the firm not be a perfect competitor?

6. If the firm increases the wage bill by two percent, how much will the efficiency of labor have to increase before the firm will stop increasing the wage bill?

7. The production function of the simple real business cycle model is given as

$$y_t = Z_t F(K_t, N_t).$$

What are the differences, if any, of this production function and the original classical production function?

8. In the insider-outsider models, explain the cause of persistent high unemployment.

9. There are two possible interpretations of the real business cycle theory. Explain these interpretations.

10. The key element in efficiency wage models is an explanation of why the efficiency of workers depends on the real wage. Within this context, explain the shirking model and the gift exchange model.

11. What role is there for monetary policy in a real business cycle model?

CHAPTER 13

MACROECONOMIC MODELS: A SUMMARY

OVERVIEW

This chapter gives an overview of the theories considered in the earlier chapters in Part II and attempts to clarify the areas of agreement and disagreement among various schools of macroeconomic theory. As was done throughout these earlier chapters, the different models are represented within the aggregate demand-aggregate supply framework, as illustrated in Figure 13.1. The analysis is divided into theoretical issues (Section 13.1) and policy issues (Section 13.2).

It is argued that the two important theoretical differences between the Keynesians and classical frameworks are:

(1) In the classical model, output and employment are completely supply-determined, whereas in the Keynesian theory, in the short run, output and employment are determined jointly by aggregate supply and demand. In the Keynesian system, aggregate demand is an important determinant of output and employment.

(2) Aggregate demand in the classical model is determined solely by the quantity of money. In the Keynesian system, money is one of a number of factors that determined aggregate demand.

The major controversy between the monetarists and the Keynesians concerns point 2, the degree to which monetary factors dominate the determination of aggregate demand. The issue dividing the new classical economists and the Keynesians concerns point (1) above, the nature of the relationship between aggregate demand and real output.

On policy issues, the noninterventionist policy conclusions of the classical economists, monetarists, and new classical economists are contrasted with the activist position of the Keynesians.

Techniques in Depth

1. Using Economic Data

Economic data can be located and used at low cost. This exercise presents two historical series for real GDP and for the money supply and shows you what can be done with a little bit of data. A proper presentation of the data can help us to see regularities or patterns in the behavior of a variable. First, we present the data in tabular form:

Year	Real GDP in $ billions		Money Supply in $ billions	
	Level	(rate)	Level	(rate)
1966	$2208.3	5.8%	$172.1	2.5%
1967	2271.4	2.9	183.3	6.5
1968	2365.6	4.1	197.5	7.7
1969	2423.3	2.4	204.0	3.3
1970	2416.2	−0.3	214.5	5.1
1971	2484.8	2.8	228.4	6.5
1972	2608.5	5.0	249.4	9.2
1973	2744.1	5.2	263.0	5.5
1974	2729.3	−0.5	274.4	4.3
1975	2695.0	−1.3	287.6	4.8
1976	2826.7	4.9	306.5	6.6
1977	2958.6	4.7	331.4	8.1
1978	3115.2	5.3	358.7	8.2
1979	3192.4	2.9	386.1	7.6
1980	3187.1	−0.2	412.2	6.8
1981	3248.8	1.9	439.1	6.5
1982	3166.0	−2.5	476.4	8.5
1983	3279.1	3.6	522.1	9.6
1984	3501.4	6.8	551.9	5.7
1985	3168.7	3.4	620.1	12.4
1986	3721.7	2.8	725.4	17.0
1987	3847.0	3.4	750.8	3.5
1988	4029.1	4.7	790.3	5.3

From this tabular presentation, we can learn several things about output and money. For example, the general levels of both series are much higher in 1988 than they were in 1966. The level of the money supply has never fallen, though the level of real GDP fell in five of the 23 years presented.

We often find these variables reported as annual rates of growth rather than as levels. Knowing that GDP was $4029.1 billion may not be meaningful, but hearing that it grew by 4.7 percent in 1988 conveys information understandable to more people. It also helps us to see more vividly the highly cyclical nature of these variables.

The table shows that real GDP has risen as fast as 6.8 percent (in 1984) and has fallen as much as 2.5 percent (in 1982) on a yearly basis. We also see that the recessionary years (negative growth rates) are interspersed between healthier periods. Since the money supply has never fallen since 1966, we have no negative growth rates. We do see that there have been periods of relatively slow money growth and periods of relatively rapid growth.

Charts or graphs are pictures that communicate these kinds of facts very quickly. Below, we chart both the rates of growth of money and real GDP. Let us see what else we can learn here.

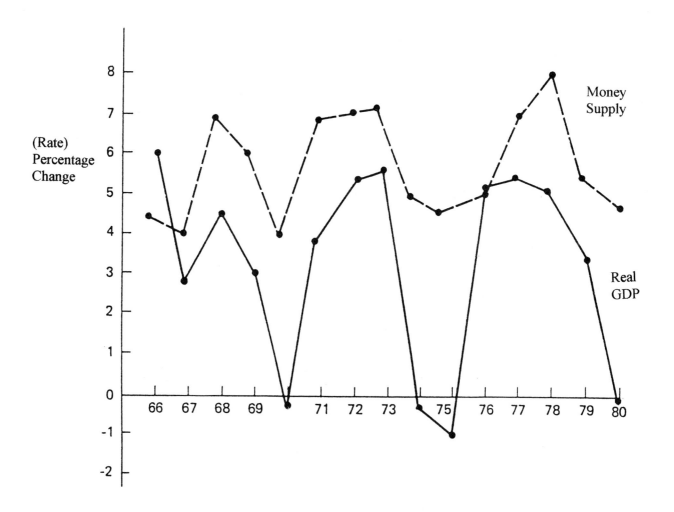

The preceding chart visually portrays the variability of these two economic variables. One interesting aspect not discussed, but revealed by the graph, concerns the shared behavior of the two series. Note that the large reductions in the growth rate of real GDP in 1969-70 and 1974-75 were accompanied by sizeable yearly reductions in the growth of money. The student should consider how this data supports or conflicts with the various macroeconomic theories summarized and contrasted in Chapter 13 of the text.

Self-Tests

Multiple-Choice Questions:

1. In the real business cycle theory, the labor market is always in equilibrium—all unemployment is:
   a. cyclical
   b. voluntary
   c. structural
   d. involuntary
   e. frictional

2. In the new Keynesian model:
   a. supply factors influence output
   b. monetary factors influence aggregate demand
   c. aggregate demand influences output
   d. all of the above

3. The fundamental difference between the monetarists and the Keynesians is:
   a. the degree to which monetary factors dominate aggregate demand
   b. whether or not the aggregate supply schedule slopes upward to the right in the short run
   c. the extent to which aggregate demand influences output
   d. all of the above

4. Which of the following theory or theories advocates policy intervention? In particular, which advocates aggregate demand management to stabilize output and employment?
   a. Monetarist theory
   b. Monetarist and Keynesian theories
   c. Real business cycle theory and new classical theory
   d. Keynesian theory
   e. None of the above

5. In macroeconomics, the controversy concerning policy issues is between:
   a. the new classical theorists and the Keynesians
   b. the noninterventionists and interventionists
   c. the real business cycle theorists and the monetarists
   d. the Keynesians and the monetarists
   e. both a and b

6. The real business cycle theory is a modern version of the:
   a. classical theory
   b. new classical theory
   c. Keynesian theory
   d. monetarist theory

7. The Keynesian aggregate supply schedule:
   a. is horizontal
   b. is vertical
   c. slopes upward to the right
   d. slopes downward to the left

8. According to the classical model, output is:
   a. completely supply determined
   b. completely demand determined
   c. determined by supply and demand factors
   d. none of the above

9. The macroeconomic model that dominated macroeconomic analysis from the early post-World War II years until the late 1960s was the:
   a. new classical model
   b. classical model
   c. monetarist model
   d. Keynesian model

10. In the new classical model, unanticipated changes in aggregate demand:
    a. shift the aggregate demand schedule only
    b. shift the aggregate supply schedule only
    c. shift both the aggregate demand and aggregate supply schedules
    d. none of the above

11. When considering the demand side, the simple Keynesian model excludes:
    a. taxes
    b. autonomous investment
    c. government spending
    d. monetary factors
    e. all of the above

12. In the new classical model, the aggregate supply schedule depends on:
    a. the expected level of the money stock
    b. the expected values of fiscal policy variables and other possible determinants of aggregate demand
    c. the expected price level
    d. Both a and b
    e. all of the above

13. In the classical system:
    a. neither output nor employment are self-adjusting to the supply-determined full-employment levels
    b. both output and employment are self-adjusting to the supply-determined full-employment levels
    c. only employment is self-adjusting to the supply-determined full-employment levels
    d. only output is self-adjusting to the supply-determined full-employment levels

14. According to the monetarists:
    a. only anticipated monetary policy actions will affect output and employment in the short run
    b. only unforeseen monetary policy actions will affect output and employment in the short run
    c. both anticipated and unanticipated monetary policy actions will affect output but not employment in the short run
    d. both anticipated and unanticipated monetary policy actions will affect both output and employment in the short run

15. The Keynesian aggregate supply schedule:
    a. slopes downward to the left
    b. slopes upward to the right
    c. is vertical
    d. is horizontal

16. The Keynesian orthodoxy was challenged by:
    a. monetarists
    b. real business cycle theorists
    c. new classicists
    d. both a and c
    e. both b and c

17. In the new classical system, an unanticipated increase in the money stock:
    a. will only shift the aggregate supply schedule
    b. will only shift the aggregate demand schedule
    c. will shift both the aggregate demand and aggregate supply schedules
    d. none of the above

18. In the Keynesian model, increases in aggregate demand:
    a. will increase price and decrease output
    b. will increase output and decrease price
    c. will decrease both price and output
    d. will increase both price and output

19. The quantity theory provides a:
    a. proportional relationship between the exogenous quantity of money and the level of nominal income
    b. disproportional relationship between the exogenous quantity of money and the level of nominal income
    c. proportional relationship between the endogenous quantity of money and the level of real income
    d. disproportional relationship between the level of prices and the money in circulation

20. In the real business cycle model, output and employment are:
    a. entirely demand determined
    b. determined by real supply-side variables
    c. determined by supply and demand factors
    d. none of the above

21. In the classical model, changes in aggregate demand:
    a. affect the price level but have no effect on output
    b. affect output but not the price level
    c. affect both output and the price level in the short run
    d. affect neither the price level nor output

Problems and/or Essay Questions:

1. Below, we present yearly historical data for a variety of economic variables. Does money growth appear to cause inflation? Does wage growth appear to lag inflation? What relationship does there seem to be between government deficits, inflation and output? Consider these relationships in light of the following data (money and real GDP data have already been presented in the previous section).

Year	Rate of Price Change (GDP Deflator)	Rate of Change of Compensation	Federal Government Deficit (billions)
1966	3.6%	6.9%	$ 3.7
1967	2.6	5.4	8.6
1968	5.0	7.9	25.2
1969	5.6	7.0	−3.2
1970	5.5	7.3	2.8
1971	5.7	6.4	23.0
1972	4.7	6.4	23.4
1973	6.5	8.3	14.5
1974	9.1	9.5	6.1
1975	9.8	9.7	53.2
1976	6.4	8.9	73.7
1977	6.7	7.8	53.6
1978	7.3	8.5	59.2
1979	8.9	9.7	40.2
1980	9.0	10.5	73.8
1981	9.7	9.2	78.9
1982	6.4	7.8	127.9
1983	3.9	4.2	207.8
1984	3.7	4.1	185.3
1985	3.0	4.5	212.3
1986	2.7	4.3	221.2
1987	3.3	4.0	149.7
1988	3.4	4.8	155.1

2. The student should fill in the following tables (use a plus sign if the effect of money on a given variable is positive, a minus sign if the effect is negative):

Theory	THEORETICAL EFFECTS Short-Run Effect of Money on:			
	Y	P	W/P	r
Classical				
Keynesian				
Monetarist				
New Classical				

Theory	THEORETICAL EFFECTS Long-Run Effect of Money on:			
	Y	P	W/P	r
Classical				
Keynesian				
Monetarist				
New Classical				

3. Construct two more similar tables. This time, title the tables the short-run and long-run effects of the government deficit on Y, P, W/P, and r.

4. It has been stated that the real business cycle theory is a modern version of the classical theory. Explain how this is the case.

5. Why can the controversies among the various schools of macroeconomic thought not be resolved?

6. Compare the role of aggregate demand in determining output and employment and the relative importance of monetary and other factors as determinants of aggregate demand in the classical model with the Keynesian system.

PART III: EXTENSIONS OF THE MODELS

CHAPTER 14

CONSUMPTION AND INVESTMENT

OVERVIEW

This is the first chapter in Part III that considers extensions of the models discussed in Part II. This first chapter examines the determinants of the private sector's demand for output: consumption and investment spending.

The section on consumption spending begins with an examination of the early empirical evidence on the Keynesian consumption function. The conflicts between the implications of short-run time series data and data from cross-section budget studies on the one hand, and long-run time series on the other, are explained. The erratic short-run movements in consumption relative to income are also noted as background to a consideration of the modern theories of consumption. Next, the life cycle hypothesis about consumption and the policy implications of this hypothesis are explained. Milton Friedman's permanent income hypothesis about consumer behavior is also discussed. The central element of both the life cycle and the permanent income hypothesis concerning consumption is the assumption that consumption depends on some concept of lifetime average income. Both theories imply that consumption will respond to changes in current measured income in a much less mechanical way than was implied by the simple Keynesian consumption function (the absolute income hypothesis) which was employed in the models of Part II. Furthermore, if household saving is affected by the bequest motive or if their expectations are rational, the income-saving link has extra dimensions.

The second section of the chapter analyzes investment demand, beginning with business fixed investment. The relationship between the level of business fixed investment and the rate of change in output, the so-called accelerator relationship, is developed. The influence of the cost of capital on the level of investment is also explained, where the relevant cost of capital variable depends on the nominal interest rate, the expected inflation rate, the depreciation rate, and the tax treatment of investment (an investment tax credit, for example). The determinants of the other components of investment spending: residential construction expenditure and business inventory are discussed. Finally, a distinction is made between consumption of durable goods and consumer purchases of durable goods that are a form of household investment. The determinants of such consumer durable goods expenditures are examined. This analysis of the other components of investment demand suggests additional channels by which monetary policy might affect aggregate demand.

Techniques in Depth

1. The Consumption Function

In this chapter, we deal again with linear functions like the consumption function. For example, the absolute income hypothesis states:

$$C = a + bY_D$$

This is the equation for a straight line with intercept equal to "a" and slope equal to "b." Assume that:

$$a = 50$$

$$b = .90$$

Therefore, for the following values of Y_D, we can calculate corresponding values of C, since

$$C = 50 + .9Y_D$$

The following table presents data generated from this consumption function:

Y_D	C
0	50
100	140
200	230
300	320

The APC is defined as C/Y_D. So, if $C = 50 + .9Y_D$, then

$$C/Y_D = 50/Y_D + .9$$

Add a column for the APC:

Y_D	C	APC
0	50	$50/0 + .9$ = undefined
100	140	$50/100 + .9 = 1.40$
200	230	$50/200 + .9 = 1.15$
300	320	$50/300 + .9 = 1.07$

Consumption and Investment   160

Notice that as Y_D gets larger, the *APC* falls. This means that as a family's income grows, it spends more, but the percent of all income spent falls. Therefore, it is saving a larger percent of its income.

The *MPC* is defined as $\Delta C/\Delta Y$. So, if $C = 50 + .9Y_D$, then

$$\Delta C/\Delta Y_D = .9$$

That means that for every $100 increase in Y_D, consumption rises by $90. Add the *MPC* to the table:

Y_D	C	APC	MPC
0	50	Undefined	
100	140	1.40	90/100 = .9
200	230	1.15	90/100 = .9
300	320	1.07	90/100 = .9
500	?	?	?
800	?	?	?
1000	?	?	?

The student should fill in the rest of the table. Then, take the following consumption functions and build similar tables. Explain why they are so different.

$$C = .9Y_D$$

$$C = -25 + .9Y_D$$

$$C = 50 + .5Y_D$$

2. Calculating Real After-Tax Returns

An important concept to any investor is the real after-tax rate of return. Any investment will have an expected or a sure nominal rate of return. For example, a one-year bond might promise the investor a 9 percent nominal return. Therefore, at the end of one year, if the bond costs $1,000, one earns a return of $90. The nominal return, i, equals $90/$1,000, or 9 percent.

Of relevance to the investor is the buying power of the return. If the inflation rate rose 6 percent over the same year, then a bundle of goods costing $1,000 would cost $1,060 at the end of the year. It takes an extra $60 just to buy the same bundle of goods. The real rate of return before taxes, r_b, then equals ($90 − $60)/$1,000 or 3 percent. Notice that the real return received equals the nominal interest rate minus the actual inflation rate. In our example, the real return is 9 percent minus 6 percent. Similarly, the expected real return before taxes is the expected nominal return (in the case of a bond, this is the promised nominal return) minus the expected inflation rate. Suppose in the preceding example, one entered a transaction with an anticipated inflation rate equal to 3 percent. Therefore, the expected (or *ex ante*) real return was 6 percent (9 percent minus 3 percent), whereas the actual (or *ex post*) real return was 3 percent (9 percent minus 6 percent). In this case, the investor would have been unpleasantly surprised.

Individuals must pay taxes on all nominal income received, including investment income. If one's marginal tax bracket is 30 percent, then on this 9 percent investment, which grossed $90, one must pay $27 (30 percent of $90) in income taxes. Therefore, the after-tax nominal return is really ($90 − $27)/$1,000 or 6.3 percent. However, the <u>after-tax real</u> return, assuming inflation is 6 percent, is only ($90 − $60 − $27)/$1,000 or .3 percent. The point of this exercise is to show how misleading the nominal interest rate can be. A prudent investor must look at the *ex ante* real after-tax return when deciding upon investment alternatives.

Self-Tests

Multiple-Choice Questions:

1. Household consumption expenditures account for about what percent of gross domestic product?
    a. 33%
    b. 67%
    c. 99%
    d. 10%

2. Which of the following attributes typifies the Keynesian consumption function?
    a. A nonproportional relationship between income and consumption
    b. A falling APC with rising income
    c. A constant MPC
    d. All of the above

3. Evidence pertaining to the absolute income hypothesis suggests:
    a. its validity in the long run
    b. its validity during every quarter in the short run
    c. its validity, on the average, in the short run
    d. all of the above

4. The simple form of the life cycle hypothesis on consumption (equation 14.5) for a person expected to live 50 years implies that a temporary rise in income of $100 raises consumption:
    a. by approximately $2 in the first year
    b. by approximately $75 in the first year
    c. by approximately $100 in the first year
    d. by approximately $0 in the first year

5. According to the life cycle hypothesis, a temporary tax rebate, especially designed for higher income (mostly 35- to 50-year-old) people, would:
    a. have a large effect on current consumption
    b. have a small effect on current consumption
    c. increase the liquidity constraint
    d. lower saving

6. According to the permanent income hypothesis, higher income families have relatively lower APC's because:
   a. they already have most of the things they need
   b. they consume based on previous peak income
   c. they are likely to be experiencing transitory income gains which do not affect consumption
   d. people with lower incomes have a higher probability of having positive transitory income gains

7. The accelerator theory of investment says that investment rises whenever:
   a. output rises at an increasing rate
   b. output rises at a decreasing rate
   c. the capital stock rises
   d. the expected inflation rate falls
   e. the economy is at less than full capacity

8. The user cost of capital depends upon:
   a. the real interest rate
   b. the depreciation rate
   c. the nominal interest rate
   d. all of the above

9. Investment spending constitutes about 10.5 percent of GDP, but it is very important to policymakers, because:
   a. it fluctuates so much
   b. it determines stock prices
   c. it causes interest rates to change
   d. without it federal taxes would be too low

10. The average propensity to save (APS):
    a. is equal to $(1 - APC)$
    b. is the ratio of consumption to income
    c. is the ratio of saving to income
    d. a and c only
    e. all of the above

11. In an effort to support the absolute income hypothesis, data was collected from 1869 to 1938. This data demonstrated that in the long run:
    a. the absolute income hypothesis was supported
    b. the consumption function was shown as a proportional relationship in which MPC = APC
    c. the consumption function was shown to be the same as that in the short run
    d. the consumption function was horizontal

12. A criticism of the life cycle hypothesis is that:
    a. it does not acknowledge liquidity constraints
    b. it does not reconcile the short-run and long-run consumption data
    c. it does not explain why quarter-to-quarter movements in consumption do not closely mirror movements in income
    d. it does not explain why higher-income families have a lower APC than lower-income families

13. A modification made to the simple accelerator model in order to make it more realistic was to:
    a. allow for adjustment costs
    b. develop a partial adjustment mechanism
    c. allow for a flexible accelerator
    d. all of the above

14. In determining the level of residential construction, for a given stock of houses, the price and quantity of new homes produced will depend on:
    a. housing demand
    b. factors that affect the flow supply schedule
    c. credit conditions
    d. all of the above

15. The Keynesian consumption function can be shown as:
    a. $C = a/Y_D - b$
    b. $C = b + Y$
    c. $C = a/Y_D + b$
    d. $C = a + bY_D$

16. The ratio of saving to income is:
    a. the average propensity to save
    b. the marginal propensity to save
    c. the average propensity to consume
    d. the marginal propensity to consume

17. If a company borrows money at a nominal interest rate of 13 percent, and the average price level is expected to rise by 13 percent, then the real interest rate will be:
    a. 13 percent
    b. 26 percent
    c. 6.5 percent
    d. zero

18. The marginal propensity to consume is equal to:
    a. the change in consumption divided by the change in saving
    b. the change in income divided by the change in consumption
    c. consumption divided by income
    d. the slope of the consumption function
    e. none of the above

19. According to the life cycle hypothesis, consumption is primarily determined by:
    a. current income
    b. wealth
    c. past income
    d. expected lifetime income
    e. both b and d

20. In the Keynesian consumption function, $C = a + bY_D$, the parameter b:
    a. is the marginal propensity to consume
    b. is the marginal propensity to save
    c. is the average propensity to save
    d. measures consumption at a zero level of disposable income

21. The absolute income hypothesis relates consumption to:
    a. past income
    b. future income
    c. current income
    d. past and future income

22. Investment in the national income accounts includes:
    a. residential construction expenditures
    b. changes in business inventories
    c. purchases of durable equipment and structures
    d. both a and b
    e. all of the above

23. In the original Keynesian consumption function the:
    a. MPC was larger than the APC
    b. APC was larger than the MPC
    c. APC was necessarily less than one
    d. multiplier was equal to one

24. The flexible accelerator model of investment can be shown as:
    a. $I_{n,t} = \lambda(\alpha Y_t - K_{t-1})$
    b. $I_{n,t} = \lambda(\alpha Y_t - K_{t+1})$
    c. $I_{n,t} = \lambda(\alpha Y_t + K_{t-1})$
    d. $I_{n,t} = \lambda(\alpha Y_t + K_{t+1})$

25. Which of the following is considered a leakage from the circular flow of income and expenditure?
    a. Consumption
    b. Saving
    c. Governmental purchases of goods and services
    d. Investment
    e. All of the above

26. According to the life cycle hypothesis, a one-time or transient change in income:
    a. has little impact on consumer behavior
    b. has the same effect as a change in wealth of the same amount
    c. has no effect on future expected income
    d. All of the above
    e. None of the above

27. According to the permanent income hypothesis, consumption is:
    a. proportional to permanent income
    b. proportional to transitory income
    c. disproportional to permanent income
    d. unrelated to permanent income

28. According to the life cycle hypothesis, as wealth increases over time:
    a. the long-run proportional consumption function shifts upward to depict the short-run nonproportional consumption/income relationships
    b. the short-run nonproportional consumption function shifts upward and depicts the long-run proportional consumption/income relationships
    c. there is an absence of a relationship between the short-run nonproportional and long-run proportional consumption functions
    d. none of the above

29. Which of the following are adjustment costs?
    a. The extra costs of speeding plant construction
    b. The disruption of production if management concentrates solely on expediting investment projects
    c. Plant shutdowns
    d. The hiring of overtime labor to install equipment
    e. All of the above

Problems and/or Essay Questions:

1. Assume researchers found the following consumption function for the Falkland Islands:

$$C = 8.0 + .90Y_D.$$

   a. What is the MPC? MPS?
   b. If $Y_D = 200$, what is the APC? APS?
   c. If $Y_D = 300$, what is the APC? APS?
   d. How did the APC change when Y_D rose to 300? Explain what this means in words.
   e. Graph this consumption function.
   f. What does the 8.0 in the function tell you?

2. Explain in words the basic features of the life cycle hypothesis about consumption. This hypothesis explains why the short-run consumption-income relationship is nonproportional, while the consumption-income relationship is proportional in the long run. How is this reconciliation of the evidence possible? Is this theory without criticism? What are its weaknesses?

3. The permanent income hypothesis says consumption is a function of permanent income, or

$$C = KY^P$$

Assume:

$$k = .70 \text{ and}$$

$$Y^P = .50Y^D + .30Y^D_{-1} + .20Y^D_{-2}$$

Where Y^D_{-1} is disposable income last period and Y^D_{-2} is disposable income two periods back. Assume a family receives in period one a $100 tax cut, and describe the impact on the economy of this temporary tax cut over a three-year period. How would these results differ under the absolute income hypothesis?

4. The effective cost of capital to the firm is given by:

$$CC = (1 - \pi)(i - \hat{P}_e\delta)$$

One feature of supply-side economics is the view that lowering corporate taxes can be beneficial. Another form gives firms accelerated depreciation allowances. In the context of the above expression, explain why such programs would be successful. Then explain why they might not. For example, if lower taxes generate larger government deficits, what does this equation say might happen to the cost of capital?

5. For this investment problem, assume the following:

nominal interest rate = 18%
expected interest rate = 14%
profits tax rate = 25%
depreciation rate = 2%

   a. What is the *ex ante* real cost of capital before taxes?
   b. What is the *ex ante* cost of capital after taxes?
   c. Assume the government decides to tax <u>real</u> profits instead of nominal profits. In the case above, how would that affect the after-tax cost of capital?
   d. Redo parts (a), (b), and (c), assuming the actual inflation rate was 16 percent. What are the relevant *ex post* calculations?

6. If the bequest motive were very strong, which of the following programs for raising the national saving rate would you favor? Explain.
   a. Reduce the tax on capital gains.
   b. Tax the elderly's Social Security benefits.
   c. Reduce inheritance taxes.
   d. Raise inheritance taxes.

7. Since saving ultimately leads to capital formation, the declining U.S. personal saving rate has become an issue of great concern. What are some of the explanations that have been offered for this decline?

8. Explain why inventory investment, a small component of total output, is of concern to policymakers.

9. By utilizing statistical techniques and annual data for a short period, Keynesian economists obtained the following estimate for the consumption function

$$C = 26.5 + 0.75Y_D.$$

Utilize this equation to calculate the average propensity to consume when the income level is 400 and 600. What does this equation imply?

10. Explain the implications of the rational expectations assumption for the permanent income hypothesis.

11. Explain the user cost of capital. What elements comprise this user cost of capital?

# CHAPTER 15

MONEY DEMAND

OVERVIEW

Money demand was discussed in the chapters in Part II that considered macroeconomic models. This chapter provides a more detailed analysis of money demand. Prior to that, however, the question of how to define money is considered. Recent innovations in the financial sector and their implications for the question of the proper definition of money are examined. The revised definitions of the U.S. monetary aggregates are explained (see Table 15.1).

Sections 15.2 and 15.3 examine post-Keynesian developments in the theory of money demand. The inventory-theoretic approach to the theory of the transactions demand for money is explained. Then, the modern portfolio approach to the demand for money as a store of wealth—Tobin's theory of money demand as behavior toward risk—is considered. Tobin's theory provides an alternative to Keynes' theory of the speculative demand for money as a rationale for the existence of an asset demand for money. In Tobin's theory, as in Keynes', we are led to the conclusion that the asset demand for money will depend inversely on the level of the interest rate.

The instability of estimated money demand functions in the mid-1970s, the so-called "Case of the Missing Money," is analyzed. The shortfall of actual money demand relative to the levels predicted by conventional specifications of the money demand function is attributed to innovations in the financial sector. In the early 1980s, the money demand equations began <u>underpredicting</u>. NOW accounts, which are part of M1, seemed to regain popularity as the general level of interest rates fell. A final section contains a brief summary of the current state of the theory of money demand.

Techniques in Depth

1. The Inventory-Theoretic Approach to the Demand for Transactions Balances

The idea of the inventory-theoretic approach is that individuals do what amounts to a very strange thing—they hold money balances, such as in inventory, which yield no pecuniary return instead of holding a bond. Why? The answer given by this approach is that people hold such sterile money because of the uncertainty about cash flows. Recall the equation that depicts the profits one can attain by <u>not</u> holding money:

PR = (benefits from buying and selling bonds) minus (costs of buying and selling bonds)

Benefits = interest rate times average bonds held per period
$= r[(n-1)/2n]Y$

Costs = number of bonds times cost per bond transaction
$= nb$

Therefore:

$PR = r[(n-1)/2n]Y - nb$

Notice: Profits from holding the bonds are very small if: the interest rate (r) or income (Y) are very low or if transactions costs (b) are very high.

Therefore, if r and/or Y is low and b is very high, it does not pay to go to the trouble of holding bonds instead of money. It pays instead to just hold on to the money and not go through the cost and trouble of buying and selling all those bonds.

Let us consider again the decision of how much money to hold. What is important here is to calculate the number of bonds transactions (n^*) which make profits a maximum. If $n^* = 0$, then you don't hold any bonds. If $n^* > 0$, then some of a given income is held as money during the period. A numerical example will help us see the relationship between PR and n:

$$Let\ Y = \$1,000/month$$

$$r = .015/month$$

$$b = \$1.00/month$$

$$PR = \$1,000[(n-1)/2n].015 - n\$1.00$$

$$PR = 15[(n-1)/2n] - n$$

Filling in the following table:

n	PR
2	$1.75
3	$2.00
4	$1.63
5	$1.00
6	$0.25
7	−$0.57

For example,

if $n = 2$, then
$$PR = 15[(2-1)/(2 \times 2)] - 2$$
$$= 15(¼) - 2$$
$$= 1.75$$

If $n = 3$,
$$PR = 15[(3-1)/(2 \times 3)] - 3$$
$$= 5 - 3$$
$$= 2.00$$

If $n = 4$,
$$PR = 15[(4-1)/(2 \times 4)] - 4$$
$$= 5.625 - 4$$
$$= 1.63$$

If $n = 5$,
$$PR = 15[(5-1)/(2 \times 5)] - 5$$
$$= 6 - 5$$
$$= 1.00$$

If $n = 6$,
$$PR = 15[(6-1)/(2 \times 6)] - 6$$
$$= 6.25 - 6$$
$$= 0.25$$

If $n = 7$,
$$PR = 15[(7-1)/(2 \times 7)] - 7$$
$$= 6.43 - 7$$
$$= -.57$$

We can now graph the relationship between the number of bond transactions and profits:

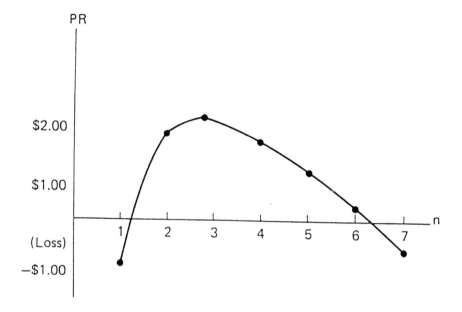

In this example, notice that when $n = 3$, the profits are maximized. In that case, the average bond holdings would be:

$$Y[(n-1)/2n] = 1,000[(3-1)/(2 \times 3)] = \$333.33$$

Interest earned per month would be:

$$.015(\$333) = \$5.00$$

The average money held would be:

$$(1/2n)Y = [1/(2 \times 3)]\$1,000 = \$166.67$$

These results show that, for this example, on the average, this individual will hold about $166.67 as money and $333.33 as bonds over the period. This will be accomplished with three bond transactions which will net the individual $5.00.

How would this result change if r were lower, say, only .010 per month? In that case:

$$PR = \$1,000[(n - 1)/2n](.010) - \$1.00n$$

The altered table is:

n	PR
2	0.50
3	0.33
4	−0.25

Notice how the lower interest rate makes bond transactions less profitable and makes the optimal number of transactions smaller, since $n^* = 2$.

The student should now calculate the average bond holdings, average money holding, and the interest earned. Did you find that the fall in r leads to a rise in money held?

Self-Tests

Multiple-Choice Questions:

1. With the Keynesian form of the money demand function:
    a. interest rates do not affect money demand
    b. income is no longer proportional to the quantity of money
    c. wealth is a primary determinant of money demand
    d. the LM curve is vertical

2. The exact definition of money is not widely agreed upon by economists because:
    a. M1 does not include some highly liquid assets
    b. M2 contains some elements of saving which are not used in transactions
    c. the theoretical concept of the transactions demand for money includes assets primarily used for spending and not for saving
    d. all of the above

3. Money market mutual funds have very low turnover rates and, therefore, should be:
    a. part of M1
    b. part of M2
    c. treated like a checking account
    d. all of the above

4. The inventory-theoretic approach to the transactions demand for money suggests that a rise in interest rates will lower the demand for money, because higher interest rates:
    a. raise the marginal revenue from bond holdings and increase the optimal number of bond transactions
    b. raise the marginal cost of bond transactions and reduce the number of bonds held
    c. make people expect future low interest rates
    d. reduce the demand for money and raise the demand for bonds

5. According to the inventory-theoretic model, a rise in income will:
   a. reduce the demand for money and bonds
   b. increase the demand for money relative to bonds
   c. increase the demand for bonds relative to money
   d. reduce the demand for money and raise the demand for bonds

6. If brokerage costs are high for buying and selling bonds, then the effect of interest rates on money demand will be lower for:
   a. groups with high incomes
   b. groups with low incomes
   c. firms
   d. none of the above

7. Credit cards generally allow individuals to postpone (at least for one month) paying for any unexpected expenditures. Therefore, it would be argued that the level of money held each month would be affected in which of these ways by the extensive use of credit cards?
   a. The monthly demand for money would rise
   b. The monthly demand for money would fall
   c. The monthly demand for money would be largely unaffected
   d. None of the above

8. According to James Tobin's modification of Keynes' theory of money demand as a store of wealth:
   a. the demand for money arises because it yields a high return
   b. the demand for money occurs because money is a risky asset
   c. the demand for money is explained as aversion to risk
   d. all of the above

9. According to Tobin, as the interest rate rises, individuals desire to hold less money because:
   a. money is intrinsically more risky
   b. the interest rate rises above the "safe-rate," and individuals expect it will fall
   c. individuals are willing to take more risky bonds at a higher return
   d. all of the above

10. The money demand equilibrium condition in equation (15.5) is expressed as $\Delta M = k\Delta Py$. This condition demonstrates that with a fixed k:
    a. changes in the quantity of money have no role in income determination
    b. fiscal policy actions have no role in income determination
    c. both <u>b</u> and <u>c</u>
    d. all of the above

11. Keynes' theory of the relationship between money and the interest rate was the theory of:
    a. the transactions demand for money
    b. the speculative demand for money
    c. money as a means of exchange
    d. money as a unit of account

12. An expression of net profits is given as

$$PR = r[(n-1)/2n]Y - nb$$

From this expression, for a given Y, the determination of the optimal money and bond holdings for the individual comes from the determination:
   a. of the optimal number of transactions (n)
   b. of the optimal brokerage fee (b)
   c. of the optimal interest rate (r)
   d. none of the above

13. In Tobin's theory of the demand for money, expected capital gain is:
   a. equal to the interest rate
   b. equal to the interest rate and some capital loss
   c. zero
   d. none of the above

14. Keynes' theory of money demand regarded the role of money:
   a. only as a medium of exchange
   b. only as a store of value
   c. both as a store of value and standard of value
   d. both as a store of value and as a medium of exchange

15. According to Keynes' theory of the speculative demand for money, the demand for money varies:
   a. only with income
   b. positively with the interest rate
   c. positively with the interest rate and income
   d. negatively with the interest rate

16. If prices and debts are measured in dollars and cents, money serves as a:
   a. store of value
   b. unit of account
   c. medium for transactions
   d. hedge against inflation

17. Classical economists concentrated on the role of money:
   a. as a store of value
   b. as a medium of exchange
   c. as a unit of account
   d. none of the above

18. The classical Cambridge version of the money demand function is shown as:
   a. $M^d = kPy$
   b. $M^d = k(P/y)$
   c. $M^d = kP/y$
   d. $M^d = P(k/y)$

19. Certificates of deposits, CDs, are included in:
    a. M1
    b. M1 and M2
    c. either M2 or M3
    d. M3 only

20. Assume that a person receives a cash income of $5,000 per month and spends this money uniformly and predictably through the month. Then, according to the inventory/theoretic approach to money demand, his or her average inventory of money will be:
    a. $1,250
    b. $2,500
    c. between zero and $5,000
    d. zero

21. According to Tobin's theory of the asset demand for money, an increase in the interest rate accompanied by a fall in uncertainty concerning bond prices:
    a. would increase the demand for bonds
    b. would increase money demand
    c. would increase both money demand and the demand for bonds
    d. might cause money demand to rise or fall

22. According to Keynes, income was the primary variable that determined the amount of money being held because of:
    a. the transactions motive but not the precautionary motive
    b. the transactions motive but not the speculative motive
    c. the speculative motive but not the transactions motive
    d. both the transactions motive and the precautionary motive

23. The M2 measure of money does not include:
    a. Time deposits on which no checks can be written
    b. Checkable deposits
    c. Term repurchase agreements at commercial banks and savings and loans associations
    d. Eurodollars

24. According to Tobin's theory of the asset demand for money, an increase in uncertainty concerning bond prices would cause the demand for:
    a. money to fall and the demand for bonds to rise
    b. bonds to fall and the demand for money to rise
    c. both money and bonds to rise
    d. both money and bonds to fall

25. Between 1995 and 1997, increases in the utilization of "sweep" accounts:
    a. did not contribute to the decline in checkable deposits
    b. was one of many factors generating a decline of 10 percent in checkable deposits
    c. was the main factor causing a decline of almost 10 percent in checkable deposits
    d. none of the above

26. According to the inventory/theoretic approach to money demand, an increase in brokerage fees:
    a. increases the optimum number of bond market transactions
    b. decreases the optimum number of bond market transactions
    c. does not change the optimum number of bond market transactions
    d. could either increase or decrease the optimum number of bond market transactions

27. The relevant definition of money as a store of wealth is:
    a. M1
    b. M2 only
    c. M3 only
    d. either M2 or M3

28. Which of the following is correct? In recent years,
    a. the government sector and households accounted for approximately two thirds of money holdings
    b. the government sector and the business sector accounted for approximately one third of money holdings
    c. households alone accounted for almost one half of money holdings
    d. the business sector and households held about one third of M1 holdings

Problems and/or Essay Questions:

1. a. Explain in detail the meaning of the following equation:

    $$PR = r[(n - 1)/2n]Y - nb$$

   b. Describe how the PR function behaves when:
      i. n changes,
      ii. r changes,
      iii. Y changes,
      iv. b changes.

2. Assume an individual has an income of $2,000/month and bond transactions cost $1.25. This month the interest rate is .01. Calculate the money and bond holdings and the number of bond transactions that maximize profits from holding money and bonds. Why wouldn't this individual hold $1.00 more in bonds? Isn't that a pretty good interest rate? The individual gets a raise and earns $2,500 next month. How does this affect his/her demand for money? What happens if the interest rate falls next month to .008? How does the higher income coupled with a lower interest rate affect the demand for money?

3. Describe how your analysis of the above question changes if we add one feature to the problem—individuals are unsure of the timing and size of all their monthly expenditures. How does uncertainty of this type affect the transactions demand for money?

4. According to Tobin's theory of the asset demand for money, what are the most important aspects of the money demand decision? Why do people hold money balances? What makes them hold more or less money?

5. Describe some of the major new financial innovations of the 1980s. What caused these changes? What trouble do they cause for measuring money? Explain why the Federal Reserve no longer "sets" M1 growth targets, favoring M2 instead.

6. Explain why money plays an important role as a means of exchange—that is, why is barter less prominent?

7. Explain the two major criticisms of Keynes' theory of the speculative demand for money.

8. What is meant by the "case of the missing money?"

9. What are sweep accounts? Why or why not did they contribute to the instability in M1 growth during the latter part of the 1990s?

10. Classical economists concentrated on the role of money as a medium of exchange. How does this differ from Keynes' theory of money demand? Compare the classical money demand function with the Keynesian money demand function.

CHAPTER 16

THE MONEY SUPPLY PROCESS

OVERVIEW

In this chapter and later in Chapter 19, monetary policy is discussed in more detail. In this chapter, the tools that the Federal Reserve uses to conduct monetary policy are described. The way in which these tools influence the money stock is examined. The question of the relative roles of the Federal Reserve, the banking sector, and the nonbank public in determining the level of the money stock is considered.

The first section of the chapter deals briefly with the institutional structure of the Federal Reserve. Then, the tools that the Federal Reserve uses to control the level of bank reserves—open-market operations, changes in the discount rate, and changes in required reserve ratios on deposits—are explained. Open-market purchases (sales) of government securities will increase (decrease) the monetary base by the amount of such open-market operations. Increases (decreases) in required reserve ratios will decrease (increase) the volume of deposits that can be supported by a given stock of bank reserves.

The next section considers the relationship between changes in bank reserves, the level of bank deposits, and the money supply. This is done, first, under a number of simplifying but restrictive assumptions and, then, for more general cases. The concept of the money multiplier is explained. The money multiplier (m) relates the monetary base to the money stock, that is:

$$M^s = m \times MB$$

where M^s is the money stock, and MB is the monetary base. The money multiplier is seen to depend on: the public's desired currency to demand deposit ratio; the bank's desired excess reserve to deposit ratio; and the required reserve ratio on checkable deposits.

The last section considers the question of "Who controls the money stock?" It is argued that uncertainty about the money multiplier creates difficulties for month-to-month control of the money stock by the Federal Reserve. For somewhat longer periods, the Federal Reserve should be able to offset undesired changes in the money multiplier by counterbalancing adjustments in the monetary base. In practice, however, since the Federal Reserve at times has had other financial goal variables, most importantly interest rate targets, the money stock has not always been closely controlled, even over such longer periods. The question of money stock versus interest rate control is returned to in Chapter 19.

Techniques in Depth

1. The Complex Version of the Money Multiplier

The money multiplier (m) relates changes in the monetary base (ΔMB) to changes in the money supply (ΔM^s):

$$m = \Delta M^s / \Delta MB$$

The Money Supply Process 178

Changes in the money supply arise from changes in currency (ΔCU) or from changes in deposits. If we are dealing with M1, then these are largely changes in checkable deposits (ΔD). If we are measuring M2, these changes in money include changes in time and saving deposits [including money market certificates ($\Delta SD + \Delta TD$)]. Therefore, we can rewrite ΔM^s as:

$$M_1^s = \Delta CU + \Delta D$$

The changes in the monetary base arise from changes in currency held by the public (ΔCU), from changes in reserves held on demand deposits (rr_d) or held on excess reserves (ΔER).

We can now show the expression for the M1 multiplier, $m1$:

$$m1 = \Delta M1/\Delta MB = (\Delta CU + \Delta D)/(\Delta CU + rr_d \times \Delta D + \Delta ER)$$

Now, divide all terms by D:

$$m1 = [(\Delta CU/\Delta D) + 1]/[(\Delta CU/\Delta D) + rr_d + (\Delta ER/\Delta D)]$$

from this expression we can easily see that:

(1) Increases in required reserves per dollar of deposit result in a fall in $m1$.

(2) When banks hold more excess reserves per dollar of deposit, this reduces $m1$.

(3) If individuals hold more deposits in saving and time deposits (and less in demand deposits), then $m1$ falls.

(4) If people hold more of their resources as currency and less as deposits, this reduces $m1$ [($\Delta CU/\Delta D$) is in both the numerator and denominator. However, the student should be able to prove that in the case above, a rise in ($\Delta CU/\Delta D$) lowers $m1$].

Self-Tests

Multiple-Choice Questions:

1. The Federal Reserve System in the United States is composed of:
    a. the Board of Governors
    b. the Federal Open Market
    c. twelve district banks
    d. all of the above

2. Monetary policy in the United States is:
    a. centralized in Washington
    b. controlled by the U.S. Treasury
    c. independently determined in each of the twelve federal reserve districts
    d. always too expansionary

3. The major asset held by commercial banks is:
   a. U.S. government securities
   b. loans
   c. other assets
   d. deposits

4. The major liability of commercial banks is:
   a. commercial loans
   b. auto loans
   c. bank reserves
   d. deposits

5. The monetary base is defined as the sum of:
   a. vault cash plus deposits
   b. loans plus deposits
   c. bank reserves plus currency held by the public
   d. deposits minus reserves

6. The Federal Reserve most directly controls:
   a. loans
   b. the monetary base
   c. saving plus time deposits
   d. the money supply

7. The three major tools that the Federal Reserve uses to control the reserves of banks are:
   a. open-market operations, the federal funds rate, and the government deficit
   b. open-market operations, the federal funds rate, and the discount rate
   c. open-market operations, legal reserve requirements, and the federal funds rate
   d. open-market operations, legal reserve requirements, and the discount rate

8. A sale of government securities in the open market will:
   a. increase bank reserves
   b. decrease bank reserves
   c. raise the money supply
   d. reduce the discount rate

9. If the money multiplier equals $1/rr_d$, then it must be true that:
   a. the public's currency holdings are changing
   b. banks do not change their holdings
   c. the federal funds rate is changing
   d. all of the above

10. The more complicated version of the money multiplier implies:
    a. the Fed has good control over M1
    b. the money supply is not completely exogenous
    c. the Fed cannot control the money supply over a period of 6 months to 1 year
    d. the public controls the money supply in the long run

The Money Supply Process   180

11. Historically, the Fed appears to have missed its annual money growth targets. This is probably mostly true because:
    a. the monetary base is uncontrollable
    b. the money multiplier shifts erratically from year to year
    c. M1 is undefinable
    d. the Fed often tries to stabilize interest rates

12. If the Federal Reserve purchases $50 million of government securities in the open market, with a 0.10 required reserve ratio, the maximum increase in deposits would be:
    a. $ 5 million
    b. $ 50 million
    c. $500 million
    d. $200 million
    e. zero

13. If the Federal Reserve were to simultaneously buy government securities in the open market and raise the legal reserve requirement on deposits:
    a. the money supply will increase
    b. the money supply will decrease
    c. the money stock will stay the same
    d. the two actions work in opposite direction, and the effect on the money supply is uncertain

14. The Open Market Committee:
    a. controls open-market operations
    b. is composed of seven members appointed by the President of the United States
    c. includes the presidents of the regional banks who all vote on a rotating basis
    d. all of the above

15. Decreases in the required reserve ratio:
    a. reduce the quantity of deposits that can be supported by a given amount of reserves
    b. increase the quantity of deposits that can be supported by a given amount of reserves
    c. will increase the purchases by the Fed of open-market securities
    d. will decrease the purchases by the Fed of open-market securities

16. Increasing the federal reserve discount rate will:
    a. contract the money supply and lower interest rates
    b. contract the money supply and raise interest rates
    c. increase the money supply and raise interest rates
    d. increase the money supply and lower interest rates

17. A $100,000 sale of government securities in the open market:
    a. increases bank reserves by that amount
    b. decreases bank reserves by that amount
    c. increases the money base by that amount
    d. increases reserve requirements by that amount

18. The money multiplier is the ratio of:
    a. bank deposits to bank reserves
    b. bank reserves to bank deposits
    c. the money supply to the monetary base
    d. the money supply to bank reserves

19. The United States system of central banking was established in:
    a. 1913
    b. 1910
    c. 1925
    d. 1950

20. Assuming the Federal Reserve raises the required reserve ratio from 20 to 25 percent, if reserves are $30 billion, then checkable deposits are:
    a. $180 billion
    b. $ 54 billion
    c. $ 24 billion
    d. $120 billion

21. Federal Reserve legal reserve requirements stipulate that banks must hold a certain percentage of their deposit liabilities:
    a. as deposits at regional Federal Reserve Banks only
    b. in currency only
    c. either in currency or as deposits at regional Federal Reserve Banks
    d. none of the above

22. In the early 1990s, reserve requirements on time and savings deposits were phased out, therefore,:
    a. increases in time and savings deposits only affect the M1 multiplier
    b. increases in time and savings deposits only affect the M2 multiplier
    c. increases in time and savings deposits affect both the M1 and M2 multipliers
    d. increases in time and savings deposits affect only the M3 multiplier

23. The most restrictive monetary policy action of the Federal Reserve is to:
    a. sell government securities, raise reserve requirements, and raise the discount rate
    b. sell government securities, raise reserve requirements, and lower the discount rate
    c. buy government securities, raise reserve requirements, and raise the discount rate
    d. sell government securities, lower reserve requirements, and raise the discount rate

24. The money multiplier would increase with:
    a. a decrease in the monetary base
    b. a decrease in the level of Federal Reserve open-market purchases
    c. a decrease in M1
    d. a decrease in the public's desired currency to checkable deposit ratio
    e. all of the above

25. An increase in the legal required reserve ratio would:
    a. reduce bank reserves
    b. reduce the money supply
    c. increase the money supply
    d. leave both bank reserves and the money supply unchanged

26. A bank creates money when it:
    a. converts its excess reserves into an interest-earning asset
    b. collects an interest payment on a loan
    c. accepts a deposit from a customer
    d. all of the above

27. If a bank has $40,000 in required reserves and the required reserve ratio is 20 percent, then demand deposits should be:
    a. $ 20,000
    b. $ 40,000
    c. $ 80,000
    d. $200,000

28. The Board of Governors of the Federal Reserve System:
    a. approves changes in the discount rate
    b. sets reserve requirements
    c. administers the discount window
    d. both a and b
    e. all of the above

29. An expansionary monetary policy by the Federal Reserve System includes:
    a. lowering reserve requirements
    b. lowering the discount rate
    c. purchasing securities in the open market
    d. all of the above
    e. none of the above

30. Assuming the Federal Reserve Bank lowers the legal reserve requirement on deposits, then:
    a. the money stock will rise
    b. the monetary base will rise
    c. both the monetary base and the money stock will rise
    d. neither the monetary base nor the money stock will rise

Problems and/or Essay Questions:

1. We generally think of the money supply as being largely exogenous or, at least, mostly governed by the Fed. Based on your knowledge of the money multiplier, explain why M1 and/or M2 might change if:
   a. incomes rise,
   b. interest rates fall,
   c. banks expect the interest rates to rise soon,
   d. inflationary expectations increase, and
   e. households fear that a severe recession will set off a rash of bankruptcies.

2. The Fed can control bank reserves and the money stock if it can control the monetary base. Explain this statement.

3. Assuming that the public's holding of currency is fixed, explain how an open-market purchase of a government security by the Fed will affect the Fed's balance sheet.

4. Explain the effects that raising or lowering the discount rate has on bank reserves.

5. The Great Depression demonstrated the extent to which banks and the public affect the money supply process. Explain how M1, the money multiplier, and the monetary base were affected by the actions of the public and the banks during this period.

6. In practice, has the Federal Reserve achieved its money growth targets? Why or why not?

7. Show the money multiplier (m) for the narrowly defined money stock (M1) and explain what m depends on.

8. How is the value of the money multiplier affected if there is:
   a. a fall in the public's desired ratio of currency to checkable deposits.
   b. a rise in the banking system's desired excess reserve to checkable deposits ratio,
   c. a fall in the required reserve ratio on checkable deposits.

9. The making of monetary policy has become centralized in Washington in two monetary policymaking groups. Who are they and what are their functions?

CHAPTER 17

LONG- AND INTERMEDIATE-TERM ECONOMIC GROWTH

OVERVIEW

Previous chapters considered only short-run movements in actual output for a given level of potential output. Here, long-run equilibrium growth in output and changes in output over what are termed "intermediate-run" time spans are considered. Such an intermediate-run period is one that is too long to be accurately represented in the short-run models of Part II, but not necessarily a period characterized by the assumptions we will make concerning long-run equilibrium growth. It is within this context of intermediate-run economic growth that the propositions of the supply-side economists are considered. Also, within this context, President Reagan's economic recovery program is examined.

The first section of the chapter examines the determinants of long-run economic growth within the framework of the aggregate production function. The determinants of such long-run growth are seen to be:

(1) technological change

(2) capital formation

(3) labor force growth

(4) education

(5) economies of scale

Edward Denison's estimates of the sources of long-run U.S. economic growth are summarized. In the next section on the determinants of intermediate-run growth, some data are reviewed on the recent slowdown in U.S. and European economic growth. The supply-side economists' explanation of this slowdown is examined. Four propositions, which are important elements of supply-side economics, are advanced.

These propositions are:

(1) Output growth in the intermediate run is predominantly supply-determined by rates of growth in factor supplies and the rate of technological change.

(2) Primarily the incentives for saving and investment determine the rate of growth of the capital input, the incentives being the after-tax returns to saving and investment.

(3) The rate of growth in the labor input, while in the long run determined by demographic factors, can also be affected significantly by incentives, in this case by changes in the after-tax real wage.

(4) Excessive government regulation of business has discouraged capital formation, contributed to the slowdown in the growth of labor productivity, and reduced the U.S. growth rate.

Next, the Keynesian critique of the supply-side position is examined.

The final sections of the chapter analyze the Reagan and Bush administrations' supply-side economic policies. The main elements of the Reagan program, termed Reaganomics, are described, some criticisms of the program are presented, and the performance of the economy during his two full terms in office is reviewed. The supply-side policies of the Bush administration are also reviewed and critiqued. Furthermore, "Clintonomics" is mentioned in this chapter presentation.

Techniques in Depth

1. Real After-Tax Returns (See TID in Chapter 14 for a similar analysis)

The supply-siders have emphasized the distinction between real after-tax returns and the marginal interest rate. Let us look at this distinction more carefully. First, consider the nominal return on a one-year bond, purchased at par ($1,000), held to maturity, and which earns $120 interest. The nominal or market return is $120/$1,000 or 12 percent. By parting with $1,000 today (buying a bond), the investor receives $1,120 one year hence and receives a return of 12 percent.

The IRS will, in general, tax the interest income. If the investor has a marginal tax rate (tax bracket) of 40 percent, then, the above investment which earns income of $120 produces a tax liability of (.4 times $120) or $48. Therefore, the after-tax return is ($120 − $48)/$1,000 or 7.2 percent. [Notice, this could have been calculated by multiplying the nominal return (12 percent) by (1 − tax rate),
(12 percent times (1 − .4) = 7.2 percent.]

The tax rate has reduced the return considerably. Inflation or loss of purchasing power, however, has yet to be considered. Assume the investor has been considering the purchase of a motorcycle. The choice was to buy one for $1,000 at the beginning of the year or for $1,100 at the end of the year (assuming motorcycle prices rise by the 10 percent inflation rate expected of all goods). Buying the bond, therefore, the investor earns $72 after taxes, but loses $100 when he purchases the motorcycle at the end of the year. Therefore, the after-tax real return is: ($120 − $48 − $100)/$1,000 or −2.8 percent. This is approximately equal to the nominal return (12 percent) times one minus the marginal tax rate (1 − .4) less the inflation rate (10 percent).

In this case, the after-tax real return is:

$$(12\%)(.6) - 10\% = 7.2\% - 10\% = -2.8\%$$

2. *Ex Ante* Versus *Ex Post* Returns

It is an interesting and sometimes frustrating economic reality that investments do not turn out as planned. No investor would willingly accept a negative 2.8 percent return. The negative sign implies one gets back in buying power less than was invested! It is true, however, that many investors receive negative returns and, in some years, most investors have encountered such negative returns. Why?

The reason is economic uncertainty. In the preceding section, we showed that the real after-tax return for a one-year bond held to maturity (no capital gain or loss) was based on three factors: the nominal return, the marginal tax rate, and the inflation rate. For most investments, there are three complicating factors that can affect the actual *ex post* yield:

(1) unexpected capital gains or losses,

(2) unexpected changes in tax status, and

(3) unexpected changes in the inflation rate.

For example, you may have hoped:

(1) to hold the bond to maturity ($i = 12\%$),

(2) your tax bracket would be .4, and

(3) the inflation rate would be 5%.

Thus, the *ex ante* after-tax real return you calculated before buying the bond was:

$$(12\%)(.6) - 5\% = 7.2\% - 5\% = +2\%$$

If the inflation rate turns out to be 10%, then your *ex post* after-tax real return is:

$$(12\%)(.6) - 10\% = 7.2\% - 10\% = -2.8\%$$

An unexpected rise in the inflation rate has changed an *ex ante* real after-tax return of +2% into an *ex post* real after-tax return of −2.8%. Similarly, unexpected changes in your tax status (due to an inheritance, for example) or the need to liquidate the investment with a resulting capital gain or capital loss would also cause the *ex post* return to differ from your *ex ante* expectation.

Self-Tests

Multiple-Choice Questions:

1. Evidence exists which supports the conclusion that technological change has largely resulted in increasing productivity of:
   a. mostly labor
   b. mostly capital
   c. both labor and capital
   d. none of the above

2. Constant returns to scale implies that if all inputs rise in proportion, output will:
   a. rise by the same dollar value
   b. rise by a greater proportion
   c. rise by an equal proportion
   d. rise by a lesser proportion

3. Diminishing returns to changes in capital per worker implies that output increases:
   a. proportionally with increases in labor and capital
   b. less than proportionally with equal increases in labor and capital
   c. at a decreasing rate when the capital-labor ratio rises
   d. at a decreasing rate when total productivity falls

4. Capital deepening refers to:
   a. more capital per worker
   b. less capital per worker
   c. a lower capital-labor ratio
   d. more capital and labor

5. In accordance with the traditional growth models, if the rate of saving in the economy falls, then:
   a. the long run steady rate of growth will fall
   b. the capital-labor ratio will rise permanently
   c. in disequilibrium, the rate of growth of output will fall below the steady-state growth rate
   d. all of the above

6. According to Edward Denison, the largest factor sustaining the secular growth rate of output of 2.9 percent was:
   a. technological change
   b. quality of labor inputs
   c. quantity of labor inputs
   d. economies of large scale

7. Feldstein and Summers argue that one reason inflation causes economic stagnation is because:
   a. inflation causes uncertainty
   b. inflation reduces pretax incomes
   c. U.S. institutions, especially tax laws, are not suited to an inflationary environment
   d. inflation induces people to save more

8. If a one-year bond of $1,000 yields a 12 percent nominal return with certainty, and during the year the inflation rate is 11 percent, then a person in the 50 percent tax bracket would earn an after-tax yield of about:
   a. -5%
   b. $+5\%$
   c. 1%
   d. $-.5\%$

9. Supply-siders favor which of the following remedies as a way to improve economic growth?
   a. Reduction in tax rates of the richest individuals so they will save more
   b. Reduction in payroll taxes to reduce the "tax wedge" to promote more employment
   c. Change rules for depreciation of capital and for valuing inventories as a way to increase capital formation
   d. all of the above

10. The supply-side theory argues that, in practice:
    a. the government budget must be balanced
    b. tax rates must be reduced
    c. there is a trade-off between balancing the budget and lowering tax rates
    d. tax rate increases imply increases in output supplied

11. Keynesians would argue that the slow growth of output during the 1970s was attributable in part to:
    a. fast monetary growth
    b. generally slow monetary growth
    c. mistimed contractions in money
    d. all of the above

12. Keynesians believe that:
    a. interest rates, for the most part, cause investment
    b. output, for the most part, causes investment
    c. investment and output are unrelated
    d. supply creates its own demand

13. According to Keynesians, a large reduction in personal income tax rates would probably:
    a. affect aggregate supply more than aggregate demand
    b. have large direct effects on the supply of labor
    c. cause output and prices to rise
    d. cause output to rise and prices to fall

14. The best supply-side policies, according to Keynesians are:
    a. reducing excise taxes or employee payroll taxes
    b. accelerated depreciation
    c. across-the-board income tax cuts
    d. wage and price controls

15. In accordance with the newer growth models, an increase in the saving rate implies:
    a. no change in the rate of capital formation
    b. a long-run decrease in the rate of capital formation
    c. a short-run increase only in the growth rate of output
    d. a long-run increase in the growth rate of output

16. In the 1970s, the income tax system:
    a. was proportional
    b. was regressive
    c. was progressive
    d. was first proportional and later regressive

17. According to James Tobin, the lower growth in the United States during the 1970s was primarily caused by:
    a. demand shocks
    b. supply shocks
    c. monetary policy "overkill"
    d. both a and c
    e. both b and c

18. According to supply-side economists, a reduction in the marginal income tax rate would cause:
    a. the price level to fall and output to remain unchanged
    b. the price level to rise and output to remain unchanged
    c. both output and the price level to rise
    d. the price level to fall and output to rise

19. An increase in the saving rate will result in:
    a. a temporary increase in capital per worker
    b. a permanent increase in capital per worker
    c. a temporary decrease in capital per worker
    d. a permanent decrease in capital per worker

20. Keynesian economists:
    a. believe that "vast increases" in labor supply will result from lowering marginal income tax rates
    b. do not believe that "vast increases" in labor supply will result from lowering marginal income tax rates
    c. believe that current income tax rates are a serious impediment to labor supply
    d. none of the above

21. According to the neoclassical model, an increase in the rate of capital formation:
    a. results in a more than proportionate increase in the output growth rate
    b. results in a less than proportionate increase in the output growth rate
    c. results in a proportionate increase in the growth rate of output
    d. none of the above

22. Steady-state growth refers to:
    a. output determination in the short run
    b. intermediate-run periods
    c. long-run equilibrium growth
    d. none of the above

23. During the first three years of a recovery from a recession:
    a. productivity, as a rule, rises relatively rapidly
    b. productivity falls slowly
    c. productivity is perplexing since it is usually unpredictable with respect to the directional change
    d. productivity usually does not change

24. The after-tax rate of return is defined as the pretax profit rate:
    a. divided by 1 minus the rate at which profits are taxed
    b. multiplied by 1 minus the rate at which profits are taxed
    c. plus investment credits
    d. minus the rate at which profits are taxed

25. According to Edward Denison, the United States has experienced:
    a. diseconomies of scale
    b. constant returns to scale
    c. economies of scale
    d. none of the above

26. An increase in the effective corporate tax rate due to increased inflation:
    a. shifts the investment schedule to the right
    b. shifts the investment schedule to the left
    c. does not shift the investment schedule
    d. shifts the saving schedule to the right

27. According to supply-side advocates, the increase in government regulatory activity in the late 1960s slowed economic growth:
    a. by increasing the cost of producing a given output
    b. by retarding the capital formation that contributes to increased productivity in terms of measured output
    c. only temporarily until there was an adequate adjustment period
    d. both a and b

28. Recent research in growth theory expands the traditional analysis by making:
    a. the rates of technological change and/or population growth exogenous
    b. the rates of population growth and/or technological change endogenous
    c. the rates of technological change exogenous and population growth endogenous
    d. the rates of population growth exogenous and technological change endogenous

29. According to the classical view, the determinants of saving, investment, and, consequently, the determination of the rate of capital formation include:
    a. productivity but not thrift
    b. thrift but not productivity
    c. the tax structure.
    d. none of the above

30. According to supply-side economists, the incentive to save during the 1970s fell due to:
    a. the U.S. tax system and inflation
    b. an increase in net export and a budget surplus
    c. the passage of the Full Employment and Balanced Growth Act of 1978 and disinflation
    d. none of the above

Problems and/or Essay Questions:

1. Compute the *ex ante* nominal return for a one-year bond held to maturity.
   Price of bond: $100
   Interest received: $ 8
   Inflation rate expected: 4%
   Marginal tax bracket: 20%

2. Using the figures given in 1,
   a. What is the *ex ante* after-tax real return?
   b. What is the *ex post* after-tax real return if:
      i. inflation turns out to be 2%?
      ii. inflation turns out to be 8%?
      iii. unexpected income loss reduces the investor's tax bracket to 18%?
      iv. unexpected income gain raises the investor's tax bracket to 30%, and inflation is 4%?
      v. the investor is forced to sell a bond at $155, and inflation is 4%?
      vi. the investor is forced to sell at $90, and inflation is 4%?
   (Assume there are no tax complications introduced by capital gains or losses.)

3. Using an aggregate demand and supply macroeconomic model as a basis for your answer, enumerate all the direct effects upon demand and supply which might arise if:
   a. Social Security taxes fall to 6% of the first $20,000 earned for all parties.
   b. firms are allowed to expense in one year all expenditures on plant, equipment, trucks, etc.
   c. firms are required to value capital and inventories at replacement cost instead of historic cost.
   After enumerating all these effects, describe which ones a typical supply-sider and which ones a typical Keynesian would stress as most relevant.

4. Consider again the experiment described in 3 part (a) above. How might the results for price and output be affected if it is known with certainty that the Fed will simultaneously contract money growth as these taxes fall?

5. Describe the behavior of the U.S. economy from 1973 to the present. How would a supply-sider explain this behavior? How would a Keynesian explain it? How is it that reasonable men can disagree?

6. Draw and then explain the Laffer curve. Of what significance is the peak of the curve to Reaganomics? Evaluate Reaganomics.

7. Interest in long-run growth models decreased during the 1970s and resurfaced in the late 1980s. Explain.

8. President Bush initially termed supply-side economics "voodoo economics." In what ways, however, were the economic policies of the Bush administration actually consistent with supply-side economics?

9. Explain the accelerated cost recovery system.

10. In 1992, the public chose a new direction in macroeconomic policy and replaced Reaganomics. What did this new program envision?

11. What is the focal point of a promising line of research that attempts to explain cross-country income differentials? Explain in detail.

PART IV: ECONOMIC POLICY

CHAPTER 18

FISCAL POLICY

OVERVIEW

The two chapters in Part IV extend the discussion of macroeconomic policy. Chapter 18 considers fiscal policy. The chapter begins with a discussion of the goals of macroeconomic policy. Two perspectives on this question are considered: that of the policymaker as minimizing a social loss function and the public-choice view of the vote-maximizing politician.

Recent trends in the level and composition of government spending are examined. The concept of automatic fiscal stabilizers is then explained. Keynesian objections to balanced budget rules (like the Gramm-Rudman-Hollings Act) are raised. They believe such rules unnecessarily limit fiscal policy, since they keep automatic stabilizers from playing their role. It would also limit the discretionary policy of Congress and the President. Keynesians are optimistic advocates despite acknowledged past failures of activist fiscal policies. The next section of the chapter considers two concepts for measuring fiscal policy. The first is the measurement of discretionary fiscal policy. Here, the concept of the structural government budget surplus or deficit is examined. The second is the cyclical component of fiscal policy. The final sections of the chapter examine the implications of the large government budget deficits of the 1980s and 1990s. Interpretations of the causes of the deficits are advanced, and a discussion follows of the relationships between government deficits, interest rates, and international trade deficits.

Techniques in Depth

1. Endogenous Taxes and the Autonomous Spending Multiplier

When we alter the simplifying assumption of all lump-sum taxes to the more realistic case of endogenous taxes, we find that the autonomous spending multiplier is lower. Let us see why in more detail and with a numerical example. First, recall that the autonomous spending multiplier reveals the change in income governed by a change in some autonomous spending component. For example:

$$\Delta Y / \Delta G$$

For our example, assume that

$$I = 50$$

$$G = 25$$

$$C = 25 + .70(Y - T)$$

$$T = 10$$

Thus, to begin with, we are dealing with lump sum taxes only. In this case, the C equation is

$$C = 18 + .70Y$$

The following table summarizes what happens if government spending rises by $10:

	Cumulative ΔY
$\Delta Y = \$10$	
	round 1 $10.00
$\Delta C = 7$	
$\Delta Y = 7$	
	round 2 $17.00
$\Delta C = 4.9$	
$\Delta Y = 4.9$	
	round 3 $21.90
$\Delta C = 3.4$	
$\Delta Y = 3.4$	
	round 4 $25.30
$\Delta C = 2.4$	
	.
	.
	.
	$33.30

The initial effect of an increase in G is to generate $10 of extra income to those factors of production supplying goods to the government. This extra income generates an extra $7 of consumption spending by those agents. This additional $7 is, however, additional income to other factors since they spend 70 percent of all additional income. The next round of additional consumption spending equals .7($7) = $4.9. Of course, this additional spending generates another $4.9 of income, and the process continues until ΔC's and ΔY's are too small to measure. If we carry this out, we converge on a cumulative Y equal to $33.3. Therefore, the multiplier equals:

$$\Delta Y/\Delta G = 33.3/10.0 = 3.3$$

Notice that this also equals:

$$1/1 - b, \text{ where } b = .7$$

To see the effect of endogenous taxes on the multiplier, assume now that:

$$T = -1 + .2Y$$

In that case, we can rewrite the C equation as

$$C = 25 + .7(Y - T) = 25 + .7Y + .7 - .14Y$$

$$C = 25.7 + .56Y$$

Compare this C equation to the lump sum version above. Notice that in this case, a dollar increase in income generates only 56 cents of additional spending. In the lump sum case, an additional dollar leads to 70 cents of spending. The difference here is that each dollar earned is taxed and less is available to be used for spending.

The implication is that since less spending occurs, the multiplier will be smaller. The same $10 government spending injection now leads to the following changes:

		Cumulative ΔY
$\Delta Y = \$10$		
	round 1	$10.00
$\Delta C = 5.60$		
$\Delta Y = 5.60$		
	round 2	$15.60
$\Delta C = 3.14$		
$\Delta Y = 3.14$		
	round 3	$18.74
$\Delta C = 1.76$		
$\Delta Y = 1.76$		
	round 4	$20.50
$\Delta C = .99$		
	.	
	.	
	.	
	.	$22.73

In this case, only $22.73 of extra income is generated. Each round of income change was made smaller as taxes were siphoned out of the economy. In this case, the multiplier is:

$$\$22.73/\$10.00 = 2.273$$

The assumption of endogenous taxes clearly makes the multiplier smaller. Notice that:

$$1/[1 - b(1 - t)] = 1/[1 - .7(1 - .2)]$$
$$= 1/(1 - .56)$$
$$= 2.273$$

What has happened to the government's budget in this case?

$$\Delta G = +\$10$$

$$\Delta T = .2(\Delta Y)$$

$$= .2(22.73) = \$4.55$$

So the budget goes into deficit but not by $10. The endogenous increase in taxes of $4.55 means that the budget goes into "the red" by only $5.45.

Self-Tests

Multiple-Choice Questions:

1. The question of optimal conduct of macroeconomic policy is one of finding the correct setting of the instruments to:
   a. keep the government budget balanced
   b. minimize a social loss function
   c. keep money growth constant
   d. maximize societal wealth

2. The behavior of policymakers as politicians coincides with the behavior of policymakers as economic stabilizers when:
   a. voters are "myopic"
   b. high unemployment generates more vote loss than high inflation
   c. voters have a bias toward deficit spending of the federal government
   d. all of the above
   e. none of the above

3. The public-choice view suggests that fiscal policymakers should:
   a. reduce deficits during economic recovery
   b. worry less about inflation
   c. be constrained by a balanced budget requirement
   d. engage in active countercyclical policies

4. The share of all goods and services produced in the U.S. going to the Federal government since 1962 has:
   a. increased
   b. decreased
   c. stayed the same

5. The net effect of a rise in the level of nominal income is:
   a. a larger deficit
   b. a smaller deficit
   c. a larger high employment deficit
   d. higher government spending

6. Assuming that taxes are endogenous and positively related to income, the autonomous expenditure multiplier is higher:
   a. the higher is the marginal tax rate
   b. the lower is the marginal tax rate
   c. if the marginal tax rate is infinite
   d. none of the above

7. We call income taxes automatic stabilizers, because:
   a. Congress legislates tax increases in recessions
   b. Congress legislates tax decreases in recessions
   c. a marginal tax rate reduces the autonomous spending multiplier
   d. the Laffer curve is concave

8. Dollar for dollar, the effect on GDP of a reduction in autonomous taxes compared to a rise in government spending is:
   a. smaller
   b. larger
   c. the same

9. The partisan theory of fiscal policy assumes:
   a. voters are myopic
   b. liberals generally favor inflation
   c. conservatives generally favor inflation
   d. election outcomes are easily predicted

10. Keynesians do not favor a strict balanced budget approach, because they believe:
    a. the government's budget acts as an automatic stabilizer
    b. policymakers should actively attempt countercyclical stabilization policy
    c. the record of politicians in the area of stabilization policy is not uniformly bad
    d. all of the above

11. If the MPC out of disposable income is .8, and the marginal income tax rate (t_1) is .25, the value of the autonomous expenditure multiplier will be:
    a. 5
    b. −4
    c. 2.5
    d. 1.05

12. If the government deficit increases by $200 billion, and the structural deficit rises by $225 billion, this implies:
    a. a mathematical error has been made
    b. automatic stabilizers are moving the budget toward surplus
    c. automatic stabilizers are moving the budget toward deficit
    d. the unemployment rate has increased

13. Keynesians believe that the Reagan policies can be characterized by:
    a. tight fiscal policy
    b. expansionary monetary policy
    c. lower interest rates
    d. larger trade deficits

14. The higher the marginal income tax rate, the:
    a. lower the autonomous expenditure multiplier
    b. higher the autonomous expenditure multiplier
    c. lower the MPC out of disposable income
    d. higher the MPC out of disposable income

15. If the tax function is given by $T = .25Y$, and the consumption is $C = 50 + .8Y_D$, then a 10-unit increase in government spending will increase equilibrium income by:
    a. 20 units
    b. 25 units
    c. 40 units
    d. 50 units

16. If there is a simultaneous reduction in income taxes and transfer payments of $100 billion, aggregate disposable income will:
    a. be lower than before
    b. be higher than before
    c. remain constant
    d. none of the above

17. If Ricardian equivalence holds:
    a. tax cuts resulting in government deficits raise interest rates
    b. tax increases to reduce the deficit lower interest rates
    c. the only important thing is the level of government spending
    d. none of the above

18. Automatic fiscal stabilizers:
    a. cause tax revenues to increase in recessionary periods
    b. keep the federal budget balanced
    c. help reduce the severity of recessions and inflationary boom periods
    d. none of the above

19. The real rate of interest is the:
    a. nominal interest rate plus the expected rate of inflation
    b. nominal interest rate minus the expected inflation rate
    c. nominal interest rate minus last year's inflation rate
    d. nominal interest rate divided by last year's inflation rate

20. The structural deficit is that portion of the deficit that:
    a. results from fluctuations in real GDP
    b. is due to nondiscretionary spending by the federal government
    c. results from the economy being at a low level of economic activity
    d. would exist even if the economy were at its potential level of output

21. According to the public-choice view:
    a. macroeconomic policymakers act to maximize their own welfare or utility rather than act for the social good
    b. policymakers in the public sector work for the public, whereas policymakers in the private sector have private interests
    c. all governments are bad and should be abolished
    d. none of the above

22. A rise in the value of the dollar:
    a. makes U.S. goods cheaper for foreigners
    b. makes U.S. exports expensive to foreigners
    c. makes foreign goods cheaper for U.S. residents
    d. means that U.S. residents have to pay more for foreign currency
    e. either b and c

23. According to the partisan theory:
    a. there is only one party, the partisan party
    b. there are two parties, the liberals and the conservatives
    c. politicians are viewed as self-centered individuals
    d. moderates and liberals share the same ideologies

24. Assume that the actual deficit is $150 billion with the economy well below potential output. If the level of economic activity rises to its potential level, tax revenues would increase by $50 billion while transfer payments fall by $20 billion. What is the structural deficit?
    a. $ 80 billion
    b. $120 billion
    c. $220 billion
    d. $180 billion
    e. $100 billion

25. Recessionary periods such as 1975, 1980, and 1981-82 were periods of significant:
    a. frictional deficits
    b. transitional deficits
    c. structural deficits
    d. cyclical deficits

26. The role of the tax-transfer system as an autonomous fiscal stabilizer requires that the budget:
    a. can have a deficit at appropriate points in the business cycle
    b. can have a surplus at appropriate points in the business cycle
    c. cannot have a structural deficit component
    d. either a or b

27. From the net tax function $T = t_0 + t_1 Y$, where $t_0 < 0$ and $t_1 > 0$, it follows that, as income rises, net tax collections increase, and the government budgetary
    a. surplus declines
    b. deficit increases
    c. deficit declines
    d. deficit does not change

28. If the tax function is given as $T = t_0 + t_1 Y$ where t_1 equals 1/3, and marginal propensity to consume out of disposable income is 3/4, then the change in GDP per unit change in $t_0 (\Delta Y / \Delta t_0)$ is:
    a. −1
    b. +1
    c. −1.5
    d. +1.5
    e. −2

Problems and/or Essay Questions:

1. A policymaker's loss function has been specified as:

$$L = a_1(U - U^*)^2 + a_2(\hat{P} - \hat{P}^*)^2 + a_3(\hat{Y} - \hat{Y}^*)^2$$

$$a_1, a_2, a_3 > 0$$

   a. What is a loss function?
   b. Define $U, U^*, \hat{P}, \hat{P}^*, \hat{Y}, \hat{Y}^*$.
   c. What does it mean about the "tastes" of policymakers if:
      $a_1 = 0, a_2 = 0, a_3 = 1.0$? What if $a_1 = 0, a_2 = 5, a_3 = 0$?
   d. Using a_1, a_2, a_3, what values of the a's might describe a Keynesian policymaker?
   e. Why is $(U - U^*)$ squared?

2. Below is a table with values for the government deficit and GDP for selected years. First, describe how the absolute size of deficits has changed over time. Second, fill in column 3, and describe how the ratio of the deficit to GDP has changed over time. Third, describe the usefulness of column 3 and how the story it tells is different from that of column 2. Note: (−) means surplus.

Year	(1) GDP	(2) Deficit	(3) Deficit/GDP
1960	555.5	(−)0.3	
1962	554.3	7.1	
1964	626.5	5.9	
1966	739.6	3.7	
1968	849.8	25.2	
1970	985.6	2.8	
1972	1145.8	23.4	
1974	1403.3	6.1	
1976	1685.1	73.7	
1978	2156.4	59.2	
1980	2644.5	73.8	
1982	3124.9	128.0	
1984	3696.7	185.4	
1986	4219.6	221.2	
1988	4810.8	155.2	
1990	5459.5	220.5	
1992	5865.0	365.2	

3. Assume the following function depicts a simple economy:

$$C = 5 + .75(Y - T)$$

$$I = 30$$

$$G = 50$$

$$T = -16 + .5Y$$

a. Calculate the autonomous spending multiplier.
b. Calculate the equilibrium level of Y.
c. If G rises to 75, describe the effect upon: Y, T, and the government deficit.
d. If t (the management tax rate) falls to .4, describe the effect upon: Y, T, and the government deficit.
e. If autonomous taxes and government spending both rise by 30, what happens to Y? What happens to the size of the government deficit? Why should such a "balanced budget" policy produce these results?

4. Comment upon the validity of the following statements:

   a. "If the unemployment rate exceeds 5.5 percent, then the high-employment budget surplus must be greater than the actual budget surplus."
   b. "The budget surplus is a poor indicator of what the government is trying to do with fiscal policy; the high-employment budget surplus is superior in that regard."
   c. "Keynesians generally prefer unbalanced federal government budgets."
   d. "The partisan view of government deficits says that right after a political election, one should be able to predict changes in the fiscal policy coming in the next year."
   e. "Reagan government deficits caused interest rates to rise and the trade deficit to worsen."

5. Explain the difference between cyclical and structural deficits.

6. In the United States, what proportion of the deficit has been cyclical, and what proportion has been structural?

7. In the 1980s, both the budget deficit and the trade deficit increased. In the early 1990s, however, the trade deficit decreased, while the budget deficit continued to rise. Explain the difference in these situations in terms of monetary and fiscal policy.

8. Explain, why, if Ricardian equivalence holds, only the level of government spending will be effective as fiscal policy.

9. At least for the short run, the U.S. federal budget deficit appears to have been eliminated. Furthermore, budget deficits in other industrialized countries have also declined substantially in the mid-1990s. How can this be explained with the public choice or partisan theories which predict a deficit bias to fiscal policy?

10. The public-choice view assumes that voter behavior is governed by "collective rationality." Explain this term. What happens when this type of "collective rationality" does not exist?

11. The original forms of the political business cycle model and the partisan model did not assume that expectations were rational and, therefore, forward-looking. How did Alberto Alesina and Jeffrey Sachs modify the partisan model of fiscal policy to assume rational expectations?

CHAPTER 19

MONETARY POLICY

OVERVIEW

The chapter begins with a brief discussion of the institutional setting for monetary policy. The degree of independence of the Federal Reserve is considered. Then the question of optimal monetary policy is examined. Two aspects of this question are considered. The first is that of the optimal strategy for monetary policy, the plan that links the policy instruments controlled by the Federal Reserve to the ultimate policy goals. The second aspect of the optimal policy question is the choice of a policy instrument or operating target in the short run, the optimal tactics of monetary policy.

The question of the optimal strategy of monetary policy leads to a discussion of intermediate targeting on a monetary aggregate. The arguments for and against such a monetary policy strategy are presented. From a purely theoretical standpoint, intermediate targeting on a monetary aggregate is shown to be an inefficient monetary policy strategy. This inefficiency results partly from the fact that the intermediate targeting approach fails to utilize all the relevant current period information. Second, the data that are used, observations on the monetary aggregate, are used inefficiently, since the intermediate targeting approach is based on the generally incorrect assumption that hitting the money stock target is equivalent to hitting the ultimate monetary policy targets. Next, practical arguments in favor of the intermediate targeting approach (as well as some practical objectives to the approach) are considered. Alternatives to intermediate targeting on monetary aggregates are examined.

In the next section on the tactics of monetary policy, an operating procedure that uses the federal funds rate to control the money stock is compared with a procedure that uses a reserve target operating procedure. Which tactic is optimal is shown to depend upon which is the major source of uncertainty in the economy: changes in money demand (the LM curve) or changes in investment spending (the IS curve). The reasons for the Federal Reserve's shifts in operating procedure in 1979, and again in 1982 are explained.

Techniques in Depth

1. Intermediate Targeting with M1

Here we show why economic uncertainty and forecast errors make it difficult for the Federal Reserve to target goal variables, like real GDP, or y. Let us rewrite the IS and LM curves in a way that reflects the uncertainty faced by policymakers

$$M/\hat{P} = \hat{c}_0 + c_1 y + c_2$$

$$y = \frac{\hat{a} - b\overline{T} + \hat{I} + \overline{G}}{1 - b} - \frac{d}{1 - b} r$$

We assume that policymakers focus exclusively achieving a value of real output equal to y^*. Federal Reserve officials know the values of G and T, the fiscal policy variables. Furthermore, they know that the value of y actually occurring will depend on these settings of G and T and upon the uncertain values of the endogenous variables ($\hat{P}$, $\hat{c}_0$, $\hat{a}$, and $\hat{I}$) and upon the values of the parameters (c_1, c_2, d, and b).

The staff at the Fed will supply the policymakers with forecasts of these variables and the most probable value of the parameters. With all this information, this yields a picture of what "could happen" in the economy without any changes in M1:

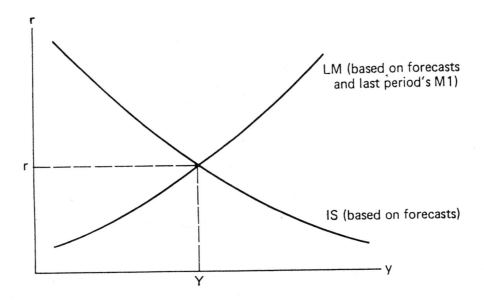

But, suppose $y \neq y^*$

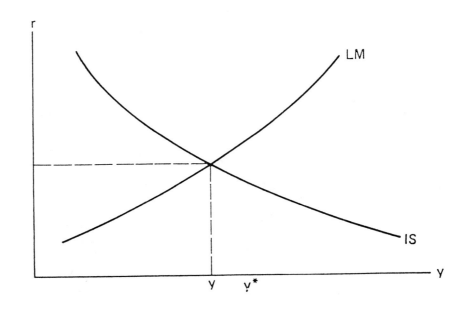

Given the knowledge, monetary policymakers can deduce the correct amount of change in M1 so as to make $y = y^*$. Notice that a rise in M1 to $M1^*$ would shift out the LM curve:

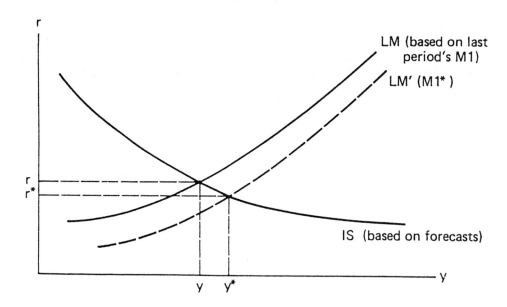

If the forecasts and knowledge of the economy were correct, then the setting of M1 at $M1^*$ brings output to its desired rate, y^*.

The student should see, however, how important information is to the correct formulation of monetary policy. The ability of policymakers to hit y^* depends crucially upon the shift factors (other than M1) acting just as predicted.

For example, suppose that, unexpectedly, firms spend much less than the forecast $\hat{I}$. In this case, the correct money setting leads to:

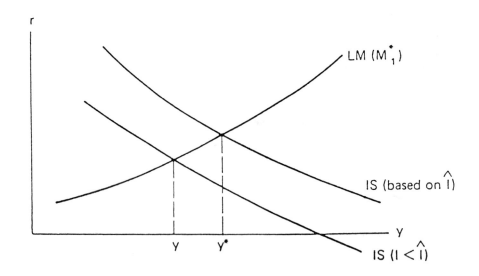

Here we see that the forecast error about I has led to recessionary conditions—i.e., undershooting the y^* goal. In order to hit the y^* with $I < \hat{I}$, a higher level of M1 above M_1^* is necessary. Strict application of monetary targeting means monitoring current money stock figures to keep M1 on its target for the current period. This will not, in general, keep y at its target level y^*.

Unanticipated shifts in the money sector can also lead to problems. For example, if c_0 turns out to be much higher than $\hat{c}_0$, or if P were higher than $\hat{P}$, either case would lead to an unexpected leftward shift in the LM curve (an unexpected excess demand for money). In that case, we would also find $y < y^*$:

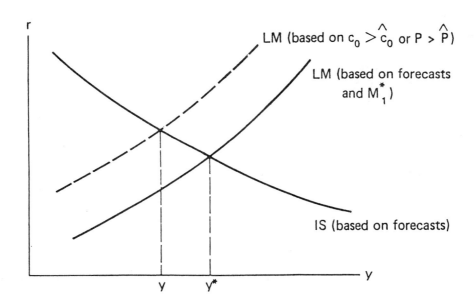

The upshot is that if monetary policymakers set M1 targets according to forecasts that turn out to be erroneous, then the policies will yield suboptimal levels of economic activity. Intermediate targeting acknowledges that interest rates and monetary aggregates can provide timely information about unexpected events and the most current requirements for target achievement. It requires that policy be responsive to current changes in either short-term interest rates or to monetary aggregates. In the chapter, more is said about which intermediate target to choose.

Self-Tests

Multiple-Choice Questions:

1. The Federal Reserve is, to a large degree, independent from the rest of the Federal government, since:
    a. all member of the Federal Reserve Board serve 14-year terms of office
    b. regional bank presidents are appointed by the Board of Governors
    c. the Federal Reserve is independent of the budget appropriation process
    d. all of the above

2. The ultimate rationale for using intermediate targets is:
   a. uncertainty and imperfect information
   b. lack of control over ultimate targets
   c. intermediate variables are more important than ultimate targets
   d. all of the above

3. Ultimate targets of the Federal Reserve include:
   a. the money supply
   b. the price level
   c. the federal funds rate
   d. bank reserves

4. M1 is a more useful intermediate target if:
   a. the IS curve is perfectly vertical
   b. money demand depends only on income
   c. money demand is inherently unstable
   d. all of the above

5. Intermediate targeting on M1 is strongly advocated by:
   a. Keynesians
   b. supply siders
   c. new classical economists
   d. monetarists

6. An alternative tactic for controlling monetary aggregates employed extensively before 1980 was to control:
   a. the federal funds rate
   b. the Treasury bill rate
   c. credit
   d. the monetary base

7. The instrument used most frequently to keep the federal funds rate at the desired level is:
   a. selling federal funds
   b. open-market operations
   c. the discount rate
   d. the reserve requirement
   e. credit controls

8. The good thing about interest rate targeting is that forecast errors:
   a. of money demand have no effect on attaining the target
   b. of money demand have no effect on the controllability of reserves
   c. of spending components have no effect on attaining the target
   d. all of the above
   e. none of the above

9. A tactic of controlling the money stock via control of the growth rate of bank reserves leads to:
   a. less of a problem of missed targets due to forecast errors
   b. less instability in the money demand function
   c. greater interest rate instability
   d. all of the above

10. If the Fed is pegging the interest rates, and money demand unexpectedly falls, then it would:
    a. lower the money supply by trying to raise interest rates
    b. raise the money supply by trying to lower interest rates
    c. use credit controls
    d. buy government bonds in the open market

11. If the great majority of shocks to our system arise from unpredictable money demand, then the preferred tactic of monetary policy is:
    a. pegging reserves
    b. pegging interest rates
    c. pegging M1
    d. pegging the supply of credit

12. The current chairperson (as of 1998) of the Board of Governors, who was appointed by President Reagan in 1987, is:
    a. Paul Volcker
    b. Arthur Burns
    c. G. William Miller
    d. Alan Greenspan

13. In the case in which the LM curve is not perfectly vertical, even if the Fed achieves its target level of the money stock, income will be below its target level if:
    a. real sector demand is actually weaker than predicted
    b. real sector demand is actually stronger than predicted
    c. real sector demand is equal to its prediction
    d. none of the above

14. Interest-rate targeting may be favored to money-stock targeting when:
    a. monetary aggregates have measurement problems
    b. there is instability in financial markets
    c. there is instability in the goods market
    d. a and b only
    e. all of the above

15. The federal funds rate:
    a. is the interest rate charged on all commercial loans
    b. is the amount of excess reserves held by all financial intermediaries
    c. is the interest rate charged on loans from one bank to another
    d. none of the above

16. Interest-rate targeting has an advantage in that it is apt to provide:
    a. stability in the monetary base
    b. stability of short-term interest rates
    c. stability in the money growth rate
    d. none of the above

17. Assuming the Fed wants to change the money stock, then it should:
    a. change the excess reserve ratio
    b. engage in open-market operations
    c. change the marginal income tax rate
    d. none of the above

18. Assuming an IS-LM framework, then if the Fed pegs the interest rate:
    a. the LM schedule slopes upward
    b. the LM schedule slopes downward
    c. the LM schedule is vertical
    d. the LM schedule becomes horizontal

19. In October of 1979, the Fed changed its operating procedure from:
    a. intermediate targeting on monetary aggregates to control of the federal funds rate
    b. pegging the interest rate to intermediate targeting on monetary aggregates
    c. control of the federal funds rate to control of reserves held by banks
    d. control of reserves held by banks to control of the federal funds rate

20. If the money stock is the intermediate target, then a positive shock to money demand:
    a. will shift the LM schedule to the right and income will rise above the target level
    b. will shift the LM schedule to the left and income falls below the target level
    c. will not shift the LM schedule and, therefore, will not displace income from the target level
    d. none of the above

21. Which of the following is not a body within the Federal Reserve System?
    a. The Open Market Committee
    b. The Board of Governors
    c. The Council of Economic Advisors
    d. Both b and c

22. Relative to fiscal policy, monetary policy:
    a. is much more independent of the political process
    b. takes longer time to implement
    c. is more closely controlled by Congress
    d. has fewer harmful side effects

23. If the money stock is targeted, then an autonomous rise in investment demand:
    a. causes income to rise, but the money stock has to be increased to accommodate the expansion
    b. increases income and money demand and lowers the interest rate
    c. causes a rise in income, money demand, and the interest rate, with a dampening effect on the expansionary process
    d. none of the above

24. Throughout the 1980s, the Federal Reserve:
    a. closely monitored the behavior of M1
    b. closely monitored the behavior of the broader aggregates, especially M2
    c. returned to a strategy of almost complete concentration on the federal funds rate
    d. de-emphasized monetary aggregates

25. If the Federal Reserve wants to change the money stock it can:
    a. change the marginal income tax rate
    b. engage in open-market operations
    c. change the required reserve ratio
    d. both b and c

26. Assuming a money supply target, then a positive shock to money demand:
    a. will shift the position of the LM schedule away from the predicted level even if the target level of the money supply is achieved
    b. will not shift the position of the LM schedule away from the predicted level even if the target level of the money supply is achieved
    c. may or may not shift the position of the LM schedule away from the predicted level even if the target level of the money supply is achieved
    d. none of the above

27. If the central bank targets the interest rate:
    a. it will guard against inflation
    b. it does not provide an anti-inflation guarantee
    c. it must increase the money supply to accommodate any increases in money demand
    d. both a and c
    e. both b and c

28. As of August of 1997, the FOMC policy directive was changed to set a specific target for:
    a. the federal funds rate
    b. checkable deposits
    c. bank reserves
    d. M2

29. According to monetarists:
    a. the LM curve is flat and money demand, as a rule, is unstable
    b. the LM curve is quite steep and money demand, at least in most circumstances, is stable
    c. the LM curve is steep, but money demand is mostly unstable
    d. interest rates are favorite targets

Problems and/or Essay Questions:

1. Policymakers learn that, because of financial innovations emerging next quarter, the demand for money will shift sharply lower. Given their desire to maintain the output rate, y^*, describe what policy directive would be sent to the open-market desk under a scheme of M1 targeting. Then, consider what might happen if they underestimated or overestimated significantly the expected drop in money demand. In the midst of all this, what complications would ensue if they predicted policy on a federal government budget deficit of $80 billion and it becomes apparent it will instead be $180 billion?

2. List and then describe the undesirable side effects of a major expansion or contraction of the money supply. Give historical examples of these from the post-World War II period.

3. Suppose that there is an unanticipated shock that decreases the level of money demanded for given levels of real income and the interest rate. Show graphically the effects of this shock for the cases where:
   a. the Federal Reserve is pegging the federal funds rate.
   b. the Federal Reserve is fixing the level of bank reserves.
   In your answer, indicate the effects of the shock on the level of the money stock, the interest rate, and the level of real income.

4. Define intermediate targeting. What has the Fed been targeting between 1979 and 1982? Since 1982? How would you describe the accuracy of this targeting?

5. Explain why money-stock targeting is desirable in the face of a potential inflationary boom.

6. Explain the Federal Reserve's intentions in the 1970s when it was decided to target the federal funds rate.

7. Discuss the situation in the late 1970s that prompted the Fed to switch from federal funds targeting to controlling bank reserves.

8. What happened to the money-income relationship in the 1980s and how did this affect monetary policy?

9. How does the time inconsistency problem arise when applied to monetary policy under discretion? What argument lends support for policy by rules?

10. Many countries want to move to inflation targeting rules. If it is not to solve the time inconsistency problem, then what other motive is there?

11. When is a money-stock target considered superior to an interest-rate target? When is an interest-rate target preferred to a money-stock target?

PART V: OPEN ECONOMY MACROECONOMICS

CHAPTER 20

EXCHANGE RATES AND THE INTERNATIONAL MONETARY SYSTEM

OVERVIEW

In this chapter, the analysis is extended to open economies. The first questions considered are those of measurement. Economic relations between the United States and other nations are discussed with reference to the major components of the U.S. balance of payments accounts: the merchandise balance, the current account, the capital account, and official reserve transactions. The foreign exchange market explains how changes in the demands and supplies of foreign currencies affect exchange rates. The changes are shown to depend on each country's demands for others' goods, services, and capital. The ways in which the exchange rate is determined under a fixed rate system, a flexible rate system, and a managed floating rate system are analyzed.

In a flexible exchange rate system, there is no central bank intervention and the exchange rate adjusts to clear the foreign exchange market, to equate the demand for and supply of foreign currency. In a fixed exchange rate system, a country's currency has a fixed par value if that country's central bank is committed to intervening in the foreign exchange market to defend the value of the currency. A managed float is a situation where the value of a country's currency is allowed to float in response to market forces, but where, at times, the central bank intervenes to prevent what are viewed as "undesirable" movements on the exchange rate.

The next section of the chapter discusses the relationships between international economic relations and the level of domestic economic activity. The effects on the level of economic activity as a result of changes in the levels of imports and exports are considered. The reverse question of the effect that the changes in the level of domestic economic activity will have on the balance of payments is also considered. Potential conflicts between domestic policy goals and goals of external balance under a fixed exchange rate are examined. The relationship between capital flows and the level of economic activity is explained. The final section of the chapter discusses the relative merits of fixed versus flexible exchange rate regimes. The arguments for and against flexible exchange rate systems are evaluated in light of the recent experience (post-1973) with greater exchange rate flexibility.

Techniques in Depth

1. Calculating the "U.S. Cost" of Foreign Items

When a U.S. citizen buys U.S. goods, he carefully watches the price of the goods. When he also buys a foreign good, he must scrutinize the exchange rate as well as the price "at home" in the foreign country. For example, assume that a German bike, purchased in Germany, costs 800 marks. What is important to the U.S. citizen is how many dollars must be given up to receive the bicycle. Given that the bike costs 800 marks, how many dollars given up depends on the exchange rate of marks for dollars. If 1 dollar exchanges for 2 marks, the exchange rate is ½ or .5. This can be stated alternatively that 1 mark costs 50 cents. If 1 dollar exchanges for 2½ marks, then the mark is worth less. We say that the mark has depreciated, while the dollar has appreciated. In this case, the exchange rate is 1/2.5 or .4; one mark costs 40 cents.

If the exchange rate is .5, 1 dollar will trade for 2 marks. To obtain 800 marks for the bike, the U.S. citizen gives up 800/2 or $400 for the bike. If, however, the mark depreciates to .4, then $400 translates into $400 times 2½ marks per dollar or 1000 marks. The U.S. citizen can receive the bike and use the extra 200 marks for something else. We can equivalently say that in dollars, the bike costs only 800/2.5 or $320 if the mark depreciates to .4.

Self-Tests

Multiple-Choice Questions:

1. The balance of payments account for any country:
   a. accounts for all earnings of the foreign activities of U.S. citizens
   b. accounts for expenditures of U.S. citizens abroad
   c. always balances
   d. all of the above

2. The U.S. current account includes:
   a. imports and exports of machinery
   b. imports and exports of government bonds
   c. foreign direct investment
   d. all of the above

3. The capital account includes:
   a. imports and exports of autos
   b. imports and exports of goods and services
   c. imports and exports of machinery
   d. imports and exports of stocks and bonds

4. When the U.S. government sends foreign aid to another country, this is recorded in the U.S. balance of payments account as:
   a. credit to the current account
   b. credit to the capital account
   c. debit to the capital account
   d. debit to the capital account

5. If autonomous transactions are in surplus by $30 billion, this implies:
   a. there is an excess supply of foreign currency
   b. there is an excess demand for foreign currency
   c. there is a current account deficit
   d. capital exports exceed capital imports

6. The higher the exchange rate, the
   a. higher the cost of imported goods, and the lower the demand for foreign exchange
   b. lower the cost of imported goods, and the lower the demand for foreign exchange
   c. lower the cost of imported goods, and the higher the demand for foreign exchange
   d. higher the cost of imported goods, and the higher the demand for foreign exchange

7. As the exchange rate rises, the supply of foreign exchange
   a. rises, if U.S. export demand is inelastic
   b. falls
   c. stays the same
   d. none of the above

8. Under a system of floating exchange rates, the exchange rate is:
   a. determined by governments
   b. market-determined
   c. both a and b
   d. neither a nor b

9. Swedish technological progress allows them to be more competitive and offer numerous products at lower prices next year. Assuming freely floating exchange rates, this should cause a U.S.:
   a. balance of payments deficit
   b. balance of payments surplus
   c. dollar depreciation
   d. dollar appreciation

10. If the United States wants to peg the price of the mark at .4 dollars when the market equilibrium rate is .3 dollars, then the U.S. central bank should:
    a. sell dollars
    b. buy marks
    c. buy dollars
    d. sell marks
    e. a and b

11. A country that pegs its exchange rate and runs persistent balance of payments deficits also runs the risk of:
    a. high unemployment
    b. running out of foreign exchange
    c. accumulating too much foreign exchange
    d. its exchange rate rising

12. The more open an economy is to foreign trade, the more likely it is that faster economic growth abroad will cause it to have:
    a. a current account deficit
    b. a current account surplus
    c. no effect
    d. no effect, especially if exchange rates are fixed

13. If a reduction in the money supply leads to a rise in interest rates and lower output, in a fixed exchange rate system:
    a. it benefits both trade and capital accounts
    b. it worsens both trade and capital accounts
    c. it increases inflation
    d. it promotes more imports of goods and services

14. When a German citizen purchases a U.S. Treasury bill and then receives an interest payment, these transactions are recorded as:
    a. a capital inflow and a service account debit
    b. a capital inflow and a service account surplus
    c. two capital inflows
    d. two capital outflows

15. The official reserve transactions balance is:
    a. negative, if the capital account is in surplus
    b. negative, if the current account is in deficit
    c. the amount of accommodating central bank transactions
    d. zero only if exchange rates are fixed

16. Assuming a system of perfectly flexible exchange rates, then a fall in the demand for U.S. exports:
    a. results in a balance of payments surplus
    b. results in a balance of payments deficit
    c. results in a rise in the exchange rate
    d. results in a fall in the exchange rate

17. Assuming a system of perfectly flexible exchange rates: then a recession abroad would cause the U.S.:
    a. exchange rate to fall
    b. exchange rate to rise
    c. to have a balance of payments surplus
    d. to have a balance of payments deficit

18. If one German mark is $.40, then three dollars trade for:
    a. 3.00 German marks
    b. 1.20 German marks
    c. 3.60 German marks
    d. 7.50 German marks

19. Alternative proposals to change the current exchange rate system are:
    a. a dirty float rate system
    b. adjustable target zones for exchange rates
    c. a new explicit system of fixed exchange rates
    d. both a and b
    e. both b and c

20. A current account deficit in a nation's balance of payments accounts suggests:
    a. that income is greater than expenditures
    b. that expenditures are greater than income
    c. that imports are equal to exports
    d. exports exceed imports

21. A reduction in U.S. official reserve assets shows up in the U.S. balance of payments accounts as a:
    a. debit
    b. credit
    c. current account entry
    d. none of the above

22. Imports from Europe are recorded as:
    a. a positive item in the current account
    b. a negative item in the current account
    c. a capital inflow item
    d. a capital outflow item

23. In a system of perfectly flexible exchange rates, an expansionary U.S. monetary policy will:
    a. lower the value of the dollar relative to foreign currencies
    b. raise the value of the dollar relative to foreign currencies
    c. not change the value of the dollar relative to foreign currencies
    d. none of the above

24. An appreciation of the dollar is:
    a. a rise in the exchange rate
    b. a fall in the exchange rate
    c. a currency crisis
    d. none of the above

25. The current international monetary system is a:
    a. fixed rate system
    b. completely flexible rate system
    c. gold standard system
    d. managed floating rate system

26. If the exchange rate rises by 5 percent, hence, the dollar volume of exports rises by 5 percent, then foreign exchange earnings:
    a. would increase by 5 percent
    b. would actually decrease by 5 percent
    c. would increase by 10 percent
    d. would not change

27. The Bretton Woods system:
    a. expected countries with persistent surpluses to devalue their currencies
    b. established fixed par values for currencies
    c. was to be a system of adjustable pegs
    d. was supposed to slow down inflation after World War II

28. If the exchange rate is flexible, an expansionary monetary policy in the foreign exchange market :
    a. will shift the demand curve for foreign exchange to the left and the supply curve of foreign exchange to the right
    b. will shift the demand curve for foreign exchange to the right and the supply curve of foreign exchange to the left
    c. will shift both the demand curve for foreign exchange and the supply curve of foreign exchange to the left
    d. will shift both the demand curve for foreign exchange and the supply curve of foreign exchange to the right

29. The statistical discrepancy:
    a. is known as the "errors and omissions term"
    b. is the amount that must be added to balance the total balance of payments
    c. is the adjusted amount to balance the capital account
    d. is the amount that has to be subtracted to balance the current account
    e. both a and b

30. Alternative proposals to change the current system of exchange rates include:
    a. a new explicit system of fixed exchange rates
    b. adjustable target zones for exchange rates
    c. a dirty float rate system
    d. both a and b

Problems and/or Essay Questions:

1. At one time, the value of the British pound was $1.84, and the yen exchanged for 43 cents. Answer the following questions:
   a. With $1.00, how many pounds or yen could a U.S. citizen obtain?
   b. If the price of a Chevrolet in the United States is $8,000, then what does it cost in pounds and in yen?
   c. If the yen appreciates by 10 percent, then how much does the car cost in yen?
   d. If the pound depreciates by 20 percent, then how much does the car cost in pounds?
   e. If you know that the price of a pound was going to rise soon, and you anticipated buying British goods later, what might you do today?

2. Explain the merits and drawbacks of both flexible and fixed exchange rate systems. Does recent world experience suggest the superiority of either of these systems? Explain.

3. Describe the implications of an autonomous increase in the Japanese demand for U.S. goods and services. Assume exchange rates are fixed, and describe what would happen to output, prices, interest rates, the U.S. demand and supply of foreign currency, the U.S. balance of payments, imports, and exports.

4. Extending your answer to 3, describe what would happen if after reading the solution described above, exchange rates were allowed to freely float. What would happen next?

5. Under fixed exchange rates, describe in detail what would be the effects on the U.S. economy if the price per unit of imported steel increased significantly. Assume that demand for steel imports is relatively price inelastic. Also, assume that steel is a major input into U.S. production. Describe the effects of the change upon output, prices, interest rates, U.S. demand and supply of foreign currency, the U.S. balance of payments, imports, and exports.

6. The behavior of the U.S. dollar can be attributed, at least partially, to the conduct of monetary policy. Explain how monetary policy can account for major changes in the value of the dollar from 1976-1984.

7. What has happened to the value of the dollar since 1988?

8. Assume a foreign recession, then explain how a flexible exchange rate insulates the domestic economy from such a shock.

9. What type of system is the European Monetary System and how long has it been in existence? What is the function of the European Exchange Rate Mechanism? Is the European Monetary System going to change in the near future?

CHAPTER 21

MONETARY AND FISCAL POLICY IN THE OPEN ECONOMY

OVERVIEW

This particular chapter encompasses monetary and fiscal policy actions in an open economy macroeconomic model. An open economy model certainly includes trade and capital flows among nations. Of special interest are the roles that such flows play in the adjustments induced by the implementation of both monetary and fiscal policy activism. Furthermore, the Mundell-Fleming model, which is often referred to as the "workhorse model" for open economy macroeconomics, is included in the chapter presentation.

The initial section provides a descriptive discussion of the Mundell-Fleming model. Specifically, this model is an open economy version of the IS-LM model that was previously considered in Chapters 6 and 7. The subsequent section considers monetary and fiscal policy actions within an open economy with respect to the case of imperfect capital mobility. Monetary and fiscal policies under fixed and flexible exchange rates are presented in a detailed analysis. With respect to the case of imperfect capital mobility, the outcome specifics are similar to those for the closed economy IS-LM model with some obvious quantitative differences.

The final section includes an analytical discussion of monetary and fiscal policy under the guise of perfect capital mobility within the framework of an open economy. The policy effects of monetary and fiscal policies are presented in an in-depth manner under the assumption of fixed and flexible exchange rates. It is important to emphasize that in the particular case of perfect capital mobility, monetary policy is "completely" ineffective, provided that the exchange rate is fixed. Alternatively, in the case of perfect capital mobility, fiscal policy is completely ineffective if the exchange rate is flexible.

Techniques in Depth

1. The Mundell-Fleming Model

The Mundell-Fleming Model is an open economy version of the IS-LM model (previously considered in Chapters 6 and 7). The following 2 equations are embodied in the closed economy IS-LM model:

(1) $M = L(Y, r)$ money market equilibrium or LM schedule

(2) $S(Y) + T = I(r) + G$ goods market equilibrium or IS schedule

The model simultaneously determines the nominal interest rate (r) and the level of <u>real</u> income (Y), with the aggregate price level held constant.

The LM schedule will not have to be changed for an open economy, since it states that the real money stock (which is assumed to be controlled by the domestic policymaker) must in equilibrium be equal to the real demand for money. With the assumption of a fixed price level, changes in the nominal money stock are changes in the real money stock as well.

The IS equation for the open economy is derived from the goods market equilibrium condition for a closed economy and by adding imports (Z) and exports (X) it becomes:

$$S + T = I + G + X - Z$$

where ($X - Z$), net exports, is the foreign sector's contribution to aggregate demand. By bringing imports over to the left-hand side and indicating the variables upon which each element in the equation depends, the open economy IS equation is:

$$S(Y) + T + Z(Y, \pi) = I(r) + G + X(Y^f, \pi)$$

Saving and investment are as in the closed economy model. Imports (see Chapter 20) depend positively on income. Import demand also depends negatively on the exchange rate (π) which is the price of foreign currency.

In addition to the IS and LM schedules, the open economy model will include a balance of payments equilibrium schedule which includes all the interest rate-income combinations that result in balance of payments equilibrium (meaning the official reserve transaction balance is zero) at a given exchange rate, π.

The equation for the BP schedule is:

$$X(Y^f, \pi) - Z(Y, \pi) + F(r - r^f) = 0$$

The first two terms comprise the trade balance (net exports), and F is the net capital inflow (the surplus or deficit in the capital account in the balance of payments).

Furthermore, the BP schedule is positively sloped in the case of imperfect capital mobility. For this case, domestic and foreign assets (i.e., bonds) are substitutes but not perfect substitutes. If domestic and foreign assets were perfect substitutes, the case of perfect capital mobility, investors would move to equalize interest rates across countries. This implies a horizontal BP schedule, that is $r = r^f$.

Self-Tests

Multiple-Choice Questions:

1. A rise in the exchange rate:
   a. makes U.S. goods more expensive to foreign residents
   b. makes U.S. goods cheaper to foreign residents
   c. increases the cost of dollars when measured in terms of the foreign currency
   d. none of the above

2. Import demand depends:
   a. negatively on the price of foreign exchange
   b. positively on the price of foreign currency
   c. negatively on income
   d. none of the above

3. A rightward shift of the IS schedule results from:
   a. a decrease in government spending
   b. a decrease in foreign income
   c. a tax cut
   d. a fall in the exchange rate

4. A leftward shift of the IS schedule results from:
   a. a decrease in government spending
   b. a decrease in foreign income
   c. a tax cut
   d. a fall in the exchange rate

5. In a system of flexible exchange rates, with perfect capital mobility, monetary policy works best through:
   a. net exports
   b. the exchange rate
   c. the interest rate
   d. both a and b
   e. all of the above

6. In a system of flexible exchange rates, a fall in the demand for U.S. exports would result in:
   a. a balance of payments deficit
   b. a balance of payments surplus
   c. a fall in the exchange rate
   d. a rise in the exchange rate

7. In a system of fixed exchange rates, an expansionary monetary policy affects the balance of payments by:
   a. worsening the trade balance but improving the balance on the capital account
   b. worsening the balance on the capital account but improving the trade balance
   c. worsening both the trade balance and the balance on the capital account
   d. improving both the trade balance and the balance on the capital account

8. With perfect capital mobility, the BP schedule is:
   a. upward-sloping
   b. downward-sloping
   c. horizontal
   d. vertical

9. With imperfect capital mobility, the BP schedule is:
   a. upward-sloping
   b. downward-sloping
   c. horizontal
   d. vertical

10. In a system of fixed exchange rates and perfect capital mobility, an increase in government spending:
    a. shifts the IS schedule to the left and the LM schedule to the right
    b. shifts the LM schedule to the left and the IS schedule to the right
    c. shifts both the IS schedule and the LM schedule to the left
    d. shifts both the IS schedule and the LM schedule to the right

11. The open economy IS equation can be shown as:
    a. $S(Y) + T + Z(Y, \pi) = I(r) + G + X(Y^f, \pi)$
    b. $S(Y) + T - Z(Y, \pi) = I(r) + G - X(Y^f, \pi)$
    c. $S(Y) + T + Z(Y, \pi) = I(r) + G - X(Y^f, \pi)$
    d. $S(Y) + T = I(r) + G + Z(Y, \pi) - X(Y^f, \pi)$

12. Which of the following will shift the BP schedule to the right?
    a. An increase in the exchange rate
    b. An exogenous rise in export demand
    c. A fall in the foreign interest rate
    d. All of the above
    e. none of the above

13. Assuming fixed exchange rates, then in the case of perfect capital mobility:
    a. monetary policy is completely ineffective, while fiscal policy is highly effective
    b. monetary policy is highly effective, while fiscal policy is completely ineffective
    c. both fiscal policy and monetary policy are completely ineffective
    d. both fiscal policy and monetary policy are highly effective

14. Assuming flexible exchange rates, then in the case of perfect capital mobility:
    a. a fiscal policy action is highly effective
    b. a fiscal policy action is completely ineffective
    c. a monetary policy action is completely ineffective
    d. none of the above

15. The open economy IS schedule is
    a. horizontal
    b. vertical
    c. downward-sloping
    d. upward-sloping

16. An autonomous decrease in import demand shifts:
    a. the IS schedule to the left
    b. the LM schedule to the left
    c. the IS schedule to the right
    d. the LM schedule to the right

17. A rise in the exchange rate is expansionary because:
    a. it decreases exports and increases import demand
    b. it increases both exports and imports
    c. it increases exports more than imports
    d. it increases exports and reduces import demand for a given level of income

18. An increase in government spending with perfect capital mobility and a fixed exchange rate system:
    a. will shift the IS schedule to the right
    b. will shift the IS schedule to the left
    c. will shift the LM schedule to the left
    d. will shift the BP schedule to the right

19. The BP schedule shifts to the right when there is:
    a. an exogenous rise in export demand
    b. an exogenous fall in export demand
    c. an increase in import demand
    d. an increase in the foreign interest rate

20. With imperfect capital mobility and fixed exchange rates, an increase in the quantity of money will:
    a. shift the IS schedule to the right
    b. shift the IS schedule to the left
    c. shift the LM schedule to the left
    d. shift the LM schedule to the right

21. With perfect capital mobility:
    a. transactions costs are negligible
    b. differential risk in assets across countries is unimportant
    c. capital moves freely between countries
    d. all of the above

22. The BP schedule will be steeper the:
    a. more responsive capital flows are to the interest rate
    b. less responsive capital flows are to the interest rate
    c. smaller the marginal propensity to import
    d. none of the above

23. The net capital inflow is:
    a. positively related to the exchange rate
    b. negatively related to the exchange rate
    c. positively related to the domestic interest rate minus the foreign interest rate
    d. none of the above

24. With perfectly flexible exchange rates, an expansionary U.S. monetary policy:
    a. will raise the value of the dollar relative to foreign currencies
    b. will cause a fall in the value of the dollar relative to foreign currencies
    c. will not change the value of the dollar relative to foreign currencies
    d. none of the above

25. Which of these factors might make assets in foreign countries less than perfect substitutes for U.S. assets?
    a. Risks due to exchange rate changes
    b. Differential risk on the assets of different countries
    c. Lack of information on properties of foreign assets
    d. All of the above
    e. None of the above

Problems and/or Essay Questions:

1. When is the BP schedule upward-sloping, and when is it horizontal?

2. Explain an increase in the money supply in the case of perfect capital mobility and a fixed exchange rate.

3. Assuming imperfect capital mobility and fixed exchange rates and, furthermore, assuming an expansionary monetary policy action, what happens to the level of income, the interest rate, and the balance of payments?

4. Assuming perfect capital mobility, fixed exchange rates, and an increase in government spending, why is an increase in government spending effective?

5. What variables shift the IS schedule to the left in the open economy model?

6. Assuming imperfect capital mobility and a fixed exchange rate, then an increase in government spending can result in either a surplus or deficit in the balance of payments deficit. Why is that so?

7. Explain an increase in government spending with flexible exchange rates and perfect capital mobility.

8. The open economy model shows another schedule in addition to the IS and LM schedules? What does this schedule represent?

ANSWER KEY

CHAPTER 1

Multiple-Choice Questions

1. e	7. b	13. b
2. c	8. b	14. c
3. b	9. c	15. d
4. a	10. d	16. d
5. c	11. b	17. b
6. c	12. c	18. a

Problems and/or Essay questions

1. To answer this question, follow the Techniques in Depth (TID) analysis for this chapter.

2. Before the 1970s, there existed a negative relationship between unemployment and inflation. Economists thus explained persistent inflation as a result of too high a level of total demand for output and explained unemployment as the result of inadequate demand. Thus, in the 1970s, economists became confused when both high inflation and unemployment existed.

3. Keynesian economics, classical economics, monetarism, new classical economics, supply-side economics, real business cycle theory, and new Keynesian economics.

4. A trade deficit is the excess of U.S. imports over exports. The fall in Asian currency values is expected to increase their exports, curtail their imports from the United States and, thus, worsen our trade deficit.

5. Between 1980 and 1997, the outstanding amount of federal government debt grew by over 500 percent. Internationally, the United States went from being the world's largest creditor nation to the world's largest debtor nation. This is a reflection of our excess spending abroad (imports) over our earnings on sales abroad (exports).

6. At first, in the 1950s and 1960s, budget deficits were small and sometimes the budget was actually in surplus. Then, in the 1970s, budget deficits increased, especially during recessions. It was in the 1980s and early 1990s that very large deficits became common. For example, each of the deficits in 1985-86 and 1991-92, were approximately 5 percent of GDP, a level unseen since World War II. Then, the deficit began to decline in 1993 and by 1997 was less than 3 percent of GDP. Projections for 1998 showed the budget moving into surplus.

CHAPTER 2

Multiple-Choice Questions

1. d	7. d	13. b	19. d	25. c
2. c	8. b	14. c	20. e	26. a
3. a	9. c	15. a	21. c	27. c
4. d	10. b	16. b	22. a	28. d
5. a	11. d	17. c	23. b	29. d
6. d	12. b	18. b	24. a	30. a

Problems and/or Essay Questions

1. In theory, yes—if transfer payments were larger than direct taxes. This seems very improbable, however.

2. GDP is the current market value of domestic goods and services produced during the year. It is final sales adjusted for inventory changes and does not include intermediate transactions.

3. 385; 365.

4. Percentage change in the price index; 3.3%; prices of a fixed bundle of goods increased by 3.3%; probably not perfect, since the cost of living is very difficult to practically measure.

5. When actual GDP is less than potential, capital and labor are not being fully utilized or employed. See the definition of potential output for why this is true. See textbook for historical examples. If the "high employment" unemployment rate rose, the gap would shrink, because potential output would be less. This assumes GDP is currently less than potential output.

6. GNP includes earnings of U.S. corporations and residents working overseas, while GDP does not. GDP includes earnings from current production in the United States by foreign-owned firms or residents, while GNP does not.

7. GDP does neither include nonmarket productive activities nor the underground economy. It also does not accurately measure welfare.

8. $[(60.3 - 55.3)/55.3] \times 100 = 9.04$.

9. The "underground economy" is made up of illegal forms of economic activities and legal activities that are not reported to avoid paying taxes. The "underground economy" is not included in gross domestic product. Examples are illegal drug trafficking, prostitution, and gambling.

10. Gross domestic product measures the production of goods and services. It is neither a measure of welfare nor a measure of material well being. A good example is leisure; GDP does not give any weight to leisure. Also, it fails to subtract some welfare costs of production. For example, production of electricity causes acid rain and, consequently, water pollution and dying forests. GDP does not subtract the economic loss from the pollution.

11. An upward bias in the CPI would mean over indexation at the cost of many billions of dollars to the U.S. Treasury. The three major possible sources of upward bias are the substitution bias, quality adjustment, and new products. The CPI measures prices of a basket of commodities with the weights given to each category fixed in a base year. These weights are changed about every 10 years. But during this time, as relative prices change, consumers shift away from items whose prices rise to items whose relative prices fall. Using weights from the base year will then overweight the items whose price has gone up the fastest and overstate inflation; this is the substitution bias. The Bureau of Labor Statistics, which maintains the CPI, tries to distinguish between changes in the underlying price of goods and changes in quality. In some cases this is relatively straightforward. But many changes in quality are hard to measure and observers believe that the CPI understates quality changes. New products often decline sharply in price in the first few years after they are introduced. However, these products are not added to the market basket until years after they came on the market and, therefore these price decreases are never recorded.

CHAPTER 3

Multiple-Choice Questions

1. d	7. b	13. d	19. d	25. c
2. a	8. a	14. d	20. b	26. a
3. c	9. d	15. b	21. c	27. c
4. e	10. d	16. c	22. d	28. a
5. d	11. e	17. d	23. d	29. c
6. c	12. a	18. a	24. b	30. d

Problems and/or Essay Questions

1. See the TID for Chapter 3 for help on this problem.

2. Same as above.

3. Same as above.

4. See Section 3.5 in the textbook.

5. A business cycle exists when actual output deviates systematically from potential output over time. A supply shock would be compatible with real business cycle models. Examples are: OPEC price increases, increases in labor force participation of the population, change in the rate of advance of technological progress.

6. Endogenous variables are determined within the model, while exogenous variables are determined outside the model. Examples in the classical model of endogenous variables include: output, employment, and the real wage. Examples in the classical model of exogenous variables include: technical change, changes in the capital stock, and population changes.

7. The labor demand curve is the marginal product of labor curve that is the slope of the production function.

8. Unlike the classical economists, the real business cycle theorists do not believe that supply-side factors change only slowly over time. Short-run fluctuations in output can be explained by changes in technology shocks, shocks that affect capital formation and labor productivity, and the prices of natural resources.

9. The first period, the classical period, is dominated by the work of Adam Smith (<u>Wealth of Nations</u>, 1776), David Ricardo (<u>Principles of Political Economy</u>, 1817), and John Stuart Mill (<u>Principles of Political Economy</u>, 1848). The second period, the neoclassical period, had as its most prominent English representatives Alfred Marshall (<u>Principles of Economics</u>, 1920) and A. C. Pigou (<u>The Theory of Unemployment</u>, 1933).

10. The labor supply curve is positively sloped; more labor is assumed to be supplied at higher real wage rates.

11. Two tenets of mercantilism that classical writers attacked were bullionism, a belief that the wealth and power of a nation were determined by the stock of precious metals, and the belief in the need for state action to direct the development of the capitalist system.

CHAPTER 4

Multiple-Choice Questions

1. b	7. d	13. c	19. c	25. d
2. d	8. d	14. c	20. b	26. c
3. d	9. d	15. c	21. e	27. d
4. b	10. c	16. d	22. a	28. d
5. c	11. e	17. e	23. d	
6. c	12. c	18. b	24. b	

Problems and/or Essay Questions

1. It is possible, depending how you interpret elements in the equation. If k is interpreted as the *ex post* reciprocal of velocity, then the equation is an identity. If instead k is interpreted as a behavioral variable symbolizing an *ex ante* determinant of money demand, then the equation can be interpreted as an equilibrium condition.

2. This increases the demand for bonds and lowers the interest rate. Aggregate demand is determined by the equation of exchange and is unaffected. The increased saving means less consumption but more investment with $g - t$ fixed.

3. Real aggregate demand remains equal to real aggregate supply. In the classical model, the latter is unaffected by monetary changes. Interest rates are determined by productivity and thrift, which also are not assumed to be affected by money.

4. If the extra government spending is financed by bonds, the private sector spending is reduced in real terms by the interest rate, and prices do not change. If the government spending is financed by an increase in money, the interest rate does not reduce real aggregate demand and the price level must increase to reduce real aggregate demand to its initial value.

5. This supply-side policy should have shifted the aggregate supply curve rightward, raising output and lowering price. From 1983 to 1985, output growth picked up, and the inflation rate fell. There is much debate, however, about what contributed most to this economic performance.

6. If the tax cut was a lump-sum cut, then only the demand side will be affected. If, however, the tax cut was in the form of a reduction in the tax rate, then there would be supply-side effects.

7. On one hand, monetary policy was important to classical economists, as stable money means stable prices. However, on the other hand, money was not important, as monetary policy cannot affect real variables such as output, employment, and the real interest rate.

8. Hyperinflation is a period when the price level simply explodes. The inflation rate reaches astronomical levels. When this occurs, the money supply always explodes as well.

9. Classical economists did not pay much attention to the supply-side effects of changes in income tax rates because, at that time, the marginal income tax rate was very low and pertained only to the relatively wealthy.

10. The first of these self-stabilizing mechanisms is the interest rate that adjusts to keep shocks to sectoral demands from affecting aggregate demand. The second set of stabilizers is freely flexible prices and money wages, which keep changes in aggregate demand from affecting output.

CHAPTER 5

Multiple-Choice Questions

1. c	7. b	13. d	19. c	25. a
2. b	8. e	14. d	20. a	26. a
3. a	9. b	15. c	21. b	27. c
4. d	10. c	16. d	22. e	28. c
5. b	11. b	17. a	23. e	29. b
6. b	12. b	18. a	24. b	

Problems and/or Essay Questions

1. See the TID for Chapter 5 for help on this question.

2. 3.33; 5.0; 2.5; not enough information to calculate.

3. $C = 85 + .9Y$.

4. Unintended inventory change is a signal which communicates to managers whether they should be raising or lowering output.

5. Aggregate demand determines output, not the opposite as in the classical model. Autonomous factors can permanently alter the level of demand, and output satisfies these changes.

6. The Kennedy-Johnson tax cut and later expansion of government military spending apparently had strong effects on aggregate demand that first stimulated output but generated inflation later.

7. An increase in exports has an expansionary effect on aggregate demand and equilibrium income, while an increase in imports has a contractionary effect.

8. With $b = 0.75$, the multiplier is equal to $1/1 - b = 1/1 - 0.75 = 1/.25 = 4$. Then, an increase in investment of $100 billion will increase equilibrium income by $400 billion.

9. The intercept a, which is assumed to be positive, is the value of consumption when disposable income equals zero. The parameter b, the slope of the function, gives an increase in consumer expenditure per unit increase in disposable income.

10. Keynes' analysis did not differ from the classical view. The level of investment is assumed to be inversely related to the level of the interest rate. At higher interest rates there are fewer investment projects that have a prospective return high enough to justify borrowing to finance them.

11. The tax multiplier is $-b/1 - b = -0.8/1 - 0.8 = -4$. The governmental expenditure multiplier can be shown as $1/1 - b = 1/1 - 0.8 = 5$. Yes, there is a relationship between the absolute values of tax and government expenditure multipliers. The effects of an increase in spending accompanied by an equal increase in taxes are a balanced budget increase.

CHAPTER 6

Multiple-Choice Questions

1. d	7. d	13. e	19. d	25. d
2. d	8. c	14. c	20. b	26. b
3. b	9. e	15. d	21. b	27. b
4. a	10. c	16. c	22. d	28. d
5. e	11. d	17. a	23. a	29. a
6. a	12. c	18. c	24. c	30. c

Problems and/or Essay Questions

1. See the TID for Chapter 6 for help in this question.

2. See the TID.

3. 6%; 10%; Yes; No.

4. See the TID.

5. In order to maintain equilibrium in the goods market, a higher (lower) interest rate implies less (more) aggregate demand (E) and a lower (higher) level of equilibrium output.

6. X_1, X_7, X_6 – Goods market equilibrium
   X_2, X_4 – ESG
   X_3, X_5 – EDG
   X_1 – Goods and money market equilibrium
   X_1, X_2, X_3, X_7 – ESM
   X_4, X_5, X_6 – EDM

7. M1 is currency held by the public, traveler's checks, demand deposits, and interest-bearing checking deposits. Because the rate on these latter accounts may change along with bond returns, investors may be less willing to move between bonds and money when bond returns change.

8. The Keynesian money demand is similar to the classical money demand when c_2 equals zero. In other words, money demand depends only on income as in the classical theory.

9. Keynes believed that, beyond the money held for planned transactions, additional money balances were held in case unexpected expenditures became necessary. Money would be held for use in possible emergencies, in order to pay unexpected medical bills or repair bills of various types. Money held for this purposed was the precautionary demand for money.

10. No, this is not what Keynes meant. A shift in the money demand function means a change in the amount of money demanded for given levels of the interest rate and income, what Keynes called a shift in liquidity preference. For instance, if very unsettled economic conditions increase the probability of firms going bankrupt and, hence, the default risk on bonds, the demand for money might increase. This is a shift in individuals' portfolios away from bonds and toward holding an increased amount of money for given levels of the interest rate and income.

11. One element of building cost is the cost of short-term borrowing to finance construction of a house. Higher interest rates mean higher cost to the builder and, other things equal, this discourages housing starts. Furthermore, an important factor determining the rate of new housing construction is the overall state of demand for houses, existing and newly constructed. Most purchases of houses are financed by long-term borrowing in the mortgage markets and high interest rates include high mortgage interest. Higher mortgage rates increase the cost of buying a house and reduce the demand for new and existing homes. This reduced demand in the housing market will lower the volume of new residential construction.

CHAPTER 7

Multiple-Choice Questions

1. a	7. d	13. a	19. d	25. b
2. d	8. d	14. d	20. c	26. a
3. c	9. d	15. c	21. a	27. c
4. c	10. d	16. d	22. b	28. c
5. c	11. d	17. a	23. c	29. a
6. c	12. a	18. a	24. a	30. d

Problems and/or Essay Questions

1. a. Monetary policy works <u>indirectly</u> upon spending by first affecting interest rates.
   b. Monetary policy works best when the LM curve is vertical and the IS curve is flat.
   c. When the interest elasticity is large, fiscal policy works best.
   d. True.

2. The autonomous reduction in M^d causes an excess supply of money. This leads to an excess demand for bonds, higher bond prices, and lower interest rates. See the TID for intermarket spillover and feedbacks to complete this answer.

3. See the TID.

4. See the TID.

5. Mr. Tobin meant that an easy fiscal policy and a loose monetary policy were offsetting in their impacts on aggregate demand and would be harmful to investment spending. President Reagan might say that his easy policy mix was a supply-side program and wasn't intended to have large effects on aggregate demand.

6. The simple Keynesian model overstates the effect of an increase in government spending, since it ignores any increase in the interest rate and decrease in investment spending caused by an increase in government spending. The IS-LM model also allows for monetary effects, from supply or demand, to affect equilibrium income.

7. With expansionary monetary policy, investment is increased. However, with expansionary fiscal policy, investment declines. Thus, expansionary monetary policy is preferred, since increased investment is important for the long-run growth of the economy.

8. The Keynesians suggest an "accommodating" monetary policy. Thus, with expansionary fiscal policy, the money supply should be increased to prevent an increase in the interest rate and, therefore, prevent crowding out of investment.

9. The crucial parameter is c_2, which measures the interest sensitivity of money demand. This parameter determines whether the LM curve is steep or flat. If c_2 is large money demand is interest-sensitive and the LM curve will be relatively flat. However, if c_2 is small money demand is interest-insensitive and the LM curve will be relatively steep.

10. Figure 7.1

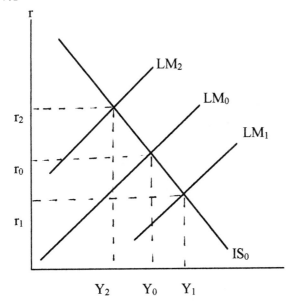

An increase in the quantity of money would shift the LM curve to the right from LM_0 to LM_1. The equilibrium level of income rises from Y_0 to Y_1 and the interest rate falls from r_0 to r_1.

11. In the case of an expansionary monetary policy the interest rate declines and investment increases. However, with an income tax cut, an expansionary fiscal policy action, the interest rate rises and investment declines.

CHAPTER 8

Multiple-Choice Questions

1. d	7. d	13. c	19. a	25. a
2. e	8. a	14. a	20. b	26. e
3. d	9. b	15. d	21. b	27. b
4. a	10. a	16. a	22. d	
5. c	11. a	17. b	23. d	
6. b	12. b	18. c	24. b	

Problems and/or Essay Questions

1. Given a fixed factor, the more variable input applied to the production process, the slower the rate of increase of output. This implies that output is increased only if the marginal product of labor falls.

2. a. Decrease in labor demand.
   b. Increase in labor demand.
   c. Increase in labor demand.
   Without diminishing returns, labor demand would not be related to changes in real wages in the example assumed in Chapter 8.

3. a. Increase in labor supply.
   b. Decrease in labor supply.
   c. Decrease in labor supply.

4. The Keynesian Y^s curve slopes up, because of imperfect information held by workers about current prices. As prices rise, firms demand more labor, and workers are willing to supply it, because they do not correctly perceive the loss in purchasing power it implies. If workers become more knowledgeable about price increases as the economy approaches potential output, the Y^s curve gets more vertical, and autonomous demand increases yield smaller output adjustments.

5. a. Because lower prices generate an ESM, lower interest rates, higher i, and more aggregate demand.
   b. Moving down means lower prices, and ESM, and lower interest rates.
   c. The nominal money stock is assumed constant; therefore, the real stock is rising as P falls.

6. See the TID for this chapter.

7. True, unless the Y^s curve is very flat. Normally, increased demand generates more employment and output only if higher prices compensate firms for higher unit costs of producing the greater output. The higher costs are due to diminishing returns and/or higher wages. Only without diminishing returns or with no wage change would output increase without price change.

8. See the TID for similar examples.

9. Demand shocks cause output and inflation to move in the same direction. Other shocks, such as the reduction in oil prices in the early 1980s, shift the aggregate supply curve rightward. This leads to higher output with lower inflation. With tight money, the output would rise less in the short run. In the long run, if lower inflation produces lower inflation expectations, this would cause the Y^s curve to shift rightward, raising output.

10. Figure 8.1

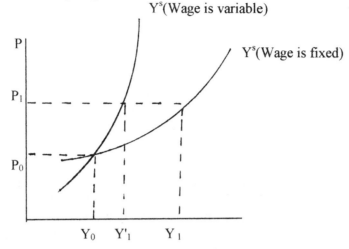

The Keynesian aggregate supply curve is steeper with a variable money wage because with a rise in price, the increase in employment and, therefore, the increase in output, is smaller.

11. The Keynesian aggregate demand curve depends on the quantity of money, and on such variables as the level of government spending, the level of tax collection, and the level of autonomous investment expenditures. The classical aggregate demand schedule depends only on the level of the money stock

12. In the Keynesian system, with a variable money wage, a given increase in aggregate demand causes output to increase by less than when the money wage is fixed. With a variable money wage, an increase in aggregate demand causes the price level to rise by more than when the money wage is fixed. Yes, there is a predictable quantitative difference. The reason being a steeper aggregate supply curve with a variable money wage than with a fixed money wage.

CHAPTER 9

Multiple-Choice Questions

1. c	7. c	13. d	19. d	25. d
2. d	8. c	14. c	20. d	26. b
3. b	9. c	15. c	21. c	27. b
4. c	10. a	16. c	22. b	28. a
5. d	11. b	17. c	23. c	29. a
6. c	12. d	18. a	24. c	

Problems and/or Essay Questions

1. The student should carefully review and synthesize Section 9.2 to answer this question.

2. The weak form essentially explains why money matters. If money demand is dominated by income rather than interest rates, however, it can be shown that only money matters (note that in this case the LM curve is vertical). This is important, because it leads to the result that only money matters for nominal aggregate demand.

3. See the TID in this chapter.

4. See the TID in this chapter.

5. See the quote from Modigliani at the end of the chapter. The car ride is analogous to potential policy mistakes, while the tub ride is Modigliani's characterization of a Friedmanesque fixed-money supply rule.

6. Much of this evidence concerns the behavior of velocity; that is, does money have a regular, largely uninterrupted, effect on nominal income? Studies of velocity suggest that velocity can change significantly and interrupt the effect of money on income. They argue that factors other than money are important determinants of income. Monetarists concede that velocity is not constant but argue that it is predictable and operates with a lag. Furthermore, they argue that money remains as the major factor affecting nominal GDP.

7. Monetarists explain the Great Depression in monetary terms. The money stock fell along with velocity, which is consistent with the quantity theory. Keynesians, however, did not adhere to this money hypothesis as the cause of the Great Depression. They believed that it was caused by a large decline in several components of aggregate demand, hence the spending hypothesis.

8. Milton Friedman and others view the instability of velocity in the 1980s as the result of a number of one-time events during that decade. One of these events was the disinflation during that decade. Another factor is the dramatic fall in interest rates in the 1980s. Other events were changes in the type of bank deposits that were available to the public and the phasing out of ceilings on deposit rates

9. When the monetary authority pegs the interest rate it surrenders the control of the quantity of money. to the private sector. In order to peg the interest rate the monetary authority must be ready to exchange money for bonds on demand. Therefore, the quantity of money will be determined by the desire of the private sector to hold bonds and not by the monetary authority.

CHAPTER 10

Multiple-Choice Questions

1. c	7. b	13. a	19. c	25. d
2. a	8. a	14. c	20. a	26. a
3. c	9. c	15. a	21. d	27. c
4. b	10. c	16. b	22. b	28. c.
5. d	11. c	17. d	23. c	29. b
6. a	12. e	18. b	24. d	

Problems and/or Essay Questions

1. The plot is self-explanatory. The student should note occasions where changes appear to be along a given Phillips curve and where shifts are occurring. It appears that u may have shifted out in the late 1970s, as there seems to be less tendency to return to a 4 percent unemployment rate.

2. Use the analysis in the TID to aid you in this question. Notice that the two policies being contrasted involve sudden unexpected changes versus gradual reductions in aggregate demand.

3. The heart of the issue is the basic stability or instability of private-sector spending. The student should reread section 10.2, then answer this question thoroughly.

4. See the TID.

5. The unemployment rate is the percent of the labor force that are unemployed. The natural rate is the noncyclical portion of the unemployment rate, and it is composed of the frictional and structurally unemployed. Since World War II, the unemployment rate has cycled around or has risen with the trend. The latter has been caused by demographic factors and, to some extent, by declining U.S. competitiveness and government transfer payments.

6. The classical economists believe that output is completely supply-determined, thus an increase in demand would cause prices to rise without affecting output. Therefore, in the classical model, changes in aggregate demand will not cause temporary fluctuations of the economy from a "natural rate."

7. The term "natural rate" implies that the output and employment levels are determined by intrinsic elements of the economic system. Although the Keynesians believe that the output and employment levels of the economy display persistence and hysteresis, they do not believe these levels are determined by intrinsic elements of the economy, and thus question any "natural levels."

8. An alternative explanation for the high European unemployment focuses on the idea that the current value of the unemployment rate may be strongly influenced by its past values. This property in a process is known as "hysteresis."

9. The Keynesian effects of a decline in autonomous investment are as follows: the aggregate demand curve will shift to the left and output will decrease in the short run. In the long run, the aggregate supply curve will shift downward as suppliers of labor come to expect a lower price level that corresponds to lower aggregate demand. The Keynesians, rather than wait for this adjustment, advocate aggregate demand management policies, i.e., an expansionary policy, to restore the level of aggregate demand to its initial level.

10. It has been attributed to different structural characteristics of labor markets in the two regions. According to this view, greater flexibility in the United States labor market, due to less regulations and lower unionization, means that increased global competition and skill-biased technological change resulted in stagnant real wages in the United States (this is especially true for low-skilled workers) instead of slower job growth and higher unemployment.

CHAPTER 11

Multiple-Choice Questions

1. c	7. c	13. c	19. a	25. c
2. c	8. c	14. d	20. d	26. c
3. a	9. c	15. e	21. d	27. c
4. e	10. d	16. b	22. a	28. a
5. b	11. d	17. d	23. b	29. d
6. b	12. c	18. d	24. c	30. b

Problems and/or Essay Questions

1. See the TID for this chapter.

2. P^e_2 would not be rational, since it systematically underforecasts the price level.

3. See the TID.

4. For a while, the lack of information would give the Fed a clear informational advantage and, thus, some ability to generate systematic short-run output changes. This should lead, however, to a new industry whose product would be "forecasts" of what was happening to money currently. This would tend to reduce the informational discrepancy and reduce the ability of the Fed to systematically affect output.

5. The new classical economists view persistently high unemployment as caused by a series of unanticipated demand events or supply shocks. They point out very large unanticipated reductions of money in the Great Depression and point to other factors, such as the banking failure, which aggravated supply problems. Nevertheless, no group seems to be fully satisfied with their explanation of the causes, severity, and persistence of the Great Depression.

6. In the early 1980s, a highly anticipated disinflationary policy reduced inflation but caused very high unemployment. The latter outcome is incompatible with the new classical economics. New classical economists argue, however, that a policy can have real effects if it is not credible, i.e., if people believe it will be abandoned in the future. Thus, the new classical economists emphasize that the policies must be anticipated and credible if they are not to cause unemployment.

7. In the Keynesian model, expectations are backward looking because the expectation of a variable such as the price level adjusts (slowly) to the past behavior of the variable. According to the rational expectations hypothesis, economic agents use all available relevant information and intelligently assess the implication of that information for the future behavior of a variable such as the price level.

8. In the auction market, the money wage is assumed to adjust quickly to clear the labor market—to equate labor supply and demand. This characterization of the auction market is found in the new classical view, as well as in the original classical theory. In the contractual view of the labor market wages are not set to clear markets, but are strongly conditioned by longer-term considerations and involve employer-worker relations. This is a Keynesian view.

9. According to the new classical view, systematic monetary and fiscal policy actions that change aggregate demand do not have any effect on output and employment, even in the short run. This is known as the new classical policy ineffectiveness postulate.

CHAPTER 12

Multiple-Choice Questions

1. b	7. d	13. b	19. a	25. b
2. d	8. c	14. c	20. d	26. a
3. d	9. d	15. a	21. d	27. b
4. d	10. e	16. c	22. c	28. d
5. b	11. c	17. b	23. d	29. c
6. b	12. d	18. a	24. c	30. c

Problems and/or Essay Questions

1. The new classical model could not explain the persistence of real world business cycles. The real business cycle model thus showed that it was the responses of optimizing agents to changes in mainly technology shocks that explain business cycles.

2. The first reason is that the empirical evidence of the role of unanticipated changes in aggregate demand and how this affects output is unclear. Also, real business cycle theorists believe that the new classical view that prediction errors cause large fluctuations in output violates the idea that agents optimize.

3. One major criticism concerns whether or not technology shocks are actually large enough to explain observed business cycles. The other major criticism is whether or not voluntary unemployment actually exists.

4. According to empirical evidence from 1984, in times of high economic activity, the percentage of voluntary unemployment (job-leavers) increases, while, in times of recession, it decreases. However, if cyclical unemployment is voluntary, the number of job-leavers should rise during a recession.

5. With perfect competition, prices are set by supply and demand—individual firms have no control over prices. Thus, markets always clear, and prices are flexible. However, with imperfect markets, such as an oligopoly, prices are not always lowered as the demand for the firm's product falls, because the firm has a given degree of market power. Thus, prices are sticky rather than flexible.

6. The efficiency of labor will have to also increase by two percent before the firm will stop increasing the wage bill.

7. The real business cycle production function includes shocks to the production process. This is represented by the term z_t. Also, in the real business cycle production function, capital stock is not fixed, whereas, in the classical production function, it was fixed.

8. During recessions, there are layoffs of insiders. Some of these layoffs are permanent, causing those insiders to leave the union. Thus, some insiders become outsiders. After the recession, the now-reduced group of insiders bargains for higher real wages. This causes unemployment of the now larger group of outsiders. This type of cycle is referred to as hysteresis.

9. One views the real business cycle theory as proposing that real supply-side factors are simply more important than nominal demand-side influences. With this interpretation, real business cycle models are just versions of the new classical model that can also incorporate supply-side shocks. When real business cycle theorists differentiate their models from new classical models, they assert a much stronger position (i.e., monetary and other nominal demand-side shocks have no significant effect on output and employment). Many real business cycle models do not even include money as a variable.

10. According to the shirking model, by setting the real wage above going market levels (i.e., a worker's next best opportunity), a firm gives a worker an incentive not to shirk or loaf on the job. If he does, he may be fired, and he knows it would be hard to get another job that pays that well. If firms can monitor job performance only imperfectly and with some cost, such a high-wage strategy may be profitable. Another explanation of why efficiency depends on the real wage centers on the moral of workers. According to this argument, if the firm pays a real wage above the market-clearing wage, this will improve morale and workers will put forth more effort. The firm pays the workers a gift of the above-market wage, and the workers reciprocate with higher efficiency.

11. Monetary policy should focus on control of the price level. A desirable monetary policy would be one that resulted in slow, steady growth in the money supply, and thus stable prices, or at least a low rate of inflation. The defining role of real business cycle models is that real, not monetary, factors are responsible for fluctuations in output and employment. Monetary policy cannot affect output and employment, and even if it could it would be suboptimal to try to eliminate the business cycle.

CHAPTER 13

Multiple-Choice Questions

1. b	7. c	13. b	19. a
2. d	8. a	14. d	20. b
3. a	9. d	15. b	21. a
4. d	10. a	16. d	
5. b	11. d	17. b	
6. a	12. d	18. d	

Problems and/or Essay Questions

No answers are provided for the first three problems in this summary chapter. Students should review the TID for this chapter and reread the chapter to answer these questions.

4. In the real business cycle model, as in the classical model, output and employment are determined completely by real supply-side variables. The labor market is always in equilibrium; all unemployment is voluntary. The role of money in the real business cycle model, as in the classical models, is only to determine the price level.

5. Because, in economics, there are no opportunities for controlled laboratory experiments aimed at settling such controversies. To test theories, events in the real world would have to be examined and many factors vary at the same time. Also, the resulting data are open to different interpretations.

6. In the classical model, output and employment are completely supply-determined. Furthermore, aggregate demand is determined solely by the quantity of money. In the Keynesian system, output and employment are determined jointly by aggregate supply and demand in the short run. In this system, aggregate demand is an important determinant of output and employment. Furthermore, money is one of a number of factors that determined aggregate demand.

CHAPTER 14

Multiple-Choice Questions

1. b	7. a	13. d	19. e	25. b
2. d	8. d	14. d	20. a	26. d
3. c	9. a	15. d	21. c	27. a
4. a	10. d	16. a	22. e	28. b
5. b	11. b	17. d	23. b	29. e
6. c	12. a	18. d	24. a	

Problems and/or Essay Questions

1. See the TID for this chapter.

2. The main idea is that people always consume according to some notion of their lifetime income. When they are young, they have "temporarily" low current incomes. If spending is influenced by the higher average lifetime income, then C/Y is large. For those who are earning more than their average lifetime income, C/Y turns out lower, since they are spending according to the lower lifetime average income. They are in the high saving part of their lifetimes. One problem with the theory is that it fails to take account of liquidity constraints. Is also imparts a forward-looking rationality to the average household which might be unrealistic.

3. The change in disposable income in the first year is $100. Permanent income rises over three years by: $50, $30, and $20. Therefore, C rises in each year by: $35, $21, and $14. Under the absolute income hypothesis, the effect would be confined to the first year and would probably be larger.

4. Lower tax rates directly lower the cost of capital and raise the level for capital. If large deficits cause interest rates to rise, then this would offset at least partially the intended effects.

5. See the TID for this chapter.

6. Raising inheritance taxes implies that persons have to save more today to guarantee a given bequest value. Reducing capital gains taxes would increase saving with or without an operative bequest motive.

7. The increased Social Security benefits over the years have reduced the need to save for retirement years. Also, increased credit availability has decreased the need to save. Lastly, the number of two-income-earner families has grown, reducing the need to save for emergencies.

8. Although a small component of total output, inventory investment is a very volatile component and has, since World War II, accounted for a very substantial portion of the decline in output during recessions.

9. The APC is 0.816 (26.5/400 + 0.75). The APC is 0.794 (26.5/600 + 0.75). This equation implies that the APC declines as income rises.

10. If expectations are rational, then all information available prior to the current period will already have been utilized in making an estimate of permanent income. This implies that changes in consumption will come only because of unanticipated changes in income, which cause changes in the estimated permanent income.

11. The user cost of capital is the cost to the firm of employing an additional unit of capital for a one period. If the firm must borrow funds to finance the purchase of capital good, the interest rate is the cost of borrowing. If the capital goods are bought with previously earned profits that have not been distributed to stockholders, the interest is the opportunity cost of the investment project, since the firm could have invested its funds externally and earned that interest rate. In either case, the interest rate is an element of the user cost of capital.

CHAPTER 15

Multiple-Choice Questions

1. b	7. b	13. c	19. d	25. c
2. d	8. c	14. d	20. b	26. b
3. b	9. c	15. d	21. a	27. d
4. a	10. d	16. b	22. d	28. b
5. c	11. b	17. b	23. c	
6. b	12. a	18. a	24. b	

Problems and/or Essay Questions

1. See the TID for this chapter.

2. See the TID for this chapter.

3. This raises the demand for money, since it raises the expected cost of bond transactions.

4. Risk and returns are paramount. People hold money, because bonds are inherently risky. They hold more or less money as a way of balancing risk and return from all assets held.

5. The 1980s witnessed Super NOW accounts and money market deposit accounts. These accounts arose because nonbank institutions created accounts that allowed savers to receive market interest rates and to write checks. Banks and other depository institutions lost business and were successful in getting legislation that allowed them the new accounts. The Fed stopped targeting M1, because the measurement problem makes it hard to predict the demand for M1. Since M2 includes both M1 and M2 accounts, the demand for M2 is more stable and is easier to predict.

6. Barter requires a double coincidence of wants. Money reduces the opportunity costs involved in buying and selling by reducing the time involved in the occurrence of a double coincidence of wants.

7. Keynes' theory implied that a person held all of his or her wealth in bonds until the interest rate fell below the critical rate, at which point the investor would transfer all of his/her wealth in both money and bonds. The other criticism of Keynes' theory concerns the existence of a "normal" level of the interest rate. This normal level is consistent with data during the period from 1936 to 1950. However, since 1950, there has been an upward trend in the interest rate.

8. Beginning in the mid-1970s, predictions based on conventional money demand functions were overstated with respect to the public's holding of money. The "case of the missing money" refers to the question of why this was happening. Later, during the 1982-83 period, the conventional money demand function began to seriously underpredict the public's money demand.

9. In these accounts, used by businesses, unnecessary funds in checking accounts, which earn no interest are automatically transferred to interest bearing accounts near the end of the business day. This financial market innovation, computerized sweep accounts, did contribute to the instability of M1 growth, because the interest bearing accounts are not part of the M1 aggregate, these transfers cause declines in that measure of the money supply.

10. Classicists confined their attention to what Keynes termed the transactions demand for money. Keynes' theory of money demand considered the role of money as a store of value in addition to its role as a medium of exchange. The store-of-value function of money means that money is one possible asset in which one can hold wealth. The classical money demand function, as developed by Cambridge economists, can be expressed as $M^d = kPy$. Money demand is proportional to nominal income (the price level P times real income y). The proportion of income held in the form of money (k) was considered to be relatively stable as long as equilibrium positions were being considered. The Fisherian version of the classical theory is shown as $MV = Py$ where the velocity of money, equal to $1/k$, was assumed to be stable. An important feature of this classical analysis is that the interest rate was not important determinant of money demand. The Keynesian money demand function, $M^d = L(y, r)$, where money demand depends on the level of income and the interest rate.

CHAPTER 16

Multiple-Choice Questions

1. d	7. d	13. d	19. a	25. b
2. a	8. b	14. a	20. d	26. a
3. b	9. b	15. b	21. c	27. d
4. d	10. b	16. b	22. b	28. d
5. c	11. d	17. b	23. a	29. d
6. b	12. c	18. c	24. d	30. a

Problems and/or Essay Questions

1. a. If incomes cause people to hold a larger portion of deposits as demand deposits, this would raise the M1 multiplier and lower the M2 multiplier.
   b. If lower interest rates encourage banks to hold larger excess reserves, this reduces both multipliers. This could also induce a switch out of time deposits and into demand deposits. This raises the M1 multiplier and lowers the M2 multiplier.
   c. This might encourage banks to hold more excess reserves and cause both multipliers to be lower.
   d. This might cause people to spend more—perhaps a switch out of TDs and into demand deposits—an increase in the M1 multiplier and a decrease in the M2 multiplier.
   e. This could cause a movement into currency and out of deposits—lowering both multipliers.

2. The monetary base consists of currency and bank reserves. Since these two liabilities of the Fed provide the foundation for the money stock, bank reserves and the money stock can be controlled when the Fed's liabilities are controlled.

3. Upon purchase, the Fed's assets will be increased by the value of the security. The Fed's liabilities will also be increased by the value of the security. When the Fed buys the security, it writes a check to the owner of the security who deposits the check in a commercial bank. The commercial bank presents the check to the Fed who credits the commercial bank's account balance at the Fed, thus increasing the Fed's liabilities by the value of the security.

4. The Fed raises or lowers the discount rate to regulate the volume of loans to a bank. Thus, when the Fed lowers (raises) the discount rate, loans to banks increase (decrease), and bank reserve deposits increase (decrease).

5. During this period, the large number of bank failures caused the public to hold more assets in currency, increasing the currency/deposit ratio. The banks that did not fail held more excess reserves to protect against bank runs, increasing the excess reserves/deposits ratio. This increase in these ratios subsequently caused the money multiplier to fall. Although the monetary base increased by a small, amount, the M1 money supply still fell sharply with the decrease in the money multiplier.

6. No. The Fed's control of the money stock depends, in part, on the actions of the public and on that of the banking system. The policy's effectiveness relies on the Fed's ability to predict these actions. The Fed, however, does not concentrate all its efforts on this one policy goal, as a conflict sometimes exists between money stock targets and interest rate targets. Therefore, money growth targets may be missed in favor of achieving desirable levels of other variables.

7. The money multiplier (m) for the narrowly defined money stock (M1) is a function of the following form: $m = \Delta M^s/\Delta(MB) = m(rr_d, CU/D, ER/D)$. The money multiplier depends on: the required reserve ratio on checkable deposits (rr_d); the public's desired currency/checkable deposit ratio (CU/D); and the excess reserve/checkable deposit ratio (ER/D).

8. a. Higher money multiplier.
   b. Lower money multiplier.
   c. Higher money multiplier.

9. The Board of Governors of the Federal Reserve Bank and the Federal Open Market Committee (FOMC). The Board of Governors administers the discount rate, the interest rate charged by the Federal Reserve on its loans to banks; and the required reserve ratio. The Open Market Committee controls open-market operations.

CHAPTER 17

Multiple-Choice Questions

1. c	7. c	13. c	19. b	25. c
2. c	8. a	14. a	20. b	26. b
3. c	9. d	15. d	21. b	27. d
4. a	10. b	16. c	22. c	28. b
5. c	11. c	17. e	23. a	29. c
6. a	12. b	18. d	24. b	30. a

Problems and/or Essay Questions

1. 8.0%.

2. a. 2.4%;
   b. 4.4%; −1.6%; 2.56%; 1.6%; 14.4%; −6.0%.

3. a. Lowering payroll taxes should stimulate labor supply and consumption spending.
   b. This very rapid depreciation makes investment spending more profitable.
   c. This reduces costs of investments. Keynesians would probably favor (a) while supply-siders would advocate (a), (b), and (c).

4. Knowledge of a contraction in money growth would reduce the price level more and yield less output growth than would have occurred from the tax cut above.

5. In general, supply-siders see the erratic behavior of the economy as stemming from very low after-tax real yields caused by high and variable inflation. Keynesians believe that aggregate demand policy was tried but used improperly. Reasonable men can disagree, because cause and effect are difficult to clearly uncover in complex economic systems.

6. The Laffer curve shows government revenue collected at various tax rates. Revenue collected at zero and 100% tax rates equal zero. In between, as tax rates rise from zero, revenues rise. However, after some critical tax rate, as tax rates continue to rise, revenues begin to fall—as tax-payers begin finding both legal and illegal ways of avoiding taxes. If tax rates were above the critical value in 1980, then the tax rate reductions would increase government tax revenues. For a complete discussion of Reaganomics, see Sections 3 and 4 of the chapter in the text.

7. The growth models before the late 1980s demonstrated that the long-run equilibrium growth rate depended on two exogenous variables—the population growth rate and the rate of technological change. Since the variables were exogenous, there were no major policy implications. However, in more recent research of growth theory, these variables were made endogenous, creating renewed interest in the growth models.

8. Bush's pledge of "no new taxes" was consistent with supply-side economics, as was his initiative to lower the capital gains tax, since supply-side analysis would suggest that such a tax reduction would increase saving and, therefore, capital formation. Also consistent with supply-side economics was Bush's attempt to decrease government spending.

9. The accelerated cost recovery system is a set of accelerated depreciation allowances for business plants and equipment. This system was aimed at encouraging business investment by increasing the after-tax return to investment.

10. Reaganomics was replaced with Clintonomics. President Clinton's program saw a more activist role for government, one that recognizes both the efficiencies and imperfections of the market. President Clinton proposed a "stimulus package" that consisted of public investment in infrastructure, worker retraining and partnerships between business and government to move resource from "sunset" to "sunrise" industries.

11. A promising line of research attempting to explain cross-country income differentials focuses on human capital. According to this explanation, in order to take advantage of technological advances requires a skilled workforce, the creation of which requires investment in formal education as well as less formal training over a long period of time. Whereas more developed countries are better able to take advantage of technological advances and investors in these countries invest at home where skilled labor is available, less developed countries lack the infrastructure, both physical and legal, that would encourage massive technology transfers.

CHAPTER 18

Multiple-Choice Questions

1. b	7. c	13. d	19. b	25. d
2. d	8. a	14. a	20. d	26. d
3. c	9. b	15. b	21. a	27. c
4. a	10. d	16. c	22. e	28. c
5. b	11. c	17. c	23. b	
6. b	12. b	18. c	24. a	

Problems and/or Questions

1. a. Reveals the loss to society generated when economic goals are not reached.
   b. These are actual and goal values of the unemployment rate, inflation, and the growth rate of real GDP.
   c. Only output growth matters to policymakers; only inflation rates matter to policymakers.
   d. $a_1 > a_2$ or $a_3 > a_2$.
   e. Because actual u below and above u^* is deemed a problem.

2. Answer not given.

3. a. 1.6.
   b. 155.2.
   c. $\Delta Y = 1.6$ times $25 = 40$; $\Delta T = .5(40) = 20$; GovDef $= 25 - 20 = 5$ increase in deficit.

d. Multiplier value rises to 1.82. Consumption automatically rises by $(.75)(.1)(155.2) = 11.64$. Therefore, Y rises by $(11.64)(1.82) = 21.2$. Taxes rise by $(21.6)(.5) = 10.6$. Government deficit falls by 10.6.

e. ΔG causes $\Delta Y = 1.6$ times $30 = 48$; ΔT causes $\Delta Y = 1.6$ times $.75(30) = 36$; so, $Y = +12$. When Y rises by 12, it generates $6 more tax revenue. If $\Delta G = 30$, $\Delta T = 30 + 6$, then surplus is created equal to 6. This still allows Y to rise, because government spends all of the $30, while consumers only spend 75 percent of changes in taxable income.

4. a. True. With high employment, the actual budget has a smaller surplus, because less tax revenue is collected than at a higher employment level.

  b. True. Because the high-employment budget nets out automatic or nondiscretionary changes in the budget.

  c. True. Keynesians think of the deficit as a short-run stabilization tool. They probably would prefer a long-run policy of balanced budgets, however.

  d. True. If liberals win the election, they will put in an expansionary program. The theory says that conservatives would do the opposite.

  e. True. Some people believe the expansionary fiscal policy led the Fed into a tight monetary policy. This raised interest rates, causing more foreigners to want to buy U.S. securities. Since they had to purchase dollars first, they raised the value of the dollar and worsened the trade deficit.

5. A cyclical deficit is the portion of the deficit that results from the economy being in a downswing. However, a structural deficit is the result of policymakers' decisions.

6. Most of the deficits through the early 1980s have been mainly cyclical. However, by the mid-1980s, the deficit became structural. In 1991, a substantial portion of the deficit was again cyclical with the onset of another recession.

7. In the 1980s, the Fed believed that expansionary fiscal policy required tight monetary policy, i.e., and high interest rates. Thus, the 1980s witnessed not only a high budget deficit but also a rising trade deficit. In the early 1990s, however, during a recession, the Fed reduced interest rates, thus lowering the trade deficit.

8. If Ricardian equivalence holds, tax increases to reduce the deficit or tax cuts to induce economic activity will not be effective, as neither will affect interest rates. Ricardo's view was that private saving depended positively on the deficit. In other words, if the deficit increases, the public will save in order to pay future tax liabilities. Moreover, if the deficit decreases, private saving will also decrease. Thus, the shifts in the supply and demand for loanable funds would offset each other, and interest rates would remain unchanged.

9. It may be that voters in the United States have come to better understand the relationship between the fiscal policies that result in large budget deficits and inflation. Politicians believe they are more likely to lose votes because of the deficit. This is consistent with polls prior to the 1996 election m where voters ranked deficit reduction ahead of tax cuts as an important issue. With respect to a group of European countries, deficit reduction is mostly due to the fact that they have bound themselves to fiscal policy rules as part of the process leading up to a move to one currency. These are the so-called Maastricht guidelines agreed to in 1991. Other countries, such as New Zealand, have resorted to legislated rules for monetary and fiscal policy. Overall, supporters of the public choice and partisan view still maintain that it is important to recognize the deviation of the goals of policymakers from those of society as a whole.

10. When this type of collective rationality does not exist, the behavior of the vote-maximizing policymaker will deviate from social-welfare-maximizing behavior.

11. The economic environment assumed by them is consistent with the new classical model, in that expectations are rational, but it has the Keynesian element that money wages are set by contracts of several years' duration. Also, as before, they assume a liberal party, whose constituency is most concerned about employment, and one conservative party, whose constituency is most concerned about inflation. In such a framework, elections create uncertainty concerning the future behavior of the inflation rate, and, therefore, the money wage demands workers (or their unions) should make. For example, in the year before a general election, workers might presume that if the liberals win, the inflation rate will be high, say about 7 percent, and if the conservatives win, it will be low, say about a 3 percent. Even if expectations are rational, the best the workers can do form an expectations of inflation, that is a weighted average of the two possible outcomes. Since each of the parties could win, the rational expectation of inflation would be five percent and firms and workers would set money wages accordingly. If the liberals win the election, then the inflation rate (7 percent) will be higher than the expected inflation rate (5 percent) on the basis of which money wages were set. This will lead to rapid expansion of output as firms hire additional workers because the real wage will be unexpectedly low for firms. But if conservatives win, actual inflation (3 percent) will be lower than the expected inflation rate (5 percent) and money wages will have been set too high. This will result in a rise in unemployment and a recession may follow.

CHAPTER 19

Multiple-Choice Questions

1. d	7. b	13. a	19. c	25. d
2. a	8. e	14. d	20. b	26. a
3. b	9. c	15. c	21. c	27. e
4. b	10. a	16. b	22. a	28. a
5. d	11. b	17. b	23. c	29. b
6. a	12. d	18. d	24. b	

Problems and/or Essay Questions

1. Under monetary targeting, M1 would not be altered, because of the drop in money demanded. Instead, the interest rate is allowed to adjust (fall in this case) to restore monetary equilibrium. If the shift was underestimated, then interest rates would fall more than they anticipated. In the midst of all this, an unexpected higher deficit would lead to even higher interest rates.

2. Students should pay particular attention to the following monetary episodes: 1966, 1969, 1974-75, and 1980.

3. Under M1 targeting, the interest rate falls as the money stock is held constant. The lower interest rate raises aggregate demand and, therefore, increases output and prices. If interest rates are instead pegged, the money supply would be reduced just enough so that interest rates are unchanged. Therefore, aggregate demand prices and output are unaffected.

4. Intermediate targeting involves using a variety of variables as indicators of the progress of monetary policy in achieving ultimate targets. Since 1979, the Fed has been using monetary aggregates as the main intermediate targets. There is debate over whether one or numerous intermediate targets should be used. There are those who prefer targeting directly on nominal GDP. The Fed seems to have taken an eclectic approach since 1979—not relying on any one target exclusively. Between 1979 and 1982, they focused on bank reserves. After the recession of 1982, interest rates have become more important again, but the Federal Reserve appears to alternate targets—sometimes targeting interest rates, while at other times focusing on monetary aggregates or exchange rates. This approach serves no single goal well, but it has the advantage of being able to apply policy to specific problems.

5. By setting low money-stock targets and adhering to them, the Fed builds credibility with the public. The public then expects low inflation, and, as a result, the Fed has protection against inflation. Interest-rate targeting does not protect against inflation; in fact, it may exacerbate it.

6. The Fed intended to target a range in which the federal funds rate would fluctuate. If the Fed wanted to tighten monetary policy, the upper end of the range would be increased. If it wanted to expand monetary policy, the lower end would be reduced.

7. In 1979, the inflation rate was over 13 percent. Since targeting monetary aggregates is more conducive to reducing inflationary expectations, it was to the Fed's advantage to switch from federal funds targeting to controlling bank reserves.

8. The growth in M1 did not correspond to increases in the growth of nominal GDP after 1985. Because of these unpredictable swings in the M1 growth rate, M1 growth was not even targeted after 1987.

9. Let us suppose that the situation is one where, due to some distortions in the economy, social welfare would be increased if output were pushed above the natural rate, the level that is consistent with price and wage setters accurately predicting the price level. A possible reason for this might be that noncompetitive features of labor and product markets lead to a natural rate that is too low. Also, suppose that consistent with the rational expectations hypotheses, the monetary policymaker can push output above the natural rate by generating an unexpectedly high rate of monetary growth. Furthermore, assume that, as is reasonable, wages and prices are set at less frequent intervals (i.e., annually) than monetary policy actions are implemented (i.e., monthly). A one point, the beginning of the year, the policymaker might announce a noninflationary rate of monetary growth of zero. But later in the year, after wages and prices are set, the policymaker will find it optimal to renege on this commitment and generate "surprise" inflation. Firms and workers (or workers unions), knowing the policymaker's preferences (assuming rational expectations), will anticipate that the policymaker will cheat. There will be no output gain; there will be higher inflation than at zero money growth. Therefore, the time inconsistency problem causes an inflationary bias in monetary policy. If there were a monetary policy rule that bound the policymaker to a zero inflation policy instead, society would be better off than with policy by discretion, because the rule would give credibility to the policymaker's announcement.

10. One motivation is to reduce the effect of political pressures on central banks. Generally, the move to inflation targeting coincides with greater independence to central banks. Another motivation to inflation targeting in several countries was they experienced problems similar to the United States with monetary aggregates as intermediate targets.

11. A money-stock target is superior to an interest-rate target when the uncertainty facing the policymaker concerns the IS schedule. An interest-rate target is preferable to a money-stock target if uncertainty centers on instability in money demand.

CHAPTER 20

Multiple-Choice Questions

1. d	7. d	13. a	19. d	25. b	31. d
2. a	8. b	14. a	20. e	26. d	
3. d	9. c	15. a	21. b	27. d	
4. c	10. e	16. c	22. b	28. c	
5. a	11. b	17. c	23. b	29. b	
6. a	12. b	18. b	24. a	30. e	

Problems and/or Essay Questions

1. a. 0.54, 2.32.
   b. 4347.8, 18,604.7.
   c. 16,913.3.
   d. 5,218.5.
   e. Buy pounds today.

2. Flexible exchange rates quickly eliminate balance of payments imbalances. Therefore, long-term trade imbalances do not exist, and wild speculations of administered official exchange devaluations (or revaluations) are avoided. Furthermore, policymakers' influence is independent of trade imbalances, and the economy is insulated against demand shocks. Exchange rate changes, however, are very susceptible to market forces and may vary considerably, generating too much uncertainty for traders. Flexible exchange rates, however, have affected policymakers who often dislike large savings. When they peg, domestic policy is affected by external balances. Additionally, the domestic economy under flexible rates is not insulated from supply shocks. Fixed exchange rates offer more stability, except in cases where long-term trade imbalances threaten official exchange rate intervention. Nevertheless, recent experience suggests that pegging exchange rates is not always successful and tends not to work if macroeconomic policies are not coordinated among trading partners.

3. This would cause a U.S. trade surplus. With higher net exports, higher output, prices, and interest rates should occur. The higher output and prices should generate a decrease in exports, a rise in imports, and a reduced level of net exports. The higher interest rates should lead to a capital account surplus. Therefore, with all adjustments accounted for, there are numerous and conflicting total effects on imports, exports, and upon the supply and demand for foreign currency.

4. If the end result was a rise in net exports, then the U.S. balance of payments surplus would lead to an excess demand for dollars in world markets. This would raise the value of the dollar and make U.S. goods more expensive to the rest of the world. The appreciation of the dollar would reduce exports and raise imports—thus causing the surplus to move towards zero.

5. In this case, there would be a higher dollar volume of imports, leading to a large balance of payments deficit. There would be a downward shift in aggregate demand, since net exports would be smaller. The aggregate supply curve would also shift up, implying higher prices at all levels of output. Thus, we should find recessionary conditions (output down, but prices could be higher or lower). These recessionary conditions should reduce imports of goods and services and exports of capital (lower interest rates). The results for imports, exports, and the supply and demand for currency depend upon the relative sizes of the effects described above.

6. From 1976 to 1980, the United States followed an accommodative monetary policy, and the value of the dollar fell. The rapid money growth raised the demand for foreign goods, services, and assets. This, in turn, reduced the demand for U.S. dollars, and the value of the dollar fell. From 1981 to 1985, the monetary policy was tighter, and the opposite occurred.

7. Since 1988, there has not been another dramatic swing the value of the dollar, even so the dollar has continued to show considerable volatility. Between 1988 and 1995, there was a gradual decline in the value of the dollar. In 1995, the dollar hit record post-World War II lows against the German mark and the Japanese yen. Between 1996-1997, the value of the dollar rose and by late 1997 the value of the dollar, whether measured relative to the German mark or more broadly by the weighted average of other currencies, was back to its 1988 level.

8. A flexible exchange rate would result in an adjustment in the exchange rate. In a flexible exchange rate system, the excess demand for foreign exchange, which resulted from the foreign recession, causes the exchange rate to rise. This adjustment works to offset the contractionary effect on the domestic economy because of the recession abroad. That is how flexible exchange rates insulate an economy from certain external shocks, i.e., a foreign recession.

9. Since 1979, a number of European countries, whose current members are the Netherlands, Belgium, Luxembourg, Greece, Germany, Austria, Ireland, Denmark, France, Portugal, Spain, Italy, and the United Kingdom, have participated in a type of fixed exchange rate system, known as the European Monetary System (EMS). Central to the EMS is the European Exchange Rate Mechanism (ERM), in which all members except Italy and the United Kingdom currently participate. Countries within the ERM agree to limit fluctuations in the value of their currencies against each other. Exchange rates are not entirely fixed but the countries do commit to keep them within a band around a set rate. The exchange rate is kept within the band by means of intervention in the foreign exchange market. The exchange rates are not set permanently, when economic conditions warrant, there are periodic realignments of currency values. Yes. The EMS countries agreed, in the Maastricht Treaty in 1991, to move, in a number of stages, to a system with a single currency and a common European Central Bank.

CHAPTER 21

Multiple-Choice Questions

1. b	7. c	13. a	19. a	25. d
2. a	8. c	14. b	20. d	
3. c	9. a	15. c	21. d	
4. d	10. d	16. c	22. b	
5. d	11. a	17. d	23. c	
6. d	12. d	18. a	24. b	

Problems and/or Essay Questions

1. The BP schedule is upward sloping in the case of imperfect capital mobility and horizontal in the case of perfect capital mobility.

2. An increase in the money supply shifts the LM schedule to the right. The domestic interest rate falls below the foreign interest rate, triggering a massive capital outflow. Central bank intervention to maintain the fixed exchange rate causes the money supply to fall back to the initial level. The domestic interest rate is restored to equality with the foreign interest rate, and income is back at its initial level.

3. An increase in the quantity of money increases the level of income, decreases the interest rate, and causes a deficit in the balance of payments.

4. An expansionary fiscal policy is highly effective, because there is no rise in the domestic interest rate and, therefore, no crowding out of private-sector spending.

5. A decrease in government spending, an increase in taxes, a decrease in foreign income, a fall in the exchange rate, and an autonomous rise in import demand.

6. It depends on the BP schedule. If the BP schedule is flatter than the LM schedule, then a increase in government spending, results in a balance of payments surplus. On the other hand, if the BP schedule is steeper than the LM schedule an increase in government spending would cause a balance of payments deficit.

7. An increase in government spending is completely ineffective. The direct effect of an increase in government spending shifts the IS schedule to the right. As a result, the domestic interest rate rises above the foreign interest rate. This results in a massive capital inflow which, with a flexible exchange rate, causes the exchange rate to fall, i.e., the domestic currency appreciates. As a result, exports will fall and imports will rise shifting the IS schedule to the left. Equilibrium will be restored only when the IS schedule has shifted all the way back to its initial position and the domestic interest rate is again equal to the foreign interest rate. At this point, the capital inflow and downward pressure on the exchange rate end. Furthermore, income is back to its initial level.

8. In addition to the IS and LM schedules, the open economy model has a BP schedule. This schedule graphs all the interest rate-income combinations that result in balance of payments equilibrium at a given exchange rate.